IT'S OK TO SAY "GOD"

IT'S OK TO SAY "GOD"

- Prelude to a Constitutional Renaissance -

TAD ARMSTRONG

WESTBOW
PRESS
A DIVISION OF THOMAS NELSON

Unless otherwise indicated, scripture quotations taken from the Holy Bible, New Living Translation, copyright 1996, 2004. Used by permission of Tyndale House Publishers, Inc., Wheaton, Illinois 60189. All rights reserved.

WestBow Press books may be ordered through booksellers or by contacting:

WestBow Press
A Division of Thomas Nelson
1663 Liberty Drive
Bloomington, IN 47403
www.westbowpress.com
1-(866) 928-1240

Tad Armstrong
P.O. Box 565
Edwardsville, IL 62025
www.ellconstitutionclubs.com
1-(618) 656-6770

ISBN: 978-1-4497-2986-8 (sc)
ISBN: 978-1-4497-2987-5 (hc)
ISBN: 978-1-4497-2985-1 (e)

Library of Congress Control Number: 2011919853

Printed in the United States of America

WestBow Press rev. date: 11/14/2011

DEDICATION

I dedicate this work to my wife, Melody, and to
the American military, past and present, whose
sacrifices permit me to pursue life, liberty,
and happiness in the land of the free.

A lie told often enough becomes the truth.

Vladimir Lenin

CONTENTS

PREFACE

When a friend, business associate, or family member informs you of the law or some news story involving government, what do you do with it? Mind you, I'm not talking about gossip. We all know gossip when we hear it and all Christians should know not to fan its flames. (Psalm 15:3). No, I am referring to information people truly believe you should know in order to be a better informed citizen. Most of us do not question the original source or the accuracy of such information that comes from a friend and, even if we do harbor some doubts, we normally find ourselves passing the "news" on to others in order to keep them "informed" as well. Right?

Eventually the masses come to believe the story is true whether or not it has any basis in fact. It takes on a life of its own and, before you know it, an entire nation is thinking and acting on a foundation of fiction. It is an amazing phenomenon, not necessarily born of illicit motive. Of course, there are those who intentionally spread lies as truth so as to brainwash their victims, but many Christians with the best of intentions participate by unknowingly spreading the falsehood. Brainwashing is especially sinister because innocents become the carriers of its parasitic methodology.

I am getting better at refusing "carrier status," but it is not an exact science. I now try to recognize my own human nature and, when I do, trade it in for Christ's nature as fast as I can. That is, I attempt to verify the integrity of important "news" before passing it on because I surely do not wish to be the mouthpiece for lies or, if not lies, then just plain bad information. Heaven forbid I would ever be used again as a conduit for ignorance, for those that listen to me might act on what they hear.

There is only one antidote for ignorance and that is the power of knowledge. Do not kid yourself; it takes hard work to grow in knowledge. I am asking you to roll up your sleeves and work at learning – the stakes are high – your country calls you to this task.

I hope your time invested in this endeavor will enable you to speak with confidence when you confront two types of folks. First, you will face those with honestly held, but innocently misinformed beliefs. After you have studied this material, you may well look back on this very day and realize that you were one of them. Good people with long-standing and deeply held, but false, beliefs will be the toughest nuts to crack. Armed with the love of Christ, you will have to show them the way. Second, you will face folks who have an agenda to bury Christian virtues in the dust. The best way to beat them at their game is to stop fighting their fight for them and to stop taking on the role of victim – that is what they want you to do – it plays right into their game plan. How's that for a teaser?

I would like to think that reading this book will make you a better Christian or, in any event, a better citizen regardless of your faith or lack of faith. If you are a Christian, you will likely be a better advocate for Christ because you will better understand the true spiritual war being waged in this country, you will trade in your hate bullets and most of your lawsuit bombs (but, believe me, there are some lawsuits that should be pursued) for the awesome power of Christ's love, you will learn that honoring God's will turns sadness and anger into joy and victory regardless of the circumstances, and, if you take an activist role, you will learn where the worthy spiritual and cultural battles are being fought and how you can help win them. You will learn that too many Christians are not only fighting against themselves (if they are fighting at all), but, if you can believe it, they are fighting for the enemy and do not realize it! Simply speaking, you will learn which contemporary issues are worthy of your time, money, and prayer and which causes are not only lost, but were never worthy of anyone's attention in the first place.

If the misinformed or uninformed hearts of the Christians who most need to hear this message do not experience a renewal of purpose, I will have failed, for it is they, far more than any lawsuit-prone atheist, who are unwittingly doing the most to undermine freedom of religion, in general, and the freedoms Christians still enjoy in this country, in particular.

If you are an atheist, I have a few questions I would like you to answer. As you will see, much to your surprise, I agree with some of your causes, not because I wish to support your unbelief, but because I wish to enable Christianity to prosper. I have never understood why you would spend any time or money fighting for turf that produces no real fruit even if victorious. I could better understand a Jew fighting for a national holiday on Yom Kippur or a Hindu for a day off on Ram Navami. I get it when Jehovah's Witnesses fought and won the right for their kids to go to public school without pledging allegiance to a flag they believed to be the forbidden worship of a graven image, but I am hard pressed to understand what a person who professes the "virtues" of believing in nothing has to gain by fighting for the loss of what the rest of us "fools" hold dear. Why, for example, do you care if the majoritarian profession of trust in God remains on our coins? Why is it not counted a virtue by atheists to maintain respectful acknowledgment for what the rest of us do believe? While it is very true that the Constitution protects minorities, I suggest that even minorities could learn a lesson from those who visit Rome and, at least to a limited degree, on occasion "do as they do."

The conclusion I have been forced to reach is that we Christians in America today could be so much more effective for the cause of Christ if we would only educate ourselves and focus on what is truly important. We have all of the ingredients we need to be strong and vibrant, including a Constitution that preserves the freedom necessary to flourish. However, we must stop playing the role of helpless victims in a culture war we only partially understand. If Christians don't get this right, we will wake up one day to find that many of our causes have only served to embolden those who seek our demise. It doesn't have to be that way if we get on the right train.

Christians need to be very careful of what they ask for. If we fight the wars of worthless causes and win, in many instances all we will have won, by way of example, is the right of others to hang the principles of Buddha on the classroom walls of the schools our Christian children attend.

In 2010, I received an e-mail story (see chapter two) that ignited a passion within me to write this book. Because the well-intended message presented the very type of falsehood I am trying to overcome, instead of "passing the story on" by hitting the forward button or simply deleting it, I chose to…well…hmmm…cloister myself off from the world for who-knew-how-long-it-would-take at my computer eating nachos and cheese curls while my mail piled high, my beard grew long, and my kids forgot what I looked like, all for the purpose of writing my very first book! Why? Because I believe God wants to use this earthen vessel in some small way to help our nation heal, to further His Kingdom, and to provide words of truth to all faiths and, yes, even to those of no faith. In addition (and, in particular), I believe it is His will to use me and my wife to help Christians steer the future better by first understanding the past and, more importantly, by getting a grip on the present.

We simply can no longer permit ourselves to be used by those whose agenda is to guide us to a place where we defeat ourselves.

To our beloved pastor, Dr. Tom Hufty, at the First Baptist Church of Maryville, Illinois, I want you to know that we pay attention to your sermons. Here are some favorite "Hufty Themes":

"Live life by making God look good."

"A Christian needs to impact the culture for Christ."

"Seek to touch a day you will never see."

"Live 1 Corinthians 16:14 - 'And everything
you do must be done with love.'"

My goal is to enlighten without being condescending, to embolden without being arrogant, to persuade without leaving scars - in other words, to educate in love. I have done my best, Dr. Hufty, to live up to your challenges.

Tad Armstrong

ACKNOWLEDGMENTS

I thank my wife, Melody, for her encouragement and wise advice along the way. We have both said on countless occasions that we would go wherever God leads us and we believe with all our hearts that He has led us to this place – to this message.

My children (Ben, Beth, Ian, and Meghan) and my "children-in-law" (Unjoo, Alan, Trisha, and Brian, respectively) have helped proofread and otherwise nurture the process along. I have not asked whether they agree with the entirety of my message, but I know our hearts are one and I thank all of them.

And, my grandchildren, Gabby, Gracie, and Maddy – what can I say? A smile from them provides me with enough energy to write 'til the cows come home.

The encouragement and well-founded criticism of Pastor R.B. and Helen Hall of Kingsland, Texas, have been invaluable and words cannot express how thankful we are for the love, support, and prayers we have felt from them and from Pastor Tom and Debbie Graddy of Ashland, Missouri.

This journey began informally with my fellow citizens and Donut Palace buddies to explore the Constitution of our great land. I did not realize how much hunger existed for this knowledge. A big thanks goes out to hundreds of ELL Constitution Club members in Madison, Jersey, and St. Clair Counties of Illinois and to the charter high school club in Edwardsville, Illinois. The adults and teenagers keep coming back month after month to learn. They are a big reason this book came to be.

I am quite sure this book would not have been written without the continued success of the clubs. I want to first thank our facility providers in Madison, Jersey, and St. Clair Counties of Illinois: St. John's United Methodist Church, Glen Carbon Community Center, Southwestern Illinois College, First Bank, Korte Recreation Center, Jerseyville Public Library, Brown Realtors, Holiday Inn, Edgemont Bible Church, and Heartland Baptist Church.

My gratitude goes out to all of our lawyer-moderators in the adult clubs (Dayna Johnson, Irv Slate, Laef Lorton, Neal Wallace, John Hopkins, Mary Albert-Fritz, and Patrick King) and Carol Wilkerson at the high school. Our financial sponsors clearly provided our foundation. Thanks to Cassens Dodge Chrysler, R.P. Lumber, Hortica Insurance Company, Korte Construction, GCS Federal Credit Union, The Bank of Edwardsville, Chuck West Agency, The Illinois State Bar Association, The Alton-Wood River Bar Association, and the law firm of Callis, Papa, Hale, Szewcyk & Danzinger, P.C. A very special thanks must go out to Bill Shaw, Allen and Linda Cassens, Tom Holloway, Robert McClellan, Pete Fornof, Mona Haberer, Kari Barton, Bob and Pat Hulme, Harry and Carol Windland, Jack Klobnak, Robert Plummer, Mark Holshouser, Bob Hart, Rev. Charlie Sward, Tom Hill, Dr. William K. Drake, Dr. Joe Helms, Dr. Mike Firsching, Mark Spengler, Norm Bohnenstiehl, Dennis Cramsey, and Edwardsville School District Superintendent and Assistant Superintendent, Dr. Ed Hightower and Dr. Lynda Andre, respectively.

I pray to God that His message gets through and that He is pleased with this attempt. I could never ask for more.

Chapter One

A ROADMAP

Hold on, my friends, to the Constitution and to the Republic for which it stands. Miracles do not cluster and what has happened once in 6,000 years may not happen again. Hold on to the Constitution, for if the American Constitution should fail, there will be anarchy throughout the world.

Daniel Webster

After the Bible, Torah, Koran, or other fundamental teaching of a respective faith, the United States Constitution, as interpreted by the Supreme Court of the United States, is likely the next most relevant writing in the lives of United States citizens. If you are not already cognizant of that reality, perhaps this book will persuade.

Article V of its provisions allow Americans to amend it whenever they wish to do so, assuming they wish to do so in sufficient numbers. By definition, then, it is as relevant today as the people it governs care to make it. It is the essence of contemporary relevance.

The focus of our Constitution is the preservation of freedom. July 4th of every year is a good time to witness just how deficient our nation is in our knowledge of our founding document. News anchors ask trivia questions to help bring the Constitution to life around that time. For example, they will ask their audience, "How many freedoms granted by the First Amendment can you name?" Typical answers are the freedom of speech or religion or the press. Some have named the freedom to own a pet.

However, the correct answer is "none." Don't believe me? The First Amendment states that "Congress shall make no law respecting an establishment of religion, or prohibiting the free exercise thereof; or abridging the freedom of speech, or of the press; or the right of the people peaceably to assemble; and to petition the Government for a redress of grievances."

Do you see any freedoms being "granted" by that language? I don't. All I see written there is that Congress is forbidden from making any laws that prohibit or abridge the freedoms being referenced. Therefore, here's a heads-up: The Constitution does not grant the freedoms of speech, religion, press, or assembly. Neither does the Declaration of Independence.

However, as expressed in the Declaration, the Founders understood that freedom comes from a higher power. "We hold these truths to be self-evident, that all men are created equal, that they are endowed by their Creator with certain unalienable rights, that among these are life, liberty and the pursuit of happiness…"

Christianity seems to be under attack and many Christians believe the Supreme Court is the key opponent in the culture wars we all face every day as we try to show our children the virtues of Christ-like living in the land of the free. While this nation is still a land of hope, it is also a broken part of a larger broken world.

We are going to explore the very decisions of our Supreme Court that shape the meaning of the religion clauses of the First Amendment. These are rulings that affect our lives in very meaningful ways. I believe you are going to be surprised when you discover the truths these decisions hold.

In chapter six, I introduce a fictional Christian family. In subsequent chapters, their story will help bring the issues addressed by our Constitution to life and, hopefully, straight into your home and community. Please help me spread the word.

After the cases on a particular topic (arranged by chapters) are presented, I provide a summary of them and my take on what they mean in our daily lives and how I believe we should respond as Christians.

I will wrap up the lessons in chapter sixteen and bare my soul in the afterword, where my hope of hopes is to spawn (with your help) a much needed Constitutional Renaissance in this land.

I would like to encourage you to discuss these powerful topics with your teenage children and friends. Many enemies of this great nation likely know our Constitution better than we do. Knowledge will forever rule ignorance, so we must gain the knowledge necessary to, once again, govern as intended by those who designed this marvelous document. The stakes are very, very high.

God bless you and your family as you take this important journey. Oops! I said "God." And, guess what? It's OK.

Chapter Two

OUR WORST ENEMY IS ...

The only thing more expensive than education is ignorance.
Benjamin Franklin

I'm afraid our worst enemy is ourselves, not because we are masochists, but because we "know not what we do." We are willing to be misled by lies told so often that they become truths. I know this is so because I have done my homework. I will show you concrete examples.

In 2010, I received one of those sometimes-maddening, sometimes-enlightening e-mails we all get. Because it was forwarded by a dear lady at our church, the First Baptist Church in Maryville, Illinois, and was sent to our Bible study group, I did not automatically delete it. Here it is:

To: All who love the Lord

Today I [Helen] went to visit the new WWII Memorial in Washington, D.C. I got an unexpected history lesson. Because I'm a baby boomer, I was one of the youngest in the crowd. Most were the age of my parents, veterans of "the greatest war." It was a beautiful day, and people were smiling and happy to be there. Hundreds of us milled around the Memorial, reading the inspiring words of Eisenhower and Truman that are engraved there.

On the Pacific side of the Memorial, a group of us gathered to read the words President Roosevelt used to announce the attack on Pearl Harbor:

Yesterday, December 7, 1941 – a date which will live in infamy – the United States of America was suddenly and deliberately attacked.

One elderly woman [Amanda] read the words aloud:

With confidence in our armed forces, with the abounding determination of our people, we will gain the inevitable triumph.

But as she read, she suddenly turned angry. "Wait a minute," she said, "they left out the end of the quote. They left out the most important part. Roosevelt ended the message with 'so help us God.'"

Her husband [Charley] said, "You are probably right. ***We're not supposed to say things like that now.***"

"I know I'm right," Amanda insisted. "I remember the speech." The two looked dismayed, shook their heads sadly and walked away.

Listening to their conversation, I thought to myself, "Well, it has been over 50 years; she has probably forgotten."

But Amanda had not forgotten. She was right. I went home and pulled out the book my book club is reading – "Flags of Our Fathers" by James Bradley. It's all about the battle at Iwo Jima. I haven't gotten too far in the book. It's tough to read because it's a graphic description of the WWII battles in the Pacific. But right there it was on page 58. Roosevelt's speech to the nation ends in "so help us God."

The people who edited out that part of the speech when they engraved it on the Memorial could have fooled me. I was born after the war. But they couldn't fool the people who were there. Roosevelt's words are engraved on their hearts.

Who gave them the right to change the words of history?

Send this around to your friends. People need to know before everyone forgets. People today are trying to change the history of America by leaving God out of it, but the truth is, God has been a part of this nation since the beginning. He still wants to be and He always will be!

<u>If you agree</u>, pass this on and God bless you! If not, may God forgive you!

Do I agree? Well, yes and no. According to the challenge, I suppose that means I will be blessed *and* forgiven–nothing wrong with that–I like that combo. In the greater sense, of course, since I am a Christian trying to walk the talk, I know I am blessed beyond measure and I know I have been and will be forgiven for the sins of my past and for those still in my future. However, in the narrow sense meant by Helen's conclusion, I cannot simply pass it on because, in doing so, we Christians are actually fanning the very flames that are burning us up! I will explain below.

In case you haven't noticed, the "rage" of the '90s that used to be found only on the road has slowly crept into our everyday existence. Just the other day, my local newspaper reported that two sisters beat up a middle-aged lady who had made a wide turn with her shopping cart on aisle six of the local Wal-Mart. People are on edge. "Road rage" has become "sidewalk rage." Many American Christians believe that every other faith, non-faith, and, in particular, their own government is out to destroy them. Just think. Those of the faith whose most important social command is to "love thy neighbor as thyself" are angry at their neighbors. They sincerely believe they don't have to take it anymore, and many have brought their anger into the courtrooms of our nation.

It is my contention that, once Christians have the facts in tow, most of the unwarranted skirmishes will cease and the real battles for legitimate turf (in the field as opposed to the courtroom) can then be fought with greater success. Best of all, hopefully, victimized Christians will learn to turn that misdirected anger into the love of Christ for all. That is my hope.

However, I do not expect to persuade without evidence. Stay with me. I believe I can make a believer out of you.

I pray to God that this book will enlighten you, bless you, and make a positive difference in your life. Whether you are a Christian, an atheist, or of another faith, I know this book will at least help you grow in secular knowledge, and that, in itself, is not bad, for as Thomas Jefferson said, "A democracy can never be ignorant and free."

There are numerous observations and the beginnings of some valuable lessons packed into Helen's story about Amanda and Charley. A quick survey will give you an idea of where we are headed.

The author of the WWII Memorial story is a "baby boomer" born after World War II and is one of the "youngest in the crowd." If she wrote her story around 2004, when the Memorial opened, that would have put her around fifty-five years of age at that time. She was "one of hundreds there that beautiful day." **Observation #1:** We "boomers" (I was born in 1951) have failed our children. I am hard on us because I have discovered somewhat late in life that most of us have failed in our duty to steer the ship. We are (or were) the folks in charge of our public schools for most of these post-WWII years. We certainly were in charge of our own children and grandchildren. We blew it, pure and simple. Ask yourself why "few under fifty-five" were present on such a beautiful day at the World War II Memorial. **We cannot possibly preserve freedom unless we teach our children our history.** I wonder how many young citizens understand the meaning of America. I know you will likely be overwhelmed with the eye-opening knowledge you will gain from completing this journey.

Helen said, "Who gave the engravers the right to change the words of history?" I ask you to forgive my penchant for being extraordinarily precise with the words I choose. I do so because words matter. I believe you will see what I mean as you progress through this book. That preface leads me to **Observation #2:** The engravers clearly did not "change" the words of history. They "failed to complete" the words of history. There is a difference and you might as well learn early on that I value the power of knowledge and abhor the inevitable repercussions of ignorance.

Observation #3: What was the reaction of Amanda and Charley? They "looked dismayed, shook their heads sadly, and walked away." No doubt

Helen's story has already been received in countless homes and will be received in countless homes to come. The e-mail train is hard to stop.

Observation #4: Allegedly to her credit, Helen sought to verify the accuracy of the couple's claim before writing her story that has been passed on by those who agree. If true, good for her. Accurate reporting. (Well, we shall see.) We used to call that mainstream news.

Observation #5: In response to his wife's protest that they left "so help us God" out of the quote, Charley said, "You are probably right. *We're not supposed to say things like that now.*" Really!?!

Here are some phrases that would likely qualify, according to Charley, as the "things like that" we are no longer supposed to say, beginning with "so help us God":

So help us God! (As in a speech or prayer.)

God bless you! (As in a parting and uplifting message or after a sneeze.)

God bless America! (As in every president's closing of a speech I can recall in my lifetime.)

So help me God! (As in the last phrase of an oath.)

In God we trust! (Look on your coins.)

Praise God! (A declaration of joy.)

God help us! (Definitely, a prayer.)

Under God! (As in the Pledge of Allegiance.)

Who do you think Charley meant by the "we" in "we're"? At a minimum, he was speaking of himself and his wife. However, in the broader sense, he was likely speaking of Americans in general. One could take a cynical approach and limit his intended universe of "we" to Christian or Jewish Americans, but I prefer the all-encompassing universe of all United States citizens who believe in a higher power. Oh, what the heck, let's include atheists whom I will bet call on God from time to time in their moments of great need.

I wonder where this kind soul of the greatest generation came up with the conclusion that "we're not supposed to say things like that now?" This man was defeated in spirit and likely has done his part to pass on his story and his conclusion far and wide.

Observation #6: What if Charley was wrong in his assessment that we can't say "God" today? What if the engravers of the words on the Pacific side of the Memorial were no better informed than Charley? Are important national "steering" decisions being made out of ignorance, albeit with the best of intentions?

The sad news is that, when it comes to the culture war I admit is raging in the land of the free, Christians seem somehow prone to loving misery. It is so easy to assume the role of victim. Victims do not have to get up off the floor and do anything. In fact, their lifeblood is to perpetuate the science of "victimology" by whining and seeking the warm embrace of caring folks who are willing to lend a shoulder or an ear.

Ironically, the reason religion flourishes in this country and that we of faith will be able to say "God" and worship freely ("freely" being a relative term to be explored later) in America's tomorrow (just as we can today) is that we cannot (metaphorically) say "God" anywhere anytime in any manner we wish. If these concepts appear to be at cross-purposes, please reserve judgment until you have reached the last chapter.

The good news is that Charley was wrong, for as God as my witness, *It's OK to Say "God"* in America "almost" anywhere "almost" anytime in "almost" any manner you wish. And, as I hope to prove to all open minds (and, perhaps, even to some that are presently closed), our Supreme Court has been far friendlier to religion and things of God than you likely believe. After all is said and done, who is it exactly that started the rumor that *we're not supposed to say things of God in today's America*? Could it have been a Christian? I know it was not a president or any of the justices of the Supreme Court of the United States. However, it does appear that everyone who has hit the "send" button has contributed to spreading it hundreds of thousands of times by now. If Charley's conclusion was false, does that give you pause? This would be a superb topic of discussion with your family. Just ponder the ramifications.

Helen said, "People today are trying to change the history of America by leaving God out of it, but the truth is, God has been a part of this nation since the beginning. He still wants to be and He always will be!" She then closed her story with this challenge:

> If you agree, pass this on and God bless you! If not, may God forgive you!

I do not believe anyone should alter history, no matter the topic. The truth is that God has been far more than a "part of this nation" since the beginning.

God is all powerful:

> **Then I heard again what sounded like the shout**
> **of a huge crowd,**
> **or the roar of mighty ocean waves,**
> **or the crash of loud thunder: Hallelujah!**
> **For the Lord our God, the Almighty, reigns.**
>
> **Revelation 19:6**

God is everywhere:

> **I can never escape from your spirit!**
> **I can never get away from your presence!**
> **If I go up to heaven, you are there;**
> **if I go down to the place of the dead, you are there.**
> **If I ride the wings of the morning, if I dwell by the farthest oceans,**
> **even there your hand will guide me, and**
> **your strength will support me.**
>
> **Psalm 139:7-10**

And, God is all knowing:

> **God would surely have known it,**
> **for He knows the secrets of every heart.**
>
> **Psalm 44:21**

My wife and I believe that Jesus Christ gave His life for you and for every human being that has ever been conceived around the globe. He is not just the God of Americans. He is the Savior of the world. He wants to be our friend and invites you to be His.

I ask different questions in this book than Helen asked of her e-mail recipients. Do you perceive yourself as just another victim of crimes against Christianity? What if those crimes are imagined? Or, if crimes have been committed, what if they turn out not to be the crimes you once thought were perpetrated against you? Against Christians? Are you fighting the wrong fight? Are you fighting at all? Do you care about the truth? Enough to search for it? To slightly alter a phrase from Helen:

> If you do, read this book and pass its message on and may God bless you! If you do not, may God still bless you!

The next and last observation regarding the WWII Memorial story describes a primary reason why I wrote this book.

Observation #7: Helen, Amanda, and Charley could not have been real people. Helen's story had to be created out of thin air, for the inscription they quote does not exist at the WWII Memorial and the story is otherwise misleading. First, some of the alleged inscription Amanda supposedly read aloud ("With confidence in our armed forces, with the abounding determination of our people, we will gain the inevitable triumph") does not appear in the inscription at all, although it does appear in the speech. Second, although the phrase "so help us God" was part of the speech, it did not conclude the speech. And, third, the clear implication in the e-mail message is that leaving out the mention of God was not just a simple oversight, but an exceptionally glaring and intentional omission, given the additional misleading implication that most of the remainder of the speech was, in fact, inscribed.

The entire speech of President Franklin Delano Roosevelt (all 480+ words) is worthy of reciting here, not only for its historical value, but also as a further example of how misleading stories foster false beliefs. It is set forth below. Note that the actual portions inscribed at the Memorial are few and in **bold** print and the reference to God, admittedly omitted from the inscription, is <u>underlined</u>.

> **Yesterday, December 7, 1941 – a date which will live in infamy** – the United States of America was suddenly and deliberately attacked by naval and air forces of the Empire of Japan.
>
> The United States was at peace with that nation and, at the solicitation of Japan, was still in conversation with its Government and its Emperor looking toward the maintenance of peace in the Pacific. Indeed, one hour after Japanese air squadrons had commenced bombing in Oahu, the Japanese Ambassador to the United States and his colleague delivered to the Secretary of State a formal reply to a recent American message. While this reply stated that it seemed useless to continue the existing diplomatic negotiations, it contained no threat or hint of war or armed attack.
>
> It will be recorded that the distance of Hawaii from Japan makes it obvious that the attack was deliberately planned many days or even weeks ago. During the intervening time the Japanese Government has deliberately sought to deceive the United States by false statements and expressions of hope for continued peace.
>
> The attack yesterday on the Hawaiian Islands has caused severe damage to American naval and military forces. Very many American lives have been lost. In addition American ships have been reported torpedoed on the high seas between San Francisco and Honolulu.
>
> Yesterday the Japanese Government also launched an attack against Malaya. Last night Japanese forces attacked Hong Kong. Last night Japanese forces attacked Guam. Last night Japanese forces attacked the Philippine Islands. Last night the Japanese attacked Wake Island. This morning the Japanese attacked Midway Island.
>
> Japan has, therefore, undertaken a surprise offensive extending throughout the Pacific area. The facts of yesterday speak for

themselves. The people of the United States have already formed their opinions and well understand the implications to the very life and safety of our nation.

As Commander-in-Chief of the Army and Navy, I have directed that all measures be taken in our defense.

Always we will remember the character of the onslaught against us. **No matter how long it may take us to overcome this premeditated invasion, the American people in their righteous might will win through to absolute victory.**

I believe I interpret the will of the Congress and of the people when I assert that we will not only defend ourselves to the uttermost but will make very certain that this form of treachery shall never endanger us again.

Hostilities exist. There is no blinking at the fact that our people, our territory and our interests are in grave danger.

With confidence in our armed forces – with the unbounded determination of our people – we will gain the inevitable triumph – so help us God.

I ask that the Congress declare that since the unprovoked and dastardly attack by Japan on Sunday, December seventh, a state of war has existed between the United States and the Japanese Empire.

There you have it. Even if the e-mail story had accurately portrayed President Roosevelt's speech, do you believe Charley's conclusion would be fair? Someone wants Christians to spread a rumor – a rumor that we can't talk about things of God like we used to. Sad to say, good Christians are, indeed, doing just that by unwittingly hitting "send" and, if not challenged, guess what? Lies will eventually morph into truths.

For sure, there are some parts of Helen's story that are worth sending. For example, "People today are trying to change the history of America by leaving God out of it." It is unquestionably true that there is a move afoot to take God out of our culture, not so much to change the past, but to change the future. We must resist by first understanding that the fundamental culprit is not the judiciary, but a segment of our society bent on transforming America into something it was never intended to be - a godless society.

It is because of what I have learned that I am driven to help right this ship of lies by equipping Christians with the sweet wind of truth to help fill our sails and bring us out of the valley we have been in for some time now.

Assuming you do not belong to "The First Church of Non-Taxpayers" or "The Church of Wife Beaters Forever" or "The Religion of Armed Robbers Today," the First Amendment to my second-most-favorite-writing in the world says that your government cannot make any law that prohibits your freedom to worship as you please. That has been the law since 1791 with respect to Congress as it relates to the "free exercise" and "establishment" clauses, since 1940 with respect to local and state government as it relates to the "free exercise" clause, and since 1947 with respect to local and state government as it relates to the "establishment" clause. All of this will be explained in due time by reading the provisions and cases that made history. It is the law today. We will be exploring what it means and the circumstances, if any exist, that limit your freedom to exercise your religion or, in metaphoric terms, that prohibit you from saying "God."

We are still free to enter upon this study in these United States, thank God! There you go. I said "God" and it's OK. You'll see!

Chapter Three

"WE, THE PEOPLE"
ARE SO MISINFORMED

Self-governing begins at age 18. Education to prepare for life ends there for many. Education to live life begins there for all – and never ends unless and until defeat finds a home at your house.
Tad Armstrong - 2011

"We, the People" are so misinformed and uninformed about many, many things. Certainly our individual storehouse of knowledge is far less than the human library of knowledge. I have knowledge to try a lawsuit, hang drywall, frame a house, paint a bit, play a little guitar, etc. I could not begin to meaningfully join in a conversation about the engine of my car and I always tell my "computer guy" to avoid using foreign language when he tries to explain how my PC works.

When it comes to the law, no layperson can be faulted for lacking in knowledge of contract, tort, or real estate law and, thus, the need for lawyers. However, relatively few have a clue about our own form of self-government, with particular emphasis on "self." We have failed as a nation to maintain our knowledge of our government and our Constitution. Indeed, this is the one area of the law we all have an obligation to learn.

One cannot defend that which he does not understand. A famous naturalized United States citizen considered the Constitution of utmost importance:

> **The strength of the Constitution lies entirely in the determination of each citizen to defend it. Only if every single citizen feels duty bound to do his share in this defense are the constitutional rights secure.**
>
> **Albert Einstein**

Most employers would believe it imperative to know what their employees are doing and, well, we are the employers of our leaders.

Before I answer the numerous questions relating to where we stand today in regard to the interplay between religion (specifically, Christianity) and government, I will explain how I have made the journey from ignorance to the empowering position of knowledge in this area.

It all began at The Donut Palace in Edwardsville, Illinois. You know the kind of place I am describing. A place not unlike countless venues around the nation where donuts, coffee, newspapers, and the internet fuel discussions that lead to resolution of the world's problems on a daily basis. Our dear friends from India, Pete and Pallavi Patel, own this fine café where dreams and tragedies of daily living are shared as family. I remember teaching Pallavi one word of English a day for years when she was trying to assimilate into our culture. My, how I admire folks who can move to an unfamiliar land and survive in business, let alone in raising children, both of which they have done quite admirably.

Anyway, I am proud of being a lawyer in Edwardsville, Illinois, U.S.A., in spite of in-your-face relentless criticism of the profession, judges, and the law in general. I expressed my frustration to a local businessman. "Bill, I don't mind constructive criticism, but every day I come into this coffee shop and overhear people with the best of intentions who believe they know the law feed other good people a line of malarkey. No wonder folks are fed up with the law. Much of what they believe about it doesn't come close to reality."

"That's your fault, Armstrong. You lawyers have done a poor job of educating the rest of us. It's as if lawyers think they have to keep it from us unless they can charge a fee for it!"

I saw red and the challenge was on to do something, but what? I wanted people to learn the law, but the law is such a vast landscape. I would need to narrow the topic to something manageable. My coffee shop buddies claimed to be experts at running the country, but, in reality, what did they know about the bottom-line fundamentals, such as the Constitution? And, honestly, I was in the same boat. Aside from one course in law school, my 30-years-of-practicing-everything-but-constitutional-law knowledge of the Constitution was based on the same source as everyone else – the media! What if the media was inaccurate or misleading or just did not have enough space or time to educate us adequately? What if my friend, Bill, was right? What if "We, the Lawyers" had failed "We, the People"? Should the citizens of this great country have to pay lawyers to learn of the promises, responsibilities, and meaning of the world's most revered legal document – ironically, a document primarily drafted by, guess who? Lawyers! The answer kept haunting me and it was a clear "No!" The challenge was on! Little did I know where it would lead!

I put a note in my church bulletin and a flyer at the coffee shop. One hundred people showed at the first meeting. "I'm not exactly sure how we are going to do this," I said, "but if you are willing to put forth the effort, so am I. Let's meet every month and take a journey through the United States Constitution. Together, I am betting we will learn something about who we claim to be." We must have done something right. As of October, 2011, we have held 80 consecutive monthly meetings of the ELL charter club and the end is not in sight!

At our first anniversary, Mandy St. Amand, a journalist with the St. Louis Post-Dispatch, took notice and wrote an article about our club. Were it not for that publicity, perhaps the charter club would be the only club and we would be content to continue the journey alone.

After Mandy's article hit the streets, I started getting calls from around the St. Louis Metropolitan area from people eager to know when ELL would be starting a club in their hometown. The response was unexpected, unsolicited, and problematic. Now what? To that point in time, all of the educational material I had prepared, as well as all of my time, was provided free of charge to club members. They offered compensation and I declined. My reward was their response to what had become my passion. And, miracle of miracles, they kept coming back month after month!

I could not begin to meet monthly in all of the communities that responded and I knew I would not be able to handle the administration of a large number of clubs without compensation. After all, I had a law practice to run and a living to make – still do. As a result, the "ELL Concept" was born and ELL took its show on the road.

Thomas Jefferson believed education was the key to the success of a democracy. He was concerned that an uneducated electorate stood to lose the promises of freedom. Because ELL club members continually express how this experience has opened their eyes, I know that "We, the People" have not heeded Jefferson's warning. The nation is hungry to learn. Folks routinely blame our elementary and secondary education system. I do not know enough about that to respond. However, even if that is true, I believe Jefferson was more concerned that we continually work throughout our lives to gain the knowledge necessary to govern ourselves. The need for knowledge does not stop at age eighteen. In fact, that is when "self-governing" begins. We are 310,000,000 strong and growing. How can "We, the People" meet Jefferson's challenge?

The ELL concept brings five components into a uniquely American winning combination.

1. Hometown moderators. I do not require moderators to be lawyers, but they are certainly welcome to offer their guidance free of charge to study ELL material and meet once per month with citizens. To date, all moderators are passionate about being a part of the ELL movement. I am betting ELL can find a lawyer-moderator (or a non-lawyer-moderator) in every community where citizens want to learn.

2. Hometown benefactors of freedom. Local businesses and individuals finance the materials and services of ELL. I have found all of our sponsors to be more excited about helping to educate Americans than they are about reaping the benefits of advertising.

3. Hometown facilities. Our clubs meet in churches, libraries, universities, city halls, and businesses free of charge. They are happy to be a part of this grand vision by lending us their space.

4. Hometown Americans. Of course, if citizens do not respond to Jefferson's challenge and he was right, this country would likely be in great danger. However, Americans have responded favorably in every community where ELL has spawned a club. They spend valuable time reading Supreme Court opinions and attending monthly meetings.

5. Our home base prepares educational material, provides binders and monthly handouts to each club, and creates new clubs on an ongoing basis.

ELL seeks to impart the truth through uniquely American sacrifices to hometown Americans across the nation who are willing to respond to freedom's challenge.

What "Truth"?

The truth about what the United States Constitution says and how the United States Supreme Court has interpreted what it says about the freedoms and rights we claim (and the responsibilities we have) as United States citizens.

What "Challenge"?

Countless thousands have fought and died or sustained serious injury and countless more have given up their loved ones to **Earn** our original freedom, to sustain our nation as one, and to protect and preserve the freedoms enshrined in our Constitution. To those who sacrificed so much for us and to those who will come after us, "We, the People" have an obligation to at least **Learn** what they died for. And, if we do not meet freedom's challenge, we stand to **Lose** all they gained.

And, thus, on February 1, 2005…

Earn It, **L**earn It, or **L**ose It. (ELL)

Constitution Clubs were born!

**CONSTITUTION
CLUBS**

See the Afterword to learn how to start a new ELL
Constitution Club in your community!

Because the Supreme Court is faced with litigation bearing upon the religion clauses on an ongoing basis, this law is ever in a state of flux. If you wish to keep up with the most current decisions, please visit the ELL Constitution Clubs web site at:

www.ellconstitutionclubs.com.

I will endeavor to keep it up-to-date with commentary as new opinions are issued by the High Court.

Chapter Four

GOD, SHOW US THE WAY

Your word is a lamp for my feet and a light for my path.
Psalm 119:105

Is there a culture war raging in this country? A war between the principled and unprincipled? Right and wrong? Morality and relativism? Religion and atheism? Christianity and other faiths? Some might say there is a war and it pits Christianity against all of the above. Is there a war going on between religion and government? And, if so, is Christianity in the cross-hairs?

I imagine there are a few nuggets of truth in affirmative answers to each of these questions.

Most of us can likely agree there is a war being waged, atheists are not in the line of fire, and Christians are (or at least seem to be) the target.

If we Christians feel like our values are being attacked, what are our options? Not unlike Amanda and Charley, we can bemoan our circumstance, shake our heads sadly, and walk away. In other words, we can give up. Some of us surrender because we are apathetic or we just do not know what we can do to help.

Or, we can first arm ourselves with knowledge and, then, either defend the turf we still have or retake the hill.

Well, I am not a quitter and my moving parts are still working, so I am going for option two.

Many believe our own government to be our greatest enemy. If you are one of these, perhaps you should reserve judgment until you arrive at the end of this journey. Is it possible many of us have been waging the wrong battles?

We are going to explore how the Supreme Court has interpreted (or misinterpreted, as the case may be) the religion clauses of the First Amendment to the United States Constitution. Based upon what my ELL Constitution Club members tell me, I am betting most of you are going to be very surprised at what you find. It is not likely going to fit with what you have been told by the media. That might be a bit harsh. Perhaps it is more accurate to say it is not likely going to fit with the headlines you have read and the sound bites you have heard. Most of us do not get beyond the bare minimum when it comes to the news – there is so much of it. However, I know that you now want to learn the truth or you would not have come this far.

I say "interpreted or misinterpreted" because, unless and until we, once again, decide as a body of citizens to get behind the wheel and steer the ship, we have to live with the incorrect interpretations as well as the correct ones. For, you see, by definition, until altered by one or more means, the Supreme Court majority is always "right." That means we need to know when they are "wrong" even if they are "right"!?!?!?

We need to start with the religion clauses and then somehow climb over or break through the "wall of separation" you have no doubt run across in those headlines and sound bites. Or, maybe that is the wrong approach. Maybe, just maybe, we need to see it for what it is – not so much a "wall" as a "short fence," but definitely some form of partition.

I present to you the religion clauses of the First Amendment to the United States Constitution:

> Congress shall make no law respecting an establishment of religion, or prohibiting the free exercise thereof...

So as to be perfectly clear, then, there are two clauses in the Constitution dealing with the subject of religion. To paraphrase, we have –

The Establishment Clause:

Congress shall make no law respecting an establishment of religion.

AND

The Free Exercise Clause:

Congress shall make no law prohibiting the free exercise of religion.

Let us begin with some basic observations. The Constitution does not specifically address prayer. It does not tell us a thing about when we can pray, where we can pray, how we can pray, or, indeed, whether we can pray at all.

It does not speak of nativity scenes on courthouse lawns or the Ten Commandments of the Old Testament. It does not address atheism or any particular faith. It does not speak to any denomination, ministry, or cult. It does not define "establishment," "religion," or "free exercise."

Of course, our Constitution was never intended to answer all questions within its four corners. If it had been so intended, it would never have been ratified, for the Framers' descendants would still be negotiating its terms today in Philadelphia and if a conclusion was eventually reached, its pages would fill a library. Our Constitution sets the course and defines limits of power through the use of broad principles. It does not offer detailed recipes for the resolution of specific issues.

Our Constitution very definitely does not use the word "wall" or "separation," and, hold on to your seat, it does not, therefore, use the phrase "wall of separation." You probably knew that. You may also believe all of the hoopla over this metaphor actually matters.

"You, the People" can do this! You can accomplish anything you want to accomplish! If you believe this country and its original ideals are worth preserving, you *will* study this material. After all, New York farmers studied the highly intellectual Federalist Papers published in their newspapers prior to the ratification of the Constitution. The Constitution was never meant for lawyers' eyes only! As I say, you can do this.

Hoping I have you hooked by now, let us begin the journey and arm ourselves with the knowledge it will take to climb out of the pit of ignorance into the sunshine of knowledge and…

WIN THIS WAR!

Chapter Five

FREE EXERCISE

Preach the Gospel at all times and when necessary use words.
St. Francis of Assisi

The vast majority of the judicial decisions interpreting the religion clauses of the First Amendment deal with the establishment clause and that study will take us some considerable time to complete. However, first, we explore the body of free exercise decisions. Perhaps the paucity of cases interpreting this clause is a tribute to this freedom; in other words, the freedom to exercise one's religion must be very real if litigation in support of that freedom or challenging that freedom has been so relatively minimal.

Are we completely free to worship as we please? Yes, as a matter of conscience - no, as a matter of deed. It is important to understand the difference.

For emphasis, the First Amendment does not "grant" us any freedoms. Let's take a closer look at the "free exercise" clause:

Congress shall make no law
prohibiting the free exercise of religion.

Hmmm! Congress shall not prohibit this freedom, but where does it come from? Once more, for emphasis, you will not find it "granted" anywhere in the Constitution. The Framers had the notion that there are just some elements of the human condition that government has no authority over, at least in theory. These "freedoms" are broadly couched in terms of "unalienable rights" discussed in the Declaration of Independence. Where

27

do you think those who signed the Declaration thought these freedoms or rights come from? Take a look yourself:

> We hold these Truths to be self-evident, that all Men are created equal, that they are endowed by their **Creator** with certain unalienable Rights, that among these are Life, Liberty, and the Pursuit of Happiness...

> Declaration of Independence, second paragraph.

So, "life, liberty, and the pursuit of happiness" are "among" the "unalienable rights" – rights that belong to humankind that cannot be transferred. The rest of these rights are not mentioned specifically, but since they all emanate from a "Creator," clearly the freedom of religion would be included either as another right or at least within the subset of "life, liberty, and the pursuit of happiness."

Many believe that, historically, the United States Supreme Court has been hostile to religion. Perhaps we should keep score and re-evaluate that belief at the end of the journey.

My reference to The First Church of Non-Taxpayers, The Church of Wife Beaters Forever, and The Religion of Armed Robbers Today in chapter two vividly admonishes us that nothing in this temporal world is literally "free." If the freedom to exercise religion included the right to withhold taxes from government based upon the sincerely held belief that God forbids man to financially support a secular government, membership in the FCNT would likely include every citizen in the nation, and government would collapse. So, what is "religion" and just how "freely" may it be "exercised"?

There is one and only one way to confidently find answers to these questions. They can be found only within the four corners of the Supreme Court opinions that interpret the Constitution. You are about to begin that journey.

A few tips are provided. With few exceptions, the "style" or name of a case is always presented as you would see it on the official decision of the Supreme Court to impress upon you that, except as otherwise defined, what you are going to read are the actual words of the respective justices. I earlier criticized all of us for running on the watered-down fuel of headlines and sound bites. Even if we read every newspaper article and listen intently to radio and television, the Fourth Estate has failed us miserably. Media outlets that report fairly, ethically, and accurately are few and far between. That is why the actual words of the justices themselves are so very important. These decisions are our primary tool of learning in ELL and in this book. You can trust what you read in these decisions and, if you do not, go to the original opinion and verify. I rarely present lower court decisions because the Supreme Court is the final arbiter of these issues. It is what they determine that counts for the nation. I will use our first case "style" as an example to explain each line:

REYNOLDS v. UNITED STATES
SUPREME COURT OF THE UNITED STATES
98 U.S. 145
January 6, 1879
[9 – 0]

The first line names the parties to the case, the second line names the court, the third line provides the "citation" (technical location where you can find the original decision), the fourth line provides the date of the decision, and the fifth line provides the vote count. Because there were nine justices on the Court for every decision we explore, unless one or more of them did not take part in the decision, the score will always add to nine. They do not vote in a case if they have a conflict of interest or, on occasion, perhaps illness prevents them from voting. The number on the left represents the number of justices favoring the victorious position and the number on the right reflects the number of justices who disagreed with the majority outcome.

I can save you a great deal of time by summarizing some parts of a decision. So, if what you read is in [brackets], that represents my summary. Otherwise, what you read are the actual words of the Court. When there is something of particular importance to learn, my comments appear in a textbox. Occasionally, much of what the Court has to say is either redundant or irrelevant to the constitutional issues we are studying. Therefore, when you see an ellipsis (...), that means the intervening material has been excised from the presentation. And, finally, I sometimes provide **bold formatting** or underlining to emphasize something worth remembering.

Please note that in many instances, the Court provides a good bit of history. Often, it is provided to reveal the "original intent" of the Framers for the provision in the Constitution that is being interpreted.

For our first "free exercise" case, we go to Salt Lake City, Utah.

REYNOLDS v. UNITED STATES
SUPREME COURT OF THE UNITED STATES
98 U.S. 145
January 6, 1879
[9 – 0]

[George Reynolds was charged with the crime of bigamy (having two spouses at the same time) in the Territory of Utah. He was a member of the Church of Jesus Christ of Latter-Day Saints, commonly called the Mormon Church, and believed, in accord with their teaching of that era, that the duty to practice polygamy (having more than one spouse at the same time) was of divine origin and that the penalty for failure to do so was "damnation in the life to come." The Court had to determine whether the Utah Territory punishment of Reynolds for practicing bigamy was a violation of his freedom to exercise his religion.]

The word "religion" is not defined in the Constitution. We must go elsewhere, therefore, to ascertain its meaning, and nowhere more appropriately, we think, than to the history of the times in the midst of which the provision was adopted. **The precise point of the inquiry is, what is the religious freedom which has been guaranteed?**

> I cannot exaggerate how important it is to understand where we have been in order to understand where we are now. You will learn a great deal of our nation's history in these cases. The Court is about to describe the place of religion in our early years. Most of you have heard that one of the reasons our ancestors fled England was to escape religious persecution by the government-run Church of England. Some of this history, therefore, will likely be surprising.

Before the adoption of the Constitution, attempts were made in some of the colonies and States to legislate not only in respect to the establishment of religion, but in respect to its doctrines and precepts as well. The people were taxed, against their will, for the support of religion, and sometimes for the support of particular sects to whose tenets they could not and did not subscribe. Punishments were prescribed for a failure to attend upon public worship, and sometimes for entertaining heretical opinions. The controversy upon this general subject…seemed…to culminate in Virginia.

> The colonists fled from religious persecution in England and proceeded forthwith to set up their own respective brand of religious persecution in America! I guess it is the nature of human beings to test whether it's good to be king if the opportunity arises.

[In 1784, three years before the Constitution was sent to the states for ratification, the Virginia legislature was considering legislation that would tax the people to pay the salaries of teachers of the Christian religion. There was considerable opposition. As a response to this attempt, James Madison prepared a document he titled **"Memorial and Remonstrance"** that presented the argument against public funding of religious education.]

> I will be referring to the "Memorial and Remonstrance" from time to time. You can find it in its entirety in the Appendix.

Madison demonstrated "that religion, or the duty we owe the Creator," was not within the cognizance of civil government. [Not only was the bill defeated, but a bill drafted by Thomas Jefferson for establishing religious freedom passed.]

In the preamble of [Jefferson's bill]...religious freedom is defined; and after a recital "that to suffer the civil magistrate to intrude his powers into a field of opinion, and to restrain the profession or propagation of principles on supposition of their ill tendency, is a dangerous fallacy which at once destroys all religious liberty," it was declared "that it is time enough for the rightful purposes of civil government for its officers to interfere when principles break out into overt acts against peace and good order." **In these two sentences is found the true distinction between what properly belongs to the church and what to the State.**

> Translation: Government has no right to affect religious thought and can only impose its will when religious principles result in actions that disrupt peace and good order.

In a little more than a year after the passage of this [Virginia] statute the convention met which prepared the Constitution of the United States. **Of this convention Mr. Jefferson was not a member, he being then absent as minister to France.** As soon as he saw the draft of the Constitution proposed for adoption, he...expressed his disappointment at the absence of an express declaration insuring the freedom of religion..., but was willing to accept it as it was, trusting that the good sense and honest intentions of the people would bring about the necessary alterations...

> Jefferson was disappointed that the original Constitution did not include the promise of religious freedom. Of course, that promise came in the First Amendment of the then soon-to-be-ratified Bill of Rights. One often reads where Jefferson was not a religious man. Really?

[After the Bill of Rights was adopted], in reply to an address to him by a committee of the Danbury Baptist Association...[Mr. Jefferson] took occasion to say:

> Believing with you that religion is a matter which lies solely between man and his god; that he owes account to none other for his faith or his worship; that the legislative powers of the government reach <u>actions only</u>, and <u>not opinions</u>, - I contemplate with sovereign reverence that act of the whole American people which declared that their legislature should "<u>make no law respecting an establishment of religion or prohibiting the free exercise thereof</u>," <u>thus building a wall of separation between church and state</u>. Adhering to this expression of the supreme will of the nation in behalf of the rights of conscience, I shall see with sincere satisfaction the progress of those sentiments which tend to restore man to all his natural rights, convinced he has no natural right in opposition to his social duties.

Jefferson first used the phrase "wall of separation" in this letter. Because the "wall of separation" deals more with the concept of an "establishment of religion" and not so much the concept of the "free exercise of religion," we will get to it in later cases.

Coming as this does from an acknowledged leader of the advocates of the measure, it may be accepted almost as an authoritative declaration of the scope and effect of the amendment thus secured. **Congress was deprived of all legislative power over mere <u>opinion</u>, but was left free to reach <u>actions</u> which were in violation of <u>social duties or subversive to good order</u>.**

Because Jefferson was a powerful influence over the drafting of the "free exercise" clause, his words that define its terms can be relied upon as a fair indication of the overall intent of those that adopted the Bill of Rights. So, it is clear that if one truly believes that paying taxes to government is a sin, he is free to have that belief, but the failure to pony up would bring consequences for violating his social duty. Now, the Court is going to explore whether or not the act of polygamy (bigamy) is "subversive of good order."

[The Court notes that polygamy was practiced almost exclusively in Asia and Africa and that from the earliest history of England, a second marriage was always void and was treated as an offense against society. In fact, in early England, as well as in many of the American colonies, the penalty was death. **Significantly, after the Constitution was ratified, Virginia adopted the <u>death penalty</u> for polygamy.**]

```
╔══════════════════════════════════════════════════════╗
║                                                      ║
║                     Surprised?                       ║
║                                                      ║
╚══════════════════════════════════════════════════════╝
```

...From that day to this we think it may safely be said there never has been a time in any State of the Union when polygamy has not been an offense against society...In the face of all this evidence, it is impossible to believe that the constitutional guaranty of religious freedom was intended to prohibit legislation in respect to this most important feature of social life. Marriage, while from its very nature a sacred obligation, is nevertheless, in most civilized nations, a civil contract, and usually regulated by law. Upon it society may be said to be built, and out of its fruits spring social relations and social obligations and duties, with which government is necessarily required to deal...Professor Lieber says, polygamy leads to the patriarchal principle, and which, when applied to large communities, fetters the people in stationary despotism, while that principle cannot long exist in connection with monogamy...An exceptional colony of polygamists under an exceptional leadership may sometimes exist for a time without appearing to disturb the social condition of the people who surround it; but, there cannot be a doubt that, unless restricted by some form of constitution, it is within the legitimate scope of the power of every civil government to determine whether polygamy or monogamy shall be the law of social life under its dominion.

In our opinion, the statute immediately under consideration is... constitutional and valid...The only question which remains is whether those who make polygamy a part of their religion are excepted from the operation of the statute. If they are, then those who do not make polygamy a part of their religious belief may be found guilty and punished, while those who do, must be acquitted and go free. This would be introducing a new element into criminal law. Laws are made for the government of actions, and while they cannot interfere with mere religious belief and opinions, they may with practices. Suppose one believed that human sacrifices were a necessary part of the religious worship, would it be seriously contended that the civil government under which he lived could not interfere to prevent a sacrifice?...

Can a man excuse his practices to the contrary because of his religious belief? To permit this would be to make the professed doctrines of religious belief superior to the law of the land, and in effect to permit every citizen to become a law unto himself. Government could exist only in name under such circumstances...When the offense consists of a positive act which is knowingly done, it would be dangerous to hold that the offender might escape punishment because he religiously believed the law which he had broken ought never to have been made. No case...can be found that has gone that far. [The conviction stands.]

At the outset, the *Reynolds* Court defined the "precise" inquiry as a search to determine what religious freedom had been guaranteed and said they must go elsewhere for the definition of religion because it was not defined in the Constitution.

In truth, the Court never does define "religion" in the decision, does it? It does not even search for a definition. And, contrary to providing answers to the meaning of "religious freedom," it is far more accurate to say that this Court, at most, told us what "religious freedom" is not; i.e., it does not include the freedom to practice polygamy.

In time, we will see that the *Reynolds* Court was wrong to suggest it would be a mockery to permit a religious belief to trump a criminal statute. However, after all, this 1879 case was the very first one to explore the meaning of the free exercise clause.

This is a good place to take a look at common sense. If a criminal statute is to be considered constitutional merely because Congress passed it, then Congress could pass anything and, by definition, it would always prevail over a conflicting religious activity. This, of course, cannot be. So, understand that there are two ways in which a criminal statute may not be the end-all be-all of the question.

First, the statute itself could exceed constitutional boundaries. Although you will see plenty of real life extremes in the cases to come, I like to use extreme hypotheticals to make a point. Suppose, for example, that a legislative body made it a crime to own a Bible. This would be a clear example of an unconstitutional criminal statute, it would be struck down and a conviction of the persons challenging the statute would be reversed.

Second, the statute itself may well be constitutional, but an exception is made for those persons whose religious actions are protected by the exercise of religious freedom as defined by the Court. For example, those who prove their "conscientious objection" to war is based on their sincerely held religious beliefs may legally avoid induction into the military. Conscription is constitutional, but as applied in certain situations, imposing criminal sanctions would be unconstitutional.

The question for the judiciary in these types of cases does not normally center upon whether a criminal statute has been violated. It likely has or the case would not be before the Court. Rather, it is whether the criminal law itself is constitutional or whether the religious act should be protected by the First Amendment's promise of "free exercise" in spite of the violation of an otherwise constitutionally sound statute. In other words, if the statute itself is valid, the next question to be answered is whether the religious act violates social duties or is subversive of good order. If it does neither, one presumes that in spite of its violation of a criminal statute, the religious act would be constitutionally protected from punishment by government.

What does this first test of the free exercise clause tell us? Well, although the limits of this freedom will have to be defined through the years on a case-by-case basis, at this early stage we know that the Court did not protect polygamy as a religious exercise.

However, does the *Reynolds* Court ever really explain how polygamy violates social duty or how it is subversive of good order? Please understand that I do not address abuse of minor girls or women when I address the broader question and all would agree with punishing those actions. I am speaking only to the practice of polygamy. And, while I am a Christian who believes a marriage should be between one man and one woman, **our Constitution was never meant to preserve freedom for just one sect of Christianity or for just Christianity itself.** Some Christians believe that only Christianity was meant to enjoy the "free exercise of religion" and, therefore, that government is entitled to favor Christianity over other faiths – even to the point of not recognizing the freedom of other faiths to exercise their particular brand of religion. That version of America would invite the type of bloodshed too well known by the citizens of Northern Ireland. Believe me, it is not a place we want to go.

Those that drafted the Bill of Rights did not use the word "sect" or "denomination" or "Christianity." They used the word "religion." What did they mean by the free exercise of "religion"? Did they mean only Christians were to enjoy this freedom? I believe the most likely answer is that the freedom to exercise one's religion belongs to all who profess a belief in a higher being – **any** higher being. Before I tell you why I believe that, take a look at some of James Madison's notes from the Virginia Convention of 1788:

> [Freedom of religion] arises from that multiplicity of sects, which pervades America, and which is the best and only security for religious liberty in any society. For where there is such a variety of sects, there cannot be a majority of any one sect to oppress and persecute the rest. Fortunately for this commonwealth, a majority of the people are decidedly against any exclusive establishment – I believe it to be so in other states. There is not a shadow of right in the general government to intermeddle with religion. Its least interference with it, would be a most flagrant usurpation. I can appeal to my uniform conduct on this subject, that I have warmly supported religious freedom…The United States abound in such a variety of sects, that it is a strong security against religious persecution, and it is sufficient to authorize a conclusion, that no one sect will ever be able to outnumber or depress the rest.

James Madison was most responsible for drafting the Constitution proper and George Mason was his counterpart for the Bill of Rights (the first ten amendments). It seems rather clear to me that if Madison or Mason had intended this freedom only for Christians, the First Amendment would have made it clear that only Christians had the right to free exercise. They would have used "sect" or "Christian sect," not "religion" as the subject matter of the stated freedom. In addition, Madison's notes, above, do not ring true for any other intent. There were approximately 2,000 Jews in the colonies and many of them fought in the Revolutionary War. I cannot imagine Madison, Jefferson, and Mason did not believe Jews were entitled to their own religious freedom and I cannot imagine the representatives of Christianity today to be so arrogant as to suggest that no other faith can participate.

Lastly, as we have already discovered, the First Amendment does not grant this freedom; it only protects it from government intrusion. The freedom to exercise one's religion is one of those unalienable rights of which all men are endowed by their Creator. Not their Creator as in the God of Abraham, but their Creator as in "a" supreme being. And, when it came to religion, I do not believe for a moment that Jefferson, author of the Declaration of Independence, defined "all men" as only "all Christian men."

It is also clear that our nation was founded upon Christian principles. Indeed, we are an unofficial Christian nation. We are not "officially Christian" for the very same reason our ancestors left England. I would think that should be clear. The reason why Christianity has fared well in America is the same reason why all religions have fared well in America.

The constitutional test is not whether polygamy violates the tenets of Christianity. Rather, the test, as we discussed, is whether having more than one wife violates a social duty or is subversive of good order. I am betting this issue will be addressed again by the High Court someday and, when it is, social duty and good order, as these standards relate to polygamy, will be explored in much greater detail before a decision is rendered.

Let's take a look at our "Religious Clause Scoreboard." Mainstream Christians would look upon this result as favoring the principles of Christianity. However, we are scoring victories for or against religion in general; therefore, since the Mormons lost, our scoreboard stands as follows:

First Amendment Scoreboard

Rulings "for" Religion: 0 --- Rulings "against" Religion: 1

Oddly enough, one of the most important cases favoring religion does not specifically discuss the religion clauses at all. Today, many Christians homeschool their children. Those of you who do will be thankful for the outcome of this next case from the state of Oregon.

PIERCE v. SOCIETY OF SISTERS
SUPREME COURT OF THE UNITED STATES
268 U.S. 510
June 1, 1925
[9 – 0]

[An Oregon statute not only compelled education for children, but also required every parent to send their child to a **public** school. Enforcing the statute would destroy the Catholic schools, other private religious schools and private military schools.]

[The Court held this statute to be unconstitutional.] The Act unreasonably interferes with the liberty of parents to direct the upbringing and education of children under their control. Rights guaranteed by the Constitution may not be abridged by legislation which has no reasonable relation to some purpose within the competency of the State. The fundamental theory of liberty excludes any general power of the State to standardize its children by forcing them to accept instruction from public teachers only. The child is not the mere creature of the State; those who nurture him and direct his destiny have the right, coupled with the high duty, to recognize and prepare him for additional obligations.

The year was 1925, a time when the Supreme Court unanimously fostered "the liberty of parents to direct the upbringing and education of children under their control." Let me repeat that. This case is living proof that the highest court in the land at one time supported the role of parents as the predominant authority in the raising of their own children. That conclusion sounds so obvious that it should not need saying. Is it still true today? You would need to join one of our ELL Constitution Clubs to find out whether the majority of the Supreme Court honors the views of parents at all when it comes to the abortion of their minor daughter's child.

Getting back to the religion clauses, the National Household Education Surveys Program, conducted by the U.S. Department of Education's National Center for Education Statistics in 2007, found that the top three reasons why parents homeschool are they want to provide religious or moral instruction, they are concerned about the environment of public schools (safety, drugs, peer pressure), and they are dissatisfied with academic instruction in public schools. As I say, even though the Court does not specifically address the free exercise of religion in *Pierce*, I think all would agree we should chalk this one up "for" religion.

First Amendment Scoreboard

Rulings "for" Religion: 1 --- Rulings "against" Religion: 1

We should thank the Jehovah's Witnesses. They have fought and won many victories for religion. This next case out of New Haven, Connecticut, is a good example.

CANTWELL v. CONNECTICUT
SUPREME COURT OF THE UNITED STATES
310 U.S. 296
May 20, 1940
[9 – 0]

[Newton Cantwell and his two sons, Jesse and Russell, members of a group known as Jehovah's Witnesses and claiming to be ordained ministers, were arrested in New Haven, Connecticut, and each was charged with crimes.]

On the day of their arrest the Cantwells were…going…from house to house on Cassius Street…with a bag containing books and pamphlets on religious subjects, a portable phonograph and a set of records, each of which, when played, introduced, and was a description of, one of the books. [The Cantwells] asked the persons who responded to their call for permission to play one of the records. If permission was granted [they] asked the person to buy the book described and, upon refusal, [they] solicited such contribution towards the publication of the pamphlets as the listener was willing to make. If a contribution was received, a pamphlet was delivered upon condition that it would be read…

[Jesse Cantwell stopped two men in the street, asked, and received, permission to play a phonograph record, and played the record "Enemies," which attacked the Catholic religion. Both were incensed by the contents of the record and were tempted to strike Cantwell unless he went away. On being told to be on his way he left their presence. There was no evidence that he was personally offensive or entered into any argument with those he interviewed.]

[All were charged with violating a statute that provides:]

> No person shall solicit money…for any alleged religious, charitable or philanthropic cause…unless such cause shall have been approved by the secretary of the public welfare council. Upon application of any person in behalf of such cause, the secretary shall determine whether such cause is a religious one or is a bona fide object of charity or philanthropy and conforms to reasonable standards of efficiency and integrity…

…The State Supreme Court…declared the legislation constitutional as an effort by the State to protect the public against fraud…

We hold that the statute…deprives the Cantwells of their liberty without due process of law in contravention of the Fourteenth Amendment. The fundamental concept of liberty embodied in that Amendment embraces the liberties guaranteed by the First Amendment.

> Please note that the First Amendment forbids **Congress** from making a law prohibiting the free exercise of religion. But, these folks were charged with violations of state statutes, not federal laws. What gives?

The First Amendment declares that Congress shall make no law... prohibiting the free exercise [of religion.] The Fourteenth Amendment has rendered the legislatures of the states as incompetent as Congress to enact such laws...

> *Cantwell* is the first case to hold that the "free exercise clause" of the First Amendment, applicable to Congress, also applies to the states and other governmental bodies through the "incorporation" of the First & Fourteenth Amendments. That can be a difficult concept. Just know that the effect of incorporation is to make all levels of government subject to the same limitations the First Amendment imposes upon Congress.

The First Amendment embraces two concepts: freedom to believe and freedom to act. The first is absolute but, in the nature of things, the second cannot be. Conduct remains subject to regulation for the protection of society...[But, the power to regulate must not unduly infringe upon the protected freedom.] No one would contest the proposition that a State may not, by statute, wholly deny the right to preach or to disseminate religious views. Plainly such a previous and absolute restraint would violate the terms of the guarantee [of religious freedom.] It is equally clear that a State may by general and non-discriminatory legislation regulate the times, the places, and the manner of soliciting upon its streets, and of holding meetings thereon; and may in other respects safeguard the peace, good order and comfort of the community, without unconstitutionally invading the liberties protected by the [First Amendment].

> In other words, religious freedom does not give a minister the right to preach over a loudspeaker at 3:00 a.m. on a public residential street.

The Cantwells are right in their insistence that the Act in question is not [a proper regulation]…[and] urge that to require them to obtain a certificate as a condition of soliciting support for their views amounts to a prior restraint on the exercise of their religion within the meaning of the Constitution. The State insists that the Act… merely safeguards against the perpetration of frauds under the cloak of religion. Conceding that this is so, the question remains whether the method adopted by Connecticut to that end transgresses the liberty safeguarded by the Constitution.

The general regulation, in the public interest, of solicitation, which does not involve any religious test and does not unreasonably obstruct or delay the collection of funds, is not open to any constitutional objection, even though the collection be for a religious purpose. Such regulation would not constitute a prohibited previous restraint on the free exercise of religion or interpose an inadmissible obstacle to its exercise.

It will be noted, however, that the Act requires an application to the secretary of the public welfare council of the State; that he is empowered to determine whether the cause is a religious one, and that the issue of a certificate depends upon his affirmative action. If he finds that the cause is not that of religion, to solicit for it becomes a crime…His decision… involves appraisal of facts, the exercise of judgment, and the formation of an opinion…Such a censorship of religion as the means of determining its right to survive is a denial of liberty protected by the First Amendment…

Nothing we have said is intended even remotely to imply that, under the cloak of religion, persons may, with impunity, commit frauds upon the public. Certainly penal laws are available to punish such conduct. Even the exercise of religion may be at some slight inconvenience in order that the State may protect its citizens from injury. Without doubt a State may protect its citizens from fraudulent solicitation by requiring a stranger in the community, before permitting him publicly to solicit funds for any purpose, to establish his identity and his authority to act for the cause which he purports to represent. The State is likewise free to regulate the time and manner of solicitation generally, in the interest of public safety, peace, comfort or convenience. But to condition the solicitation of aid for the perpetuation of religious views or systems upon a license, the grant of which rests in the exercise of a determination by state authority as to what is a religious cause, is to lay a forbidden burden upon the exercise of liberty protected by the Constitution.

> The problem here is not a requirement of registering before soliciting. It is the fact that government is requiring a religious registrant to first pass government's test of what government determines is a valid religion. This test, says the Court, is an invalid burden on religious freedom.

[Jesse Cantwell was also charged with inciting a breach of the peace.]

...The State of Connecticut has an obvious interest in the preservation and protection of peace and good order within her borders. We must determine whether the alleged protection of the State's interest...has been pressed to a point where it has come into fatal collision with the overriding interest protected by the Constitution...

The offense known as breach of the peace embraces a great variety of conduct destroying or menacing public order and tranquility. It includes not only violent acts but acts and words likely to produce violence in others. No one would have the hardihood to suggest that the principle of freedom of speech sanctions incitement to riot or that religious liberty connotes the privilege to exhort others to physical attack upon those belonging to another sect. When clear and present danger of riot, disorder, interference with traffic upon the public streets, or other immediate threat to public safety, peace, or order, appears, the power of the State to prevent or punish is obvious. Equally obvious is it that a State may not unduly suppress free communication of views, religious or other, under the guise of conserving desirable conditions. Here we have a situation analogous to a conviction under a statute sweeping in a great variety of conduct under a general and indefinite characterization, and leaving to the executive and judicial branches too wide a discretion in its application...

We note that Jesse Cantwell, on April 26, 1938, was upon a public street, where he had a right to be, and where he had a right peacefully to impart his views to others. There is no showing that his deportment was noisy, truculent, overbearing or offensive. He requested of two pedestrians permission to play to them a phonograph record. The permission was granted. It is not claimed that he intended to insult or affront the hearers by playing the record. It is plain that he wished only to interest them in his propaganda. The sound of the phonograph is not shown to have disturbed residents of the street, to have drawn a crowd, or to have impeded traffic. Thus far he had invaded no right or interest of the public or of the men accosted.

The record played by Cantwell embodies a general attack on all organized religious systems as instruments of Satan and injurious to man; it then singles out the Roman Catholic Church for strictures couched in terms which naturally would offend not only persons of that persuasion, but all others who respect the honestly held religious faith of their fellows. The hearers were in fact highly offended. One of them said he felt like hitting Cantwell and the other that he was tempted to throw Cantwell off the street. The one who testified he felt like hitting Cantwell said (in answer to the question, "Did you do anything else or have any other reaction?"): "No, sir, because he said he would take the Victrola and he went." The other witnesses testified that he told Cantwell he had better get off the street before something happened to him and that was the end of the matter as Cantwell picked up his books and walked up the street.

Cantwell's conduct...did not amount to a breach of the peace...We find...no assault or threatening of bodily harm, no truculent bearing, no intentional discourtesy, no personal abuse. On the contrary, we find only an effort to persuade a willing listener to buy a book or to contribute money in the interest of what Cantwell, however misguided others may think him, conceived to be true religion.

In the realm of religious faith, and in that of political belief, sharp differences arise. In both fields the tenets of one man may seem the rankest error to his neighbor. To persuade others to his own point of view, the pleader, as we know, at times, resorts to exaggeration, to vilification of men who have been, or are, prominent in church or state,

45

and even to false statement. But the people of this nation have ordained in the light of history, that, in spite of the probability of excesses and abuses, these liberties are, in the long view, essential to enlightened opinion and right conduct on the part of the citizens of a democracy. The essential characteristics of these liberties is, that under their shield many types of life, character, opinion and belief can develop unmolested and unobstructed. Nowhere is this shield more necessary than in our own country for a people composed of many races and of many creeds. There are limits to the exercise of these liberties. The danger in these times from the coercive activities of those who in the delusion of racial or religious conceit would incite violence and breaches of the peace in order to deprive others of their equal right to the exercise of their liberties, is emphasized by events familiar to all. These and other transgressions of those limits the States appropriately may punish…Cantwell's communication, considered in the light of the constitutional guarantees, raised no such clear and present menace to public peace and order as to render him liable to conviction of the common law offense in question. The judgment affirming the convictions…is reversed.

> The power to regulate religion may not unduly infringe the protected freedom. A State may by general and non-discriminatory legislation regulate the times, places, and manner of soliciting upon its streets and may safeguard peace, good order, and comfort of the community. A State may combat fraudulent solicitation by requiring a stranger to establish his identity and authority to act for his cause before soliciting. But, to condition solicitation for the perpetuation of religious views upon a license, the grant of which rests in the exercise of a determination by state authority as to what is a religious cause, is to lay a forbidden burden upon the exercise of liberty protected by the Constitution.

Chalk another one up "for" religion.

```
┌──────────────────────────────────────────────────────────┐
│  ┌────────────────────────────────────────────────────┐  │
│  │              First Amendment Scoreboard             │  │
│  │  Rulings "for" Religion: 2 --- Rulings "against" Religion: 1  │  │
│  └────────────────────────────────────────────────────┘  │
└──────────────────────────────────────────────────────────┘
```

The Jehovah's Witnesses will not yield to a government that oversteps its bounds. Let's go to Struthers, Ohio, and Jeannette, Pennsylvania.

In *Martin v. City of Struthers* (1943), [a city ordinance prohibited any person to knock on doors, ring doorbells, or otherwise summon occupants of any residence for the purpose of distributing handbills or circulars. Martin was convicted of violating the ordinance, but the Supreme Court reversed his conviction, finding the ordinance unconstitutional as applied to a person distributing advertisements of a religious meeting.] No one supposes a city need permit a man with a communicable disease to distribute leaflets to homes or that the First Amendment prohibits a state from preventing distribution of leaflets in a church against the will of the church authorities. We are faced here with the necessity of weighing the conflicting interests of the right of Martin as well as the right of the householder to determine whether [the householder is willing to receive the message] against the interest of the community to protect the interests of all of its citizens, whether particular citizens want that protection or not. The ordinance subjects the messenger to criminal punishment for annoying the person he calls, whether or not the recipient is glad to receive it. The ordinance seeks to prohibit the dissemination of knowledge.

In *Murdock v. Pennsylvania* (1943), [an ordinance required persons soliciting for merchandise of any kind to purchase a license to do so for a set fee per day. Jehovah's Witnesses contended the ordinance deprived them of freedom of speech, press, and religion.] <u>Freedom of speech, freedom of the press, freedom of religion are available to all, not merely to those who can pay their own way</u>. It is one thing to impose a tax on the income or property of a preacher. It is quite another thing to exact a tax from him for the privilege of delivering a sermon. The power to tax the exercise of a privilege is the power to control or suppress its enjoyment. Considerable emphasis is placed on the kind of literature which petitioners were distributing – its provocative, abusive, and ill-mannered character and the assault which it makes on our established churches and the cherished faiths of many of us. But those considerations are no justification for the license tax which the ordinance imposes. Plainly a community may not suppress, or the state tax, the dissemination of views because they are unpopular, annoying or distasteful. If that device were ever sanctioned, there would have been forged a ready instrument for the suppression of the faith which any minority cherishes but which does not happen to be in favor. That would be a complete repudiation of the philosophy of the Bill of Rights.

Preachers do not have to purchase the right to preach in America. It is free. Even if you do not support the views of Jehovah's Witnesses, their victory serves to preserve your rights, as well as theirs. Religion is not doing too bad thus far, is it? Score another two "for" religion.

> ### First Amendment Scoreboard
> Rulings "for" Religion: 4 --- Rulings "against" Religion: 1

This next case is one of my favorites. You already know the outcome. I alluded to it in the Preface. This is the case where the Jehovah's Witnesses won the right "not" to salute our flag, not out of any disrespect for our country, but based upon their Biblical understanding that doing so is the worship of a graven image and, hence, a sin. If that were all this case teaches, we could move on. However, this case has an abundance of lessons important to a sound understanding of our country. In this decision, the court overrules a case that had been decided only three years prior in *Minersville School District v. Gobitis*, where the Court upheld a Pennsylvania statute that permitted children who refused to salute the flag to be expelled from public school and allowed fines and jail sentences to be imposed upon their parents.

WEST VIRGINIA BOARD OF EDUCATION v. BARNETTE
SUPREME COURT OF THE UNITED STATES
319 U.S. 624
June 14, 1943
[6 – 3]

OPINION: Justice Jackson…Following the decision by this Court on June 3, 1940, in *Minersville School District v. Gobitis*, the West Virginia legislature amended its statutes to require all schools therein to conduct courses of instruction in history, civics, and in the constitutions of the United States and of the state "for the purpose of teaching, fostering and perpetuating the ideals, principles and spirit of Americanism, and increasing the knowledge of the organization and machinery of the government."

> So far, this sounds like a great way to attain national unity, right?

…[The Board of Education adopted a resolution based upon the *Gobitis* opinion ordering that all teachers and pupils shall be required to salute the flag. Refusal to do so was to be regarded as an act of insubordination subjecting the kids to expulsion. An expelled child was to be considered unlawfully absent and, therefore, a delinquent, subjecting parents to prosecution, fines and jail.] Objections to the salute as "being too much like Hitler's" were raised by the PTA, the Boy and Girl Scouts, the Red Cross, and the Federation of Women's Clubs…What is now required is the "stiff-arm" salute, the saluter to keep the right hand raised with palm turned up while the following is repeated: "I pledge allegiance to the Flag of the United States of America and to the Republic for which it stands; one nation, indivisible, with liberty and justice for all."

Can it be that young children in America (the home of the free) who are compelled to go to public school if they cannot afford private education are not only expelled for insubordination if they fervently believe it is sacrilegious to "worship a graven image by saluting it," but, in addition, their parents are jailed and fined unless and until their children succumb? Is this Norman Rockwell's America? I certainly believe in instilling patriotism and respect for the flag in our children, but there are limits. For those of you who dislike this outcome, but have never read it, I am betting the following will give you pause for reflection and, perhaps, reconsideration. As an aside, the phrase "under God" was not added until 1954.

Appellees…brought suit…asking for an injunction to restrain enforcement of these laws and regulations against Jehovah's Witnesses. The Witnesses… teach that the obligation imposed by law of God is superior to that of laws enacted by temporal government. Their religious beliefs include a literal version of Exodus, chapter 20, verses 4 and 5…:

> **Thou shalt not make unto thee any graven image…; thou shalt not bow down thyself to them nor serve them.**

This is the King James Version, not the New Living Translation published by Tyndale House Publishers, Inc. It is a direct quote from the Supreme Court opinion.

They consider that the flag is an "image" within this command. For this reason they refuse to salute it. Children of this faith have been expelled from school and are threatened with exclusion for no other cause. Officials threaten to send them to reformatories maintained for criminally inclined juveniles. Parents of such children have been prosecuted and are threatened with prosecutions for causing delinquency…

Do such laws have a chance of serving their purpose? Do they make children feel more (or less) likely to love their country?

The refusal of these persons to participate in the ceremony does not interfere with or deny rights of others to do so. Nor is there any question in this case that their behavior is peaceable and orderly. The sole conflict is between authority and rights of the individual. The State asserts power to condition access to public education on making a prescribed sign and profession and at the same time to coerce attendance by punishing both parent and child...

As the present Chief Justice said in dissent in the *Gobitis* case, the State may "require teaching by instruction and study of all in our history and in the structure and organization of our government, including the guaranties of civil liberty, which tend to inspire patriotism and love of country." **Here, however, we are dealing with a compulsion of students to declare a belief...**

Symbolism is a primitive but effective way of communicating ideas. The use of an emblem or flag to symbolize some system, idea, institution, or personality, is a short cut from mind to mind. Causes and nations, political parties, lodges and ecclesiastical groups seek to knit the loyalty of their followings to a flag or banner, a color or design. The State announces rank, function, and authority through crowns and maces, uniforms and black robes; the church speaks through the Cross, the Crucifix, the altar and shrine, and clerical raiment. Symbols of State often convey political ideas just as religious symbols come to convey theological ones. Associated with many of these symbols are appropriate gestures of acceptance or respect: a salute, a bowed or bared head, a bended knee. A person gets from a symbol the meaning he puts into it, and what is one man's comfort and inspiration is another's jest and scorn...

Censorship or suppression of expression of opinion is tolerated by our Constitution only when the expression presents a **clear and present danger** of action of a kind the State is empowered to prevent and punish... But here the power of compulsion is invoked without any allegation that remaining passive during a flag salute ritual creates a clear and present danger that would justify an effort even to muffle expression. **To sustain the compulsory flag salute we are required to say that a Bill of Rights which guards the individual's right to speak his own mind, left it**

open to public authorities to compel him to utter what is not in his mind…

The question which underlies the flag salute controversy is whether such a ceremony so touching matters of opinion and political attitude may be imposed upon the individual by official authority under powers committed to any political organization under our Constitution. We examine rather than assume existence of this power and, against this broader definition of issues in this case, re-examine specific grounds assigned for the *Gobitis* decision.

1st It was said [in *Gobitis*] that the flag-salute controversy confronted the Court with "the problem which Lincoln cast in memorable dilemma: 'Must a government of necessity be too strong for the liberties of its people, or too weak to maintain its own existence?'" and that the answer must be in favor of strength.

…It may be doubted whether Mr. Lincoln would have thought that the strength of government to maintain itself would be impressively vindicated by our confirming power of the State to expel a handful of children from school…If validly applied to this problem, the utterance cited would resolve every issue of power in favor of those in authority and would require us to override every liberty thought to weaken or delay execution of their policies…

To enforce [these] rights today is not to choose weak government over strong government. It is only to adhere as a means of strength to individual freedom of mind in preference to officially disciplined uniformity for which history indicates a disappointing and disastrous end…

2nd It was also considered in the *Gobitis* case that functions of educational officers in States, counties and school districts were such that to interfere with their authority "would in effect make us the school board for the country."

The Fourteenth Amendment, as now applied to the States, protects the citizen against the State itself and all of its creatures – Boards of Education not excepted…

3rd The *Gobitis* opinion reasoned that this is a field "where courts possess no marked and certainly no controlling competence," that it is committed to the legislatures as well as the courts to guard cherished liberties and that it is constitutionally appropriate to "fight out the wise use of legislative authority in the forum of public opinion and before legislative assemblies rather than to transfer such a contest to the judicial arena," since all the "effective means of inducing political changes are left free."

The very purpose of a Bill of Rights was to withdraw certain subjects from the [winds] of political controversy, to place them beyond the reach of majorities and officials and to establish them as legal principles to be applied by the courts. **One's right to life, liberty, and property, to free speech, a free press, freedom of worship and assembly, and other fundamental rights may not be submitted to a vote; they depend on the outcome of no elections...**

> That is one of my favorite quotes. In America, unalienable rights and freedoms guaranteed by the Constitution do not depend upon who is in power or how a vote is cast. They are not within the power of humans to diminish. This was the plan of the Framers.

The task of translating the majestic generalities of the Bill of Rights...into concrete restraints on officials dealing with the problems of the twentieth century is [difficult]. **These principles grew in soil which also produced a philosophy that the individual was the center of society, that his liberty was attainable through mere absence of governmental restraints, and that government should be entrusted with few controls and only the mildest supervision over men's affairs...We cannot, because of modest estimates of our competence in such specialties as public education, withhold the judgment that history authenticates as the function of this Court when liberty is infringed.**

4th Lastly,...*Gobitis*...reasons that "National unity is the basis of national security," that the authorities have "the right to select appropriate means for its attainment," and hence reaches the conclusion that such compulsory measures toward "national unity" are constitutional. Upon the verity of this assumption depends our answer in this case.

National unity as an end which officials may foster by persuasion and example is not in question. The problem is whether under our Constitution compulsion as here employed is a permissible means for its achievement…

As governmental pressure toward unity becomes greater, so strife becomes more bitter as to whose unity it shall be…Ultimate futility of such attempts to compel coherence is the lesson of every such effort from the Roman drive to stamp out Christianity as a disturber of its pagan unity, the Inquisition, as a means to religious and dynastic unity, the Siberian exiles as a means to Russian unity, down to the fast failing efforts of our present totalitarian enemies.

Those who begin coercive elimination of dissent soon find themselves exterminating dissenters. Compulsory unification of opinion achieves only the unanimity of the graveyard…We set up government by consent of the governed, and the Bill of Rights denies those in power any legal opportunity to coerce that consent. Authority here is to be controlled by public opinion, not public opinion by authority.

The pen is, indeed, mightier than the sword!

The case is made difficult not because the principles of its decision are obscure but because the flag involved is our own. Nevertheless, we apply the limitations of the Constitution with no fear that freedom to be intellectually and spiritually diverse or even contrary will disintegrate the social organization. To believe that patriotism will not flourish if patriotic ceremonies are voluntary and spontaneous instead of a compulsory routine is to make an unflattering estimate of the appeal of our institutions to free minds…

If there is any fixed star in our constitutional constellation, it is that no official, high or petty, can prescribe what shall be orthodox in politics, nationalism, religion, or other matters of opinion or force citizens to confess by word or act their faith therein...We think the action of the local authorities in compelling the flag salute and pledge transcends constitutional limitations on their power and invades the sphere of intellect and spirit which it is the purpose of the First Amendment to our Constitution to reserve from all official control. [The decision of this Court in *Minersville School District v. Gobitis* is overruled.]

CONCURRENCE: Justice Black...

> This is a "concurring opinion." In a concurrence, the justice or justices who go along with it agree with the outcome of the majority, but either base their agreement on different reasoning than the majority opinion or simply wish to add their own words of wisdom.

Words uttered under coercion are proof of loyalty to nothing but self-interest. Love of country must spring from willing hearts and free minds, inspired by a fair administration of wise laws enacted by the people's elected representatives within the bounds of express constitutional prohibitions. These laws must, to be consistent with the First Amendment, permit the widest toleration of conflicting viewpoints consistent with a society of free men. Neither our domestic tranquility in peace nor our martial effort in war depend on compelling little children to participate in a ceremony which ends in nothing for them but a fear of spiritual condemnation...The ceremonial, when enforced against conscientious objectors, more likely to defeat than to serve its high purpose, is a handy implement for disguised religious persecution and is inconsistent with our Constitution's plan and purpose.

CONCURRENCE: Justice Murphy...Emotion aroused by the flag as a symbol for which we have fought and are now fighting again [is understandable]. But there is before us the right of freedom to believe, freedom to worship one's Maker according to the dictates of one's conscience, a right which the Constitution specifically shelters. Reflection has convinced me that as a judge I have no loftier duty or responsibility than to uphold that spiritual freedom to its farthest reaches...To many it is deeply distasteful to join in a public chorus of affirmation of private belief...**Official compulsion to affirm what is contrary to one's religious beliefs is the antithesis of freedom of worship**...It is in that freedom and the example of persuasion, not in force and compulsion, that the real unity of America lies.

DISSENT: Justices Roberts and Reed...[Not provided.]

DISSENT: Justice Frankfurter...One who belongs to the most vilified and persecuted minority in history is not likely to be insensible to the freedoms guaranteed by our Constitution.

> Justice Frankfurter was Jewish and the author of the *Minersville v. Gobitis* opinion.

Were my purely personal attitude relevant I should wholeheartedly associate myself with the general libertarian views in the Court's opinion...But as judges we are neither Jew nor Gentile, neither Catholic nor agnostic. We owe equal attachment to the Constitution and are equally bound by our judicial obligations whether we derive our citizenship from the earliest or the latest immigrants to these shores. As a member of this Court I am not justified in writing my private notions of policy into the Constitution, no matter how deeply I may cherish them or how mischievous I may deem their disregard. The duty of a judge who must decide which of two claims before the Court shall prevail, that of a State to enact and enforce laws within its general competence or that of an individual to refuse obedience because of the demands of his conscience, is not that of the ordinary person. It can never be emphasized too much that one's own opinion about the wisdom or evil of a law should be excluded altogether when one is doing one's duty on the bench. The only opinion of our own even looking in that direction that is material is our opinion whether legislators could in reason have enacted such a law.

An "originalist" believes the Constitution should be interpreted in a manner most consistent with the intent of those who crafted the document. Any other method, to them, can only be some made-up version of how some unelected justice views what is best for our society. As a conservative and an originalist, I applaud Justice Frankfurter's attitude towards deference to legislation, albeit misapplied in this case. He surely does not mean that the only test of constitutional legislation is that it must be supported by "reason," for if that is so, one would have to assume an arrogance beyond belief to suggest that *any* legislation (having passed or it would not be before the Court) would ever have *no* basis in reason.

In the light of all the circumstances, including the history of this question in this Court, it would require more daring than I possess to deny that reasonable legislators could have taken the action which is before us for review. Most unwillingly, therefore, I must differ from my brethren with regard to legislation like this. I cannot bring my mind to believe that the "liberty" secured by the Constitution gives this Court authority to deny to the State of West Virginia the attainment of that which we all recognize as a legitimate legislative end, namely, the promotion of good citizenship, by employment of the means here chosen...

Saluting the flag suppresses no belief nor curbs it. Children and their parents may believe what they please, avow their belief and practice it. It is not even remotely suggested that the requirement for saluting the flag involves the slightest restriction against the fullest opportunity on the part both of the children and of their parents to disavow as publicly as they choose to do so the meaning that others attach to the gesture of salute. All channels of affirmative free expression are open to both children and parents...

Justice Frankfurter would prefer to "compel and expel" – to force a vow of "allegiance" to government that some believe a sin because, after all, these same children and their parents then have the right to tell all who are willing to listen that what they have been forced to do by their own government, all in the name of "instilling national pride and unity," is disgusting to them and to their God. I am compelled to take one more look at some of the most beautiful words ever uttered by the Supreme Court in this case. They are worthy of a bookmark to show your friends and family what the Supreme Court has said about religion. Please ponder these gems:

> One's right to life, liberty, and property, to free speech, a free press, freedom of worship and assembly, and other fundamental rights may not be submitted to a vote; they depend on the outcome of no elections.

> Those who begin coercive elimination of dissent soon find themselves exterminating dissenters. Compulsory unification of opinion achieves only the unanimity of the graveyard.

> If there is any fixed star in our constitutional constellation, it is that no official, high or petty, can prescribe what shall be orthodox in politics, nationalism, religion, or other matters of opinion or force citizens to confess by word or act their faith therein.

> There is before us the right of freedom to believe, freedom to worship one's Maker according to the dictates of one's conscience, a right which the Constitution specifically shelters. Reflection has convinced me that as a judge I have no loftier duty or responsibility than to uphold that spiritual freedom to its farthest reaches... To many it is deeply distasteful to join in a public chorus of affirmation of private belief...Official compulsion to affirm what is contrary to one's religious beliefs is the antithesis of freedom of worship.

Score yet another "for" religion.

First Amendment Scoreboard

Rulings "for" Religion: 5 --- Rulings "against" Religion: 1

In an interesting side note, the American Legion supported the outcome of the *Barnette* case.

Perhaps we should ponder this question: If the government cannot make these kids violate their religious beliefs and "bow down to the flag," how can government make them attend a public school that teaches evolution if that is contrary to their religious beliefs? Where do we draw the line? We will be looking at the evolution cases in chapter ten.

Next stop? Maryland. All aboard!

***Torcaso v. Maryland* (1961):** [Mr. Torcaso was appointed to the office of Notary Public by the Governor of Maryland but was refused his commission because he would not declare his belief in God as required by the Maryland Constitution. Claiming that this requirement violated his rights under the First and the Fourteenth Amendments, he sued in a state court to compel issuance of his commission. The Court held that this test for public office cannot be enforced...because it unconstitutionally invades his freedom of belief and religion.]

[It is true that there is much historical precedent for such laws, but when our Constitution was adopted, the desire to put the people "securely beyond the reach" of religious test oaths brought about the inclusion in Article VI of that document of a provision that "no religious Test shall ever be required as a Qualification to any Office or public Trust under the United States."]

> There is no question that many of the Framers were devout Christians. There is also no question that they included the foregoing language in Article VI of the Constitution to insure that a profession of belief in a Creator would never be a requirement to hold public office. If we seek to enforce the Constitution according to the Framers' intent, we must not look the other way if that intent conflicts with what we *thought* it would say.

The *Torcaso* Court stated: "We repeat and again reaffirm that neither a State nor the Federal Government can constitutionally force a person to profess a belief or disbelief in any religion. Neither can constitutionally pass laws or impose requirements which aid all religions as against non-believers and neither can aid those religions based on a belief in the existence of God as against those religions founded on different beliefs. In upholding the State's religious test for public office the highest court of Maryland said: 'The petitioner is not compelled to believe or disbelieve, under threat of punishment or other compulsion. True, unless he makes the declaration of belief he cannot hold public office in Maryland, but he is not compelled to hold office.' The fact, however, that a person is not compelled to hold office cannot possibly be an excuse for barring him from office by state-imposed criteria forbidden by the Constitution. This Maryland religious test for public office unconstitutionally invades Torcaso's freedom of belief and religion and therefore cannot be enforced against him."

I have to score this "for" religion, simply because it also protects a Christian from ever being forced to profess a faith other than his own as a requirement to hold public office. To put it another way, it preserves the right to keep private beliefs private.

> ### First Amendment Scoreboard
> Rulings "for" Religion: 6 --- Rulings "against" Religion: 1

We make a pit stop in New York before moving on. We will study *Walz v. Tax Commission* (1970) in chapter eleven. It presents a classic clash between the free exercise and establishment clauses. I just cannot pass by 1970 without at least mentioning its outcome. *Walz* holds that taxing churches who own real estate would inhibit their free exercise of religion and that exempting them does not serve to support an establishment of religion. Therefore, it is constitutional to exempt churches from the burden of real estate taxation. Chalk up another "for" religion!

First Amendment Scoreboard

Rulings "for" Religion: 7 --- Rulings "against" Religion: 1

We head to Washington, D.C., for a brief encounter with *Clay v. United States* (1971). Cassius Clay (later, Muhammad Ali) was convicted for refusing to submit to induction into the Armed Forces. The conviction was reversed for technical reasons not relevant to our study. However, I place it here because it sets forth the requirements for conscientious objector status. In order to qualify, a registrant must show that he is conscientiously opposed to war in any form, that this opposition is based upon religious training and belief, and that his objection is sincere. Ring the "for" bell and the end of another round – in court!

First Amendment Scoreboard

Rulings "for" Religion: 8 --- Rulings "against" Religion: 1

Are you surprised that religion is doing this well so far? I have not yet seen the Supreme Court tell us we can't say "God," have you?

The next case tells of a sect of folks that just may have the right idea about daily living. Here is an opinion that will likely make you proud to be an American. You might even conclude that the right to freely exercise one's religion really does exist in America. I do not believe we have been to Wisconsin yet. Here we go!

Don't copy the behavior and customs of this world, but let God transform you into a new person by changing the way you think. Then you will know what God wants you to do, and you will know how good and pleasing and perfect his will really is.

Romans 12:2

WISCONSIN v. YODER
SUPREME COURT OF THE UNITED STATES
406 U.S. 205
May 15, 1972
[6 – 1]

OPINION: [Justices Powell and Rehnquist did not participate.] Chief Justice Burger…The Wisconsin Supreme Court held that respondents' convictions of violating the State's compulsory school-attendance law were invalid under the Free Exercise Clause of the First Amendment…We affirm.

…Jonas Yoder and Wallace Miller are members of the Old Order Amish religion and…Adin Yutzy is a member of the Conservative Amish Mennonite Church. They and their families are residents of Green County, Wisconsin. Wisconsin's compulsory school-attendance law required them to cause their children to attend public or private school until reaching age 16 but they declined to send their children, ages 14 and 15, to public school after they completed the eighth grade. The children were not enrolled in any private school or within any recognized exception to the compulsory-attendance law…They were charged, tried, and convicted of violating the compulsory-attendance law…and were fined the sum of $5 each…The trial testimony showed that respondents believed, in accordance with the tenets of Old Order Amish communities generally, that their children's attendance at high school, public or private, was contrary to the Amish religion and way of life. They believed that by sending their children to high school, they would not only expose themselves to the danger of the censure of the church community, but, as found by the county court, also endanger their own salvation and that of their children. The State stipulated that respondents' religious beliefs were sincere…

[The respondents' experts expressed their opinions on the relationship of the Amish belief concerning school attendance to the more general tenets of their religion and described the impact that compulsory high school attendance could have on the continued survival of Amish communities as they exist in the United States today.] The history of the Amish sect was given in some detail, beginning with the Swiss Anabaptists of the 16th

century who rejected institutionalized churches and sought to return to the early, simple Christian life de-emphasizing material success, rejecting the competitive spirit, and seeking to insulate themselves from the modern world. As a result of their common heritage, Old Order Amish communities today are characterized by a fundamental belief that salvation requires life in a church community separate and apart from the world and worldly influence. This concept of life aloof from the world and its values is central to their faith.

A related feature of Old Order Amish communities is their devotion to a life in harmony with nature and the soil, as exemplified by the simple life of the early Christian era that continued in America during much of our early national life. Amish beliefs require members of the community to make their living by farming or closely related activities. Broadly speaking, the Old Order Amish religion pervades and determines the entire mode of life of its adherents. Their conduct is regulated in great detail by the Ordnung, or rules, of the church community. Adult baptism, which occurs in late adolescence, is the time at which Amish young people voluntarily undertake heavy obligations, not unlike the Bar Mitzvah of the Jews, to abide by the rules of the church community.

Amish objection to formal education beyond the eighth grade is firmly grounded in these central religious concepts. They object to the high school, and higher education generally, because the values they teach are in marked variance with Amish values and the Amish way of life; they view secondary school education as an impermissible exposure of their children to a "worldly" influence in conflict with their beliefs. The high school tends to emphasize intellectual and scientific accomplishments, self-distinction, competitiveness, worldly success, and social life with other students. Amish society emphasizes informal learning-through-doing; a life of "goodness," rather than a life of intellect; wisdom, rather than technical knowledge; community welfare, rather than competition; and separation from, rather than integration with, contemporary worldly society.

Formal high school education beyond the eighth grade is contrary to Amish beliefs, not only because it places Amish children in an environment hostile to Amish beliefs with increasing emphasis on competition in class work and sports and with pressure to conform to the styles, manners, and ways of the peer group, but also because it takes them away from their community, physically and emotionally, during the crucial and formative adolescent period of life. During this period, the children must acquire Amish attitudes favoring manual work and self-reliance and the specific skills needed to perform the adult role of an Amish farmer or housewife. They must learn to enjoy physical labor. Once a child has learned basic reading, writing, and elementary mathematics, these traits, skills, and attitudes admittedly fall within the category of those best learned through example and "doing" rather than in a classroom. And, at this time in life, the Amish child must also grow in his faith and his relationship to the Amish community if he is to be prepared to accept the heavy obligations imposed by adult baptism. In short, high school attendance with teachers who are not of the Amish faith – and may even be hostile to it – interposes a serious barrier to the integration of the Amish child into the Amish religious community. Dr. John Hostetler, one of the experts on Amish society, testified that the modern high school is not equipped, in curriculum or social environment, to impart the values promoted by Amish society...

On the basis of such considerations, Dr. Hostetler testified that compulsory high school attendance could not only result in great psychological harm to Amish children, because of the conflicts it would produce, but would also, in his opinion, ultimately result in the destruction of the Old Order Amish church community as it exists in the United States today. The testimony of Dr. Donald A. Erickson, an expert witness on education, also showed that the Amish succeed in preparing their high school age children to be productive members of the Amish community. He described their system of learning-through-doing the skills directly relevant to their adult roles in the Amish community as "ideal" and perhaps superior to ordinary high school education. The evidence also showed that the Amish have an excellent record as law-abiding and generally self-sufficient members of society...

Providing public schools ranks at the very apex of the function of a State. Yet even this paramount responsibility was, in *Pierce v. Society of Sisters*, made to yield to the right of parents to provide an equivalent education in a privately operated system...As that case suggests, the values of parental direction of the religious upbringing and education of their children in their early and formative years have a high place in our society. [The] State's interest in universal education, however highly we rank it, is not totally free from a balancing process when it impinges on fundamental rights and interests, such as those specifically protected by the Free Exercise Clause of the First Amendment, and the traditional interest of parents with respect to the religious upbringing of their children so long as they, in the words of *Pierce*, "prepare them for additional obligations."

...The essence of all that has been said and written on the subject is that only those interests of the highest order and those not otherwise served can overbalance legitimate claims to the free exercise of religion...

A way of life, however virtuous and admirable, may not be interposed as a barrier to reasonable state regulation of education if it is based on purely secular considerations; **to have the protection of the Religion Clauses, the claims must be rooted in religious belief.** Although a determination of what is a "religious" belief or practice entitled to constitutional protection may present a most delicate question, the very concept of ordered liberty precludes allowing every person to make his own standards on matters of conduct in which society as a whole has important interests. Thus, if the Amish asserted their claims because of their subjective evaluation and rejection of the contemporary secular values accepted by the majority, much as Thoreau rejected the social values of his time and isolated himself at Walden Pond, their claims would not rest on a religious basis. Thoreau's choice was philosophical and personal rather than religious, and such belief does not rise to the demands of the Religion Clauses...The record in this case abundantly supports the claim that the traditional way of life of the Amish is not merely a matter of personal preference, but one of deep religious conviction, shared by an organized group, and intimately related to daily living. That the Old Order Amish daily life and religious practice stem from their faith is shown by the fact that it is in response to their literal interpretation of the Biblical injunction from the Epistle of Paul to the Romans, "be not conformed to this world..." This command is fundamental to the Amish faith...

> This is the King James Version, not the New Living Translation published by Tyndale House Publishers, Inc. It is a direct quote from the Supreme Court opinion.

The record shows that the respondents' religious beliefs…and…"life style" have not altered in fundamentals for centuries. Their way of life in a church-oriented community, separated from the outside world and "worldly" influences, their attachment to nature and the soil, is a way inherently simple and uncomplicated, albeit difficult to preserve against the pressure to conform. Their rejection of telephones, automobiles, radios, and television, their mode of dress, of speech, their habits of manual work do indeed set them apart from much of contemporary society; these customs are both symbolic and practical.

As the society around the Amish has become more populous, urban, industrialized, and complex, particularly in this century, government regulation of human affairs has correspondingly become more detailed and pervasive. The Amish mode of life has thus come into conflict increasingly with requirements of contemporary society exerting a hydraulic insistence on conformity to majoritarian standards…The values and programs of the modern secondary school are in sharp conflict with the fundamental mode of life mandated by the Amish religion; modern laws requiring compulsory secondary education have accordingly engendered great concern and conflict. The conclusion is inescapable that secondary schooling, by exposing Amish children to worldly influences in terms of attitudes, goals, and values contrary to beliefs, and substantially interfering with the religious development of the Amish child and his integration into the way of life of the Amish faith community at the crucial adolescent stage of development, contravenes the basic religious tenets and practice of the Amish faith, both as to the parent and the child…

Compulsory school attendance to age 16 for Amish children carries with it a very real threat of undermining the Amish community…; they must either abandon belief and be assimilated into society at large, or be forced to migrate to some other and more tolerant region…

Wisconsin…argues that "actions," even though religiously grounded, are outside the protection of the First Amendment. But our decisions have rejected the idea that religiously grounded conduct is always outside the protection of the Free Exercise Clause. It is true that activities of individuals, even when religiously based, are often subject to regulation by the States in the exercise of their undoubted power to promote the health, safety, and general welfare, or the Federal Government in the exercise of its delegated powers. *Reynolds v. United States.* But to agree that religiously grounded conduct must often be subject to the broad police power of the State is not to deny that there are areas of conduct protected by the Free Exercise Clause of the First Amendment and thus beyond the power of the State to control… *Murdock v. Pennsylvania; Cantwell v. Connecticut.* This case, therefore, does not become easier because respondents were convicted for their "actions" in refusing to send their children to the public high school…

The evidence…is persuasively to the effect that an additional one or two years of formal high school for Amish children in place of their long-established program of informal vocational education would do little to serve [the interests of the state.] Respondents' experts testified at trial, without challenge, that the value of all education must be assessed in terms of its capacity to prepare the child for life. It is one thing to say that compulsory education for a year or two beyond the eighth grade may be necessary when its goal is the preparation of the child for life in modern society as the majority live, but it is quite another if the goal of education be viewed as the preparation of the child for life in the separated agrarian community that is the keystone of the Amish faith. The State attacks respondents' position as one fostering ignorance from which the child must be protected by the State.

No one can question the State's duty to protect children from ignorance but…this record strongly shows that the Amish community has been a highly successful social unit within our society, even if apart from the conventional mainstream. Its members are productive and very law-abiding members of society; they reject public welfare in any of its usual modern forms. **The Congress itself recognized their self-sufficiency by authorizing exemption of such groups as the Amish from the obligation to pay social security taxes.**

```
I didn't know that!
```

It is neither fair nor correct to suggest that the Amish are opposed to education beyond the eighth grade level. What this record shows is that they are opposed to conventional formal education of the type provided by a certified high school because it comes at the child's crucial adolescent period of religious development. Dr. Donald Erickson, for example, testified that their system of learning-by-doing was an "ideal system" of education in terms of preparing Amish children for life as adults in the Amish community, and that "I would be inclined to say they do a better job in this than most of the rest of us do."

...We must not forget that in the Middle Ages important values of the civilization of the Western World were preserved by members of religious orders who isolated themselves from all worldly influences against great obstacles. **There can be no assumption that today's majority is "right" and the Amish and others like them are "wrong." A way of life that is odd or even erratic but interferes with no rights or interests of others is not to be condemned because it is different...**

The State's argument...appears to rest on the potential that exemption of Amish parents from the requirements of the compulsory-education law might allow some parents to act contrary to the best interests of their children by foreclosing their opportunity to make an intelligent choice between the Amish way of life and that of the outside world. The same argument could, of course, be made with respect to all church schools short of college. There is nothing in the record or in the ordinary course of human experience to suggest that non-Amish parents generally consult with children of ages 14-16 if they are placed in a church school of the parents' faith.

Indeed it seems clear that if the State is empowered...to "save" a child from himself or his Amish parents by requiring an additional two years of compulsory formal high school education, the State will in large measure influence, if not determine, the religious future of the child...**This case involves the fundamental interest of parents, as contrasted with that of the State, to guide the religious future and education of their** children. The history and culture of Western civilization reflect a strong tradition of parental concern for the nurture and upbringing of their children. This primary role of the parents in the upbringing of their children is now established beyond debate as an enduring American tradition…The Court's holding in *Pierce* stands as a charter of the rights of parents to direct the religious upbringing of their children…For the reasons stated we hold…that the First and Fourteenth Amendments prevent the State from compelling respondents to cause their children to attend formal high school to age 16…Nothing we hold is intended to undermine the general applicability of the State's compulsory school-attendance statutes or to limit the power of the State to promulgate reasonable standards that, while not impairing the free exercise of religion, provide for continuing agricultural vocational education under parental and church guidance by the Old Order Amish or others similarly situated. The States have had a long history of amicable and effective relationships with church-sponsored schools, and there is no basis for assuming that, in this related context, reasonable standards cannot be established concerning the content of the continuing vocational education of Amish children under parental guidance, provided always that state regulations are not inconsistent with what we have said in this opinion. Affirmed…

DISSENT: Justice Douglas…I think the children should be entitled to be heard…[A child] may want to be a pianist or an astronaut or an oceanographer. To do so he will have to break from the Amish tradition… What we do today, at least in this respect, opens the way to give organized religion a broader base than it has ever enjoyed; and it even promises that in time *Reynolds* will be overruled…

Put another mark in the "for" column. The *Yoder* case makes one truly proud to be a citizen of this country, does it not?

> ### First Amendment Scoreboard
> Rulings "for" Religion: 9 --- Rulings "against" Religion: 1

The next case will likely surprise many of you on several fronts.

McDANIEL v. PATY
SUPREME COURT OF THE UNITED STATES
435 U.S. 618
April 19, 1978
[8 – 0]

OPINION: [Justice Blackmun took no part in the consideration of this case.] Chief Justice Burger…[The question presented by this appeal is whether a Tennessee statute barring ministers from serving as delegates to the State's limited Constitutional Convention deprived McDaniel of the right to the free exercise of religion.]

In its first constitution, in 1796, Tennessee disqualified ministers from serving as legislators. That disqualifying provision has continued unchanged since its adoption…The state legislature applied this provision to candidates for delegate to the State's 1977 limited Constitutional Convention when it enacted [a provision that required a delegate to have the same qualifications of a legislator. In other words, because a minister could not be in the legislature, he could not be a delegate to the convention.]

McDaniel, an ordained minister of a Baptist Church in Chattanooga, filed as a candidate for delegate to the Constitutional Convention. An opposing candidate, appellee Selma Cash Paty, sued…for a declaratory judgment striking his name from the ballot. The Trial Judge…held that these laws violated the First and Fourteenth Amendments to the Federal Constitution and declared McDaniel eligible for the office of delegate. Accordingly, McDaniel's name remained on the ballot and in the ensuing election he was elected by a vote almost equal to that of three opposing candidates. After the election, the Tennessee Supreme Court reversed the Trial Court, holding that the disqualification of clergy imposed no burden upon "religious belief" and restricted "religious action…only in the lawmaking process of government – where religious action is absolutely prohibited by the establishment clause…" The state interests in preventing the establishment of religion and in avoiding the divisiveness and tendency to channel political activity along religious lines, resulting from clergy participation in political affairs, were deemed by that court sufficiently weighty to justify [McDaniel's disqualification in spite of the Free Exercise Clause.]

> We will get to the Establishment Clause, but a comment here is in order. Why would a minister's political motivations serve to "establish religion" any more so than the political motivations of a non-minister believer? To be consistent, the Tennessee Supreme Court would have to exclude anyone of faith from political office which is absurd on its face.

The disqualification of ministers from legislative office was a practice carried from England by seven of the original States; later six new States similarly excluded clergymen from some political offices...The purpose of the several States in providing for disqualification was primarily to assure the success of a new political experiment, the separation of church and state. Prior to 1776, most of the 13 Colonies had some form of an established, or government-sponsored, church. Even after ratification of the First Amendment, which prohibited the Federal Government from following such a course, some States continued pro-establishment provisions...

> It is not historically accurate to suggest the Framers never intended a "separation." One does not need to consult the Jefferson "wall of separation" letter to see that states disqualified clergy from public office in order to try a new political experiment – separation of church and state. Additionally, the concept of "separation" has been the greatest reason why religion (Christianity, in particular) has flourished in this country. However, I agree that excluding ministers from public office is not appropriate. Their participation does not breach the "wall" or "short fence" of separation. It does not violate the establishment clause.

In light of this history and a widespread awareness of that period of undue and often dominant clerical influence in public and political affairs here, in England, and on the Continent, it is not surprising that strong views were held by some that one way to assure disestablishment was to keep clergymen out of public office. Indeed, some of the foremost political philosophers and statesmen of that period held such views regarding the clergy...Thomas Jefferson initially advocated such a position in his 1783 draft of a constitution for Virginia. James Madison, however...opposed clergy disqualification.

> An early disagreement between the heavyweights! This next quote of John Witherspoon dramatically demonstrates, through the use of satire, why clergy exclusion was a bad idea.

When proposals were made earlier to prevent clergymen from holding public office, John Witherspoon, a Presbyterian minister, president of Princeton University, and the only clergyman to sign the Declaration of Independence, made a cogent protest and, with tongue in cheek, offered an amendment to a provision much like that challenged here:

> No clergyman, of any denomination, shall be capable of being elected a member of the Senate or House of Representatives, because (here insert the grounds of offensive disqualification, which I have not been able to discover). Provided always, and it is the true intent and meaning of this part of the Constitution, that if at any time he shall be completely deprived of the clerical character by those by whom he was invested with it, as by deposition for cursing and swearing, drunkenness or uncleanness, he shall then be fully restored to all the privileges of a free citizen; his offense [of being a clergyman] shall no more be remembered against him; but he may be chosen either to the Senate or House of Representatives, and shall be treated with all the respect due to his brethren, the other members of Assembly.

> Witherspoon used satire to show how absurd clergy exclusion was. A minister cannot hold public office, but if he is defrocked for drunkenness, then he will qualify!?!?!?!

As the value of the disestablishment experiment was perceived, 11 of 13 States disqualifying the clergy from some types of public office gradually abandoned that limitation...Only Maryland and Tennessee continued their clergy-disqualification provisions into this century...Tennessee remains the only State excluding ministers from certain public offices...

The right to the free exercise of religion unquestionably encompasses the right to preach, proselytize, and perform other similar religious functions, or, in other words, to be a minister of the type McDaniel was found to be. Tennessee also acknowledges the right of its adult citizens generally to seek and hold office as legislators or delegates to the state Constitutional Convention. Yet under the clergy-disqualification provision, McDaniel cannot exercise both rights simultaneously because the State has conditioned the exercise of one on the surrender of the other...In so doing, Tennessee has encroached upon McDaniel's right to the free exercise of religion. "To condition the availability of benefits including access to the ballot upon this appellant's willingness to violate a cardinal principle of his religious faith by surrendering his religiously impelled ministry effectively penalizes the free exercise of his constitutional liberties."

...Tennessee asserts that its interest in preventing the establishment of a state religion is consistent with the Establishment Clause...The essence of the rationale underlying the Tennessee restriction on ministers is that if elected to public office they will necessarily exercise their powers and influence to promote the interests of one sect or thwart the interests of another, thus pitting one against the others, contrary to the anti-establishment principle with its command of neutrality. However widely that view may have been held in the 18th century by many, including enlightened statesmen of that day, the American experience provides no persuasive support for the fear that clergymen in public office will be less careful of anti-establishment interests or less faithful to their oaths of civil office than their unordained counterparts.

We hold that [this statute] violates McDaniel's First Amendment right to the free exercise of his religion…[Judgment reversed.]

CONCURRENCE: Justice Brennan…Religious ideas, no less than any other, may be the subject of debate which is "uninhibited, robust, and wide-open…" That public debate of religious ideas, like any other, may arouse emotion, may incite, may foment religious divisiveness and strife does not rob it of constitutional protection. *Cantwell v. Connecticut.* The mere fact that a purpose of the Establishment Clause is to reduce or eliminate religious divisiveness or strife, does not place religious discussion, association, and political participation in a status less preferred than rights of discussion, association, and political participation generally. "**Adherents of particular faiths and individual churches frequently take strong positions on public issues including…vigorous advocacy of legal or constitutional positions. Of course, churches as much as secular bodies and private citizens have that right.**"

Hallelujah!

The State's goal of preventing sectarian bickering and strife may not be accomplished by regulating religious speech and political association… **Government may not inquire into the religious beliefs and motivations of officeholders – it may not remove them from office merely for making public statements regarding religion, or question whether their legislative actions stem from religious conviction.** In short, government may not as a goal promote "safe thinking" with respect to religion and fence out from political participation those, such as ministers, whom it regards as over involved in religion. **Religionists no less than members of any other group enjoy the full measure of protection afforded speech, association, and political activity generally.** The Establishment Clause, properly understood, is a shield against any attempt by government to inhibit religion as it has done here. It may not be used as a sword to justify repression of religion or its adherents from any aspect of public life…The antidote which the Constitution provides against zealots who would inject sectarianism into the political process is to subject their ideas to refutation in the marketplace of ideas and their platforms to rejection at the polls. With these safeguards, it is unlikely that they will succeed in inducing government to act along religiously divisive lines...

Score yet one more "for" religion.

> ### First Amendment Scoreboard
> Rulings "for" Religion: 10 --- Rulings "against" Religion: 1

For our final "free exercise" case, we go to Florida. This one is a bit different and may surprise you. Once again, religion wins!

**...Whenever you present offerings to the Lord,
you must bring animals from your flocks and herds.
If your sacrifice for a whole burnt offering is from the herd,
bring a bull with no physical defects...**

Leviticus 1:2-3

CHURCH OF THE LUKUMI BABALU AYE, INC.
v.
HIALEAH
SUPREME COURT OF THE UNITED STATES
508 U.S. 520
June 11, 1993
[9 – 0]

OPINION: Justice Kennedy...This case involves practices of the Santeria religion, which originated in the 19th century. When hundreds of thousands of members of the Yoruba people were brought as slaves from western Africa to Cuba, their traditional African religion absorbed significant elements

75

of Roman Catholicism. The resulting syncretion, or fusion, is Santeria, "the way of the saints." The Cuban Yoruba express their devotion to spirits, called *orishas*, through the iconography of Catholic saints. Catholic symbols are often present at Santeria rites and Santeria devotees attend the Catholic sacraments…The basis of the Santeria religion is the nurture of a personal relation with the *orishas,* and one of the principal forms of devotion is an animal sacrifice…Animal sacrifice is mentioned throughout the Old Testament and it played an important role in the practice of Judaism before destruction of the second Temple in Jerusalem. In modern Islam, there is an annual sacrifice commemorating Abraham's sacrifice of a ram in the stead of his son.

According to Santeria teaching, the *orishas*…depend for survival on the sacrifice. Sacrifices are performed at birth, marriage, and death rites, for the cure of the sick, for the initiation of new members and priests, and during an annual celebration. Animals sacrificed in Santeria rituals include chickens, pigeons, etc. The animals are killed by the cutting of the carotid arteries in the neck. The sacrificed animal is cooked and eaten, except after healing and death rituals.

Santeria adherents faced widespread persecution in Cuba, so the religion and its rituals were practiced in secret. The open practice of Santeria and its rites remains infrequent. The religion was brought to this nation most often by exiles from the Cuban revolution…There are at least 50,000 practitioners in South Florida today.

The Church of the Lukumi Babalu Aye…practices the Santeria religion… Ernesto Pichardo…is the Church's priest…In April 1987, the Church leased land in the city of Hialeah, Florida,…to bring the practice of the Santeria faith, including its ritual of animal sacrifice, into the open… [The city council held a number of public sessions and adopted numerous resolutions that effectively sought to run the Santerians out of town.]

The District Court concluded that the purpose of the ordinances was not to exclude the Church from the city but to end the practice of animal sacrifice…and that the ordinances did not target religious conduct "on their face," though it noted that in any event "specifically regulating religious conduct" does not violate the First Amendment "when the conduct is deemed inconsistent with public health and welfare." Thus, the court concluded that, at most, the ordinances' effect on petitioners' religious conduct was "incidental to their secular purpose and effect." [We reverse.]

In other words, the Supreme Court unanimously held in favor of the Santerians. The opinion follows.

The District Court...found four compelling interests: (1)...Animal sacrifices present a substantial health risk...(2) There is emotional injury to children who witness the sacrifice of animals. (3) [The city has an interest in] protecting animals from cruel and unnecessary killing and... the method of killing used in Santeria sacrifice was "unreliable and not humane, and that the animals, before being sacrificed, are often kept in conditions that produce a great deal of fear and stress in the animal." (4) [The city has an interest in] restricting the slaughter or sacrifice of animals to areas zoned for slaughterhouse use...The District Court concluded the compelling governmental interests "fully justify the absolute prohibition of ritual sacrifice"...The Court of Appeals...affirmed...

The city does not argue that Santeria is not a "religion" within the meaning of the First Amendment. Nor could it. Although the practice of animal sacrifice may seem abhorrent to some, "religious beliefs need not be acceptable, logical, consistent, or comprehensible to others in order to merit First Amendment protection." Given the historical association between animal sacrifice and religious worship, petitioners' assertion that animal sacrifice is an integral part of their religion "cannot be deemed bizarre or incredible."...

At a minimum, the protections of the Free Exercise Clause pertain if the law at issue discriminates against some or all religious beliefs or regulates or prohibits conduct because it is undertaken for religious reasons. Indeed, it was "historical instances of religious persecution and intolerance that gave concern to those who drafted the Free Exercise Clause."...In *McDaniel v. Paty*...we invalidated a state law that disqualified members of the clergy from holding certain public offices, because it "imposed special disabilities on the basis of…religious status." On the same principle,…we found that a municipal ordinance was applied in an unconstitutional manner when interpreted to prohibit preaching in a public park by a Jehovah's Witness but to permit preaching during the course of a Catholic mass or Protestant church service…(*Fowler v. Rhode Island*).

The record in this case compels the conclusion that suppression of the central element of the Santeria worship service was the object of the ordinances…

It is a necessary conclusion that almost the only conduct subject to [the ordinances] is the religious exercise of Santeria church members …Ordinance 87-71…prohibits the sacrifice of animals, but defines sacrifice as "to unnecessarily kill…an animal in a public or private ritual or ceremony not for the primary purpose of food consumption." The definition excludes almost all killings of animals except for religious sacrifice and…**exempts kosher slaughter**…[This feature of the law supports our conclusion] that Santeria alone was the exclusive legislative concern. The net result…is that few if any killings of animals are prohibited other than Santeria sacrifice, which is proscribed because it occurs during a ritual or ceremony and its primary purpose is to make an offering to the *orishas*, not food consumption. Indeed, careful drafting ensured that, although Santeria sacrifice is prohibited, killings that are no more necessary or humane in almost all other circumstances are unpunished…

Ordinance 87-52…prohibits the "possession, sacrifice, or slaughter" of an animal with the "intent to use such animal for food purposes,"…[but exempts] "any licensed food establishment" with regard to "any animals which are specifically raised for food purposes," if the activity is permitted by zoning and other laws. This exception, too, seems intended to cover kosher slaughter. Again, the burden of the ordinance, in practical terms, falls on Santeria adherents but almost no others…

Ordinance 87-40's…prohibition is broad on its face, punishing "whoever … unnecessarily … kills any animal." … Killings for religious reasons are deemed unnecessary, whereas most other killings fall outside the prohibition. **The city permits…hunting, slaughter of animals for**

food, eradication of insects and pests, and euthanasia as necessary. There is no indication in the record that respondent has concluded that hunting or fishing for sport is unnecessary...

Under federal and Florida law and Ordinance 87-40,...killing an animal by the "simultaneous and instantaneous severance of the carotid arteries with a sharp instrument" – the method used in kosher slaughter – is approved as humane. The District Court found that, though Santeria sacrifice also results in severance of the carotid arteries, the method used during sacrifice is less reliable and therefore not humane. If the city has a real concern that other methods are less humane, however, the subject of the regulation should be the method of slaughter itself, not a religious classification that is said to bear some general relation to it...

The city...asserts...that animal sacrifice is "different" from the animal killings that are permitted by law. According to the city, it is "self-evident" that killing animals for food is "important"; the eradication of insects and pests is "obviously justified"; and the euthanasia of excess animals "makes sense." [This does not] explain why religion alone must bear the burden of the ordinances, when many of these secular killings fall within the city's interest in preventing the cruel treatment of animals...

The health risks posed by the improper disposal of animal carcasses are the same whether Santeria sacrifice or some nonreligious killing preceded it. The city does not, however, prohibit hunters from bringing their kill to their houses, nor does it regulate disposal after their activity. Despite substantial testimony at trial that the same public health hazards result from improper disposal of garbage by restaurants, restaurants are outside the scope of the ordinances. Improper disposal is a general problem that causes substantial health risks, but which respondent addresses only when it results from religious exercise...Under the city's ordinances, hunters may eat their kill and fisherman may eat their catch without undergoing governmental inspection. Likewise, state law requires inspection of meat that is sold but exempts meat from animals raised for the use of the owner and "members of his household and nonpaying guests and employees." The asserted interest in inspected meat is not pursued in contexts similar to that of religious animal sacrifice.

Ordinance 87-72, which prohibits the slaughter of animals outside of areas zoned for slaughterhouses,...includes an exemption for "any person, group, or organization" that "slaughters or processes for sale, small numbers of hogs and/or cattle per week in accordance with an exemption provided by state law." Respondent has not explained why commercial operations that slaughter "small numbers" of hogs and cattle do not implicate its professed desire to prevent cruelty to animals and preserve the public health. Although the city has classified Santeria sacrifice as slaughter, subjecting it to this ordinance, it does not regulate other killings for food in like manner.

...Each of Hialeah's ordinances [pursue governmental interests] only against conduct motivated by religious belief. The ordinances "have every appearance of a prohibition that society is prepared to impose upon [Santeria worshipers] but not upon itself." This precise evil is what the requirement of general applicability is designed to prevent...Respondent has not demonstrated...that...its governmental interests are compelling... Legislators may not devise mechanisms...designed to persecute or oppress a religion or its practices...[These laws are void.]

Eleven to one! Fairly impressive!

> #### First Amendment Scoreboard
> Rulings "for" Religion: 11 --- Rulings "against" Religion: 1

There are additional Free Exercise Clause cases, but these 12 are a fair representation of the entire body of this area of jurisprudence. Did you notice any hostility toward religion or, specifically, toward Christianity? Did the Court tell us we cannot say "God"? Here is a summary:

1879: In *Reynolds v. United States* we learned that Congress has no power to legislate over matters of opinion or conscience, but religious freedom ends when religious actions exceed the bounds of social duty or good order. In particular, polygamy, no matter how sincerely believed to be commanded by the God of the Mormons of that era, was nevertheless a line beyond which no one could go without criminal punishment to follow. The Court did not give us much guidance on the definition of "religion" or "social duty" or "subversion of good order," but at least we know that there are limits to religious freedom and having more than one spouse is one of them.

History Lesson: Although our ancestors fled England, in part, to free themselves from the "established" Church of England, some of the colonies and resulting States "established" religious sects of their own and taxed citizens to support them, making non-payment subject to criminal prosecution. Three years before the Constitution was signed, Madison and Jefferson turned the tide in Virginia by defeating a proposal to tax citizens to support Christian teachers. Madison believed that government had no right to tell people what to believe or what duties they owed their Creator. Jefferson was not a member of the Constitutional Convention that met in Philadelphia. He was acting as our minister to France at the time. He was frustrated that the original Constitution did not include the promise of religious freedom. That promise soon followed in the form of the First Amendment. Polygamy was considered a crime early in England's history and was punishable by death in Virginia soon after the Constitution was ratified.

1925: In *Pierce v. Society of Sisters* we learned that state government cannot force children to attend public school. Although education can be required, parents have a right to direct the upbringing of their children who, after all, are not mere creatures of the state. Private schooling, and ultimately homeschooling, is constitutional.

1940: In *Cantwell v. Connecticut* we learned that local government may not require religion to first prove it is a valid religion before soliciting membership and money on the public streets. The power to regulate religion must not unduly infringe upon the freedom of religion. Government may, by general and non-discriminatory legislation, regulate the times, places, and manner of soliciting and may safeguard the peace, good order, and comfort of the community.

1943: In *Martin v. City of Struthers* we learned that local government may not forbid solicitors of religion from knocking on doors.

1943: In *Murdock v. Pennsylvania* we learned that local government may not condition the distribution of religious material on the payment of a license fee. Freedom of speech, press, and religion are available to all, not merely to those who can pay their own way.

1943: In *West Virginia Board of Education v. Barnette* we learned that local government may not criminalize the failure of young children to salute the flag. Jehovah's Witnesses believe this to be the forbidden worship of a graven image.

Principles: "No official, high or petty, can prescribe what shall be orthodox in politics, nationalism, religion, or other matters of opinion or force citizens to confess by word or act their faith therein…There is before us the right of freedom to believe, freedom to worship one's Maker according to the dictates of one's conscience, a right which the Constitution specifically shelters…Official compulsion to affirm what is contrary to one's religious beliefs is the antithesis of freedom of worship."

History Lessons: The phrase "under God" was added to the Pledge of Allegiance in 1954.

1961: In *Torcaso v. Watkins* we learned that state government may not require a declaration of a belief in God in order to become a Notary Public (or hold any public office) as this invades the freedom of belief and religion.

History Lessons: Article VI of the Constitution states: "No religious Test shall ever be required as a Qualification to any Office or public Trust under the United States."

1970: In *Walz v. Tax Commission* we learned that the free exercise of religion forbids taxing its real estate and that such indirect subsidy does not "establish" religion.

1971: In *Clay v. United States* we learned that sincerely held religious beliefs can exempt one from military obligations.

<u>History Lessons</u>: Cassius Clay (later, Muhammad Ali) was convicted of draft evasion. The conviction was reversed on a technicality.

1972: In *Wisconsin v. Yoder* we learned that sincerely held religious beliefs exempt Amish children from two years of mandated public school. The Amish were not required "to conform to this world."

<u>Principles</u>: There can be no presumption that today's majority is "right" and that the Amish are "wrong." The primary role of parents in the upbringing of their children was established beyond debate as an enduring American tradition at the time.

<u>History Lessons</u>: The Amish are exempt from the duty to pay social security taxes and they, therefore, do not receive its benefits.

1978: In *McDaniel v. Paty* we learned that a state may not forbid clergy from holding public office.

<u>Principles</u>: "The exclusion manifests patent hostility toward, not neutrality respecting, religion and has a primary effect which inhibits religion... Religious ideas, no less than any other, may be the subject of debate which is 'uninhibited, robust, and wide-open...' That public debate of religious ideas, like any other, may arouse emotion, may incite, may foment religious divisiveness and strife does not rob it of constitutional protection...Religious discussion, association, or political participation is not a less preferred status than rights of discussion, association, and political participation generally...Churches as much as secular bodies and private citizens have the right to take strong positions on public issues... Government may not inquire into the religious beliefs and motivations of officeholders – it may not remove them from office merely for making public statements regarding religion, or question whether their legislative actions stem from religious conviction...Religionists no less than members of any other group enjoy the full measure of protection afforded speech, association, and political activity generally. The Establishment Clause, properly understood, is a shield against any attempt by government to inhibit religion as it has done here."

These principles stated in *McDaniel v. Paty* are extraordinarily supportive of people of faith, wouldn't you agree?

<u>History Lessons</u>: Ministers were disqualified from holding public office in most of the states at the time of the Constitution's ratification. They were experimenting with separation of church and state.

1993: In *Church of the Lukumi Babalu Aye v. Hialeah* we learned that a city may not target religion to its exclusion even it if practices a form of animal sacrifice.

<u>Principles</u>: Although the practice of animal sacrifice may seem abhorrent to some, "religious beliefs need not be acceptable, logical, consistent, or comprehensible to others in order to merit First Amendment protection."

<u>History Lessons</u>: The Santeria religion teaches that spirits, called *orishas*, depend for survival on animal sacrifices. In 1993, there were 50,000 members residing in Florida.

THE SUGGESTED CHRISTIAN RESPONSE

You now have a very sound knowledge of how the Supreme Court has interpreted the free exercise clause of the First Amendment. You have learned of specific court rulings, very important principles to keep in mind, and some valuable history lessons. Now what?

I will help show you where the battle lines are drawn in the present culture war and war on Christianity by first taking a brief look at the role of religion in the individual lives of some of our past and present leaders and then apply what we have learned thus far.

George Washington

"It is the duty of all nations to acknowledge the Providence of Almighty God, to obey His will, to be grateful for His benefits, and humbly to implore His protection and favor."

Thanksgiving Proclamation, 1789.

The oath of office of the President of the United States is found in the last paragraph of Article II, Section 1 of the Constitution:

I do solemnly swear (or affirm) that I will faithfully execute the Office of President of the United States, and will to the best of my Ability, preserve, protect and defend the Constitution of the United States.

When our first president took this oath, he voluntarily added "So help me God" at the end. **It was OK for him to say "God,"** along with almost every president since, so why can't we say "God" today? Who started the rumor that we can't do that anymore? If it was intentional, who took that very phrase off of the WWII Memorial quote of FDR and why?

Here are some additional Washington quotes:

"It would be peculiarly improper to omit, in this first official act, my fervent supplications to that Almighty Being who rules over the universe, and who presides in the councils of nations...No People can be bound to acknowledge and adore the Invisible Hand which conducts the affairs of men more than the people of the United States. Every step by which they have advanced to the character of an independent nation seems to have been distinguished by some token of providential agency...We ought to be no less persuaded that the propitious smiles of Heaven can never be expected on a nation that disregards the eternal rules of order and right which Heaven itself has ordained..."

Washington's Inaugural Address

"Of all the dispositions and habits which lead to a political prosperity, religion and morality are indispensable supports."

Washington's Farewell Address

John Adams

"Our Constitution was made only for a moral and religious people. It is wholly inadequate for the government of any other."

Address, 1798.

Thomas Jefferson

"Among the most inestimable of our blessings, also, is that...of liberty to worship our Creator in the way we think most agreeable to His will; a liberty deemed in other countries incompatible with good government and yet proved by our experience to be its best support."

Reply to John Thomas, 1807.

"The constitutional freedom of religion is the most inalienable and sacred of all human rights."

Board of Visitors Minutes, 1819.

James Madison

"Religion...is the basis and foundation of government...Before any man can be considered as a member of civil society, he must be considered as a subject of the Governor of the Universe."

Memorial and Remonstrance, 1785.

Abraham Lincoln

"I do not think I could myself be brought to support a man for office whom I knew to be an open enemy of, and scoffer at, religion."

Ronald Reagan

"Freedom prospers when religion is vibrant and the rule of law under God is acknowledged."

Bill Clinton

"Sometimes I think the environment in which we operate is entirely too secular. The fact that we have freedom *of* religion does not mean we need to try to have freedom *from* religion."

George W. Bush

"Freedom is the almighty God's gift to each man and woman in this world...There's a way to accomplish the separation of church and state, and at the same time, accomplish the social objective of having America a hopeful place, and a loving place."

****

Of course, I could go on and on with solid evidence supporting the fact that most, if not all, of our presidents and numerous additional leaders believed in a higher power and were not ashamed to say so. Why, then, are we ashamed to say so? Have you noticed that just when every unimaginable human activity is coming out of the closet, we seem to have put God in the closet? When did it become politically incorrect to say "God" in public? Let me show you what I mean.

In my lifetime, I recall somewhat of an uproar over President Kennedy's religion, Catholicism. And, President Bush (II) was roundly criticized for wearing his faith on his sleeve. You know the mantra: "Presidents should keep religion out of government," the naysayers shout. "They should honor separation of church and state."

However, the naysayers never understood what "separation" meant. We will be exploring that in detail in later chapters. They also do not understand the meaning of "free exercise." From what you have seen thus far, does this freedom permit presidents to speak of God?

Wouldn't you think that applies to you, as well? Of course, it does.

Now you know the good news. You know that:

> The Constitution does not demand government hostility toward religion and "religious ideas, no less than any other, may be the subject of debate which is uninhibited, robust and wide-open." *McDaniel v. Paty.*

And…

> Religious discussion, association, or political participation of religion is not a less preferred status than rights of discussion, association, and political participation in other matters and that "government may not inquire into the religious beliefs and motivations of officeholders and may not remove them from office merely for making public statements regarding religion, or question whether their legislative actions stem from religious conviction." *McDaniel v. Paty.*

And…

> People of faith (yes, even politicians) "enjoy the full measure of protection afforded speech, association, and political activity in general." *McDaniel v. Paty.*

And, now you know that all of these wonderful measures of religious freedom exist because of how the Supreme Court has interpreted the Constitution. Are you surprised? As for myself, not unlike President Lincoln, I cannot imagine electing a leader to represent me and my family who does not believe in God. Contrary to folks who complain about public servants who are not afraid to live their faith, we of faith should be supporting them with our votes. That is not a constitutionally improper road to take.

Armed with the knowledge you have gained thus far, what should you do, as a Christian, when your neighbors criticize good people in government who have the courage to live their faith in God "out loud"? Well, if the complainers have a problem with folks who add a reference to God when taking an oath or freely speaking of their faith to a journalist or praying or saying "God bless America" at the end of a speech, do not do as Amanda and Charley did. Do not agree with the misinformed that *"We're not supposed to say things of God anymore."*

Do not shake your head sadly and walk away. For, now you know the truth. Politely and in a manner pleasing to Christ, let them know they are wrong. Show them these cases and the words uttered by the Supreme Court justices. If you get a chance, how about introducing them to Jesus Christ and, oh, by the way, let them know **"It's OK to say 'God.'"**

Chapter Six

ESTABLISHMENT:
GOD HELP US GET OVER THE "WALL"

We now have arrived at our study of the "establishment clause" and, to refresh, here it is once more:

Congress shall make no law respecting an establishment of religion.

Once again, please note the Constitution does not define "respecting," "establishment," or "religion." The Supreme Court will be doing that.

The "wall of separation" is the phrase used for understanding "establishment." It is not something we need to climb over, go around, crash through, or tear down. Rather, it is a metaphor (and nothing more) that we need to "get over," as in "accept." Christians see red when confronted with what they have been led to believe is a wall constructed solely by Thomas Jefferson, but it is my considered opinion that Christians need to see it for what it is – a red herring.

To help understand what all of this really means, I now introduce you to a hypothetical family of four: Jackson Elliot, the father; Ava Elliot, the mother; Webster Elliot, the seventeen-year-old public high school senior son; and, Alyssa Elliot, the eight-year-old public elementary school daughter. Where shall we place the Elliots?

In 2005, a study released by the nonpartisan Bay Area Center for Voting Research ranked the top 25 most liberal and conservative cities in America. The study concluded that Detroit, Michigan; Gary, Indiana; and, Berkeley,

California, were the top three most liberal cities. The others included Washington, D.C., and were represented by the additional states of New Jersey, Massachusetts, Ohio, Connecticut, Maryland, Washington, Illinois, Pennsylvania, Alabama, Missouri, New York, Rhode Island, and Minnesota.

The top three conservative cities were Provo, Utah; Lubbock, Texas; and, Abilene, Texas. Andrews, Texas, my birthplace, is 100 miles south of Lubbock and 165 miles west of Abilene. Lubbock was the perfect place for Bobby Knight to end his stellar coaching career. I guess you could say I have conservative roots and I am "mighty proud" to add two more cities in Texas to that top 25 conservative list: Plano and Arlington. The other cities are represented by the additional states of Florida, Colorado, Arizona, California, Louisiana, Pennsylvania, Oklahoma, Kansas, and Alaska.

The Elliot family consider themselves to be conservative – to the right of center, but not extremist. They like the politics of Newt Gingrich and they attend the Baptist Church.

I am going to plant them in a liberal community – let us say the fictional community of Berkley, California – not the real Berkeley – I don't need them calling me. Actually, all of the Elliots were born and raised near Lubbock, but Jackson's employer offered to double his salary on the condition that he move his family to Berkley. He chose the additional income. Little did he know how unfortuitous that would be for him and his family. We will be looking in on the Elliots from time to time.

<u>It's Just a Metaphor – Get Over It</u>

That really sounds cold. How about this?: "It's Just a Metaphor – Please Understand It – And Then – Please Get Over It." Much better.

The close relationship of the government of England and the Church of England eventually convinced the persecuted colonists that separation of religion and government was necessary. All scholars can agree that the "establishment clause" was at least intended to forbid an American "established" religion or church to be run by the federal government. And, the Fourteenth Amendment, coupled with the First Amendment, would not permit a church or religion to be run by a state or local government. If such were attempted, it would be easily identifiable without the use of any metaphor.

As you will see, however, the Court has properly interpreted the clause to forbid far more than a government-run church. If the Framers had intended such a limited goal, it would have been very easy to clearly state as much in the First Amendment. They did not do so.

What happens when a legislative body passes a law to provide salaries to ministers or to school teachers of a Catholic school? What result when a county exempts churches from paying their fair share of real estate tax? These examples fall far short of "establishing a government-run church," but do help to "establish" religion, or would do so, if permitted. What if government seeks to provide money to public schools and private religious schools to operate their bus transportation system? The possibilities of government action getting into the undefined realm of "establishing religion" are endless. And, thus, the Court has been faced with numerous different fact situations whereby the justices must determine the line between government and religion that cannot be crossed.

Oops? Did I say "line"? I suppose I could have said "wall" or "line in the sand" or "hedge" or "divider" or "partition" or "fence." I could have even said "wall of separation." That is the phrase Jefferson used in a private letter he wrote that was mentioned in the *Reynolds* case, the very first case we studied in chapter five. If, instead, he had said "line in the sand," what difference would it make? None.

All would agree that this clause means there are some aspects of life wherein government should not intrude upon religion and religion should not intrude upon government. The Court is about defining where that line should be drawn (or where that wall should be erected). Some believe it should be high and impenetrable. Some believe it should be low and porous. See, more metaphors – all used to express the plain and undeniable concept that in this country, religion and government are not one and the same. We are not a theocracy. There are good reasons for that. We need to get over what we call it and focus on where the separation lies or where it should lie. However, if we must call it something, after having reviewed all of the "establishment clause" cases, I feel a more accurate description of that which "separates" is not a "wall," but rather, a "short fence" – the type of fence in Italian neighborhoods that keeps "your stuff in" and "your neighbor's stuff out," yet encourages friendly relationships.

Let us begin the "establishment journey" in our quest to see whether a short fence of separation is a good idea and whether "It's OK to say 'God.'"

Because there are far too many cases of importance to cover in detail, some of these are presented in summary form, without an official "style." All aboard the establishment train!

Chapter Seven

ESTABLISHMENT:
PRIVATE SCHOOL SUBSIDIES

Ava Elliot would work outside the home, if necessary, but as long as Jackson can support the family adequately, they both believe she needs to be home until the kids are raised. They have several concerns about public education, but cannot afford private schooling for their kids and, since public education back in Lubbock was to their liking, Ava has not equipped herself to homeschool. So, Webster will finish high school at Berkley Senior High and Alyssa will attend the local elementary public school, at least for their first year in Berkley.

Jackson had been on the school board back in Texas, so at his first opportunity, after settling in from the move, he familiarized himself with the school district and their methods of funding public education.

He obtained some material from the district office and city hall. The churches in the area represented more different types of religion than he knew existed. Welcome to California. Okay, so he expected the atmosphere to be much different than it had been in the Panhandle, but he did not expect to find that a portion of the real estate taxes he would be paying would go to fund the transportation expenses of getting school children to and from their respective *private religious* schools! He knew that some of these schools' teachings were far afield from his Christian beliefs. There was even a tax to fund the purchase of history books for these schools – history books that failed to mention anything about the Pilgrims or the Christian heritage of the Founding Fathers.

Something just did not smell right to Jackson. He couldn't afford to enroll *his* kids in private Christian-based schools, yet his tax dollars would be helping to transport *other* kids to private religious schools. How could this be? It appeared to him he was being asked to lend support to sects so foreign to his beliefs that their teachings were pure heresy.

Although he had taken an oath to uphold the Constitution of the United States when he was sworn in as an elected school board member back in Texas, Jackson really was at a loss when it came to his knowledge of what it said about private school tax subsidies. He had questions as a taxpayer and, even more so, as a Christian. Were these taxes constitutional? Was there anything he could do? "Probably not much," he thought. He had received Helen's e-mail (see chapter two) and remembered Charley saying "we're not supposed to talk about God anymore." Why spend any time on these questions?

Every person who holds public office takes an oath to support our Constitution, but few have much knowledge of what it means. Of course, even if they did, that doesn't mean they would honor their oath and most of us wouldn't know if they were or not, for we, too, are clueless. What result? Well, either through ignorance or intent, laws are sometimes enacted (indeed, taxes are passed) by local, state, or federal government that are void on their face and unconstitutional. Why do we put up with it? We can right the ship or sail wherever the wind takes us. It is our choice.

We now take a good look at five Supreme Court decisions that address questions involving financial support for private religious education. When you are finished, you will be able to help Jackson answer his questions and may even re-think your own beliefs.

The primary importance of the first case (a 5 – 4 decision) is not the outcome. I personally believe the majority got this one wrong, but I will admit it is a close call. The history lessons provided in this case are more important – indeed, they are critical – to an understanding of the "establishment clause" and, therefore, critical to an understanding of the proper Christian response. *Everson v. Board of Education* takes us on a 1947 journey that reveals how these religion clauses came to be and why the Framers were so concerned with the role of religion in the society they were attempting to craft.

All aboard! First stop – New Jersey.

EVERSON v. BOARD OF EDUCATION
SUPREME COURT OF THE UNITED STATES
330 U.S. 1
February 10, 1947
[5 – 4]

OPINION: Justice Black…[A New Jersey statute authorizes its local school districts to provide for the transportation of children to and from schools, including public and private schools, but not to and from private "for profit" schools.] Ewing Township Board of Education, acting pursuant to this statute, authorized reimbursement to parents of money expended by the parents for the bus transportation of their children on regular busses operated by the public transportation system. Part of this money was for the payment of transportation of some children in the community to Catholic parochial schools…

The only contention here is that [this transportation subsidy]…violated the Federal Constitution…[by forcing] inhabitants to pay taxes to help support and maintain schools which are dedicated to, and which…teach the Catholic Faith…

The First Amendment, as made applicable to the states by the Fourteenth Amendment,…commands that a state "shall make no law respecting an establishment of religion, or prohibiting the free exercise thereof…" These words…reflected in the minds of early Americans a vivid mental picture of conditions and practices which they fervently wished to stamp out in order to preserve liberty for themselves and for their posterity. Doubtless their goal has not been entirely reached; but so far has the nation moved toward it that the expression "law respecting an establishment of religion" probably does not so vividly remind present-day Americans of the evils, fears, and political problems that caused that expression to be written into our Bill of Rights…

> The goals of the "establishment clause" (to avoid the evils, fears, and political unrest that existed in England with respect to religion) are easily forgotten today because, in large part, they have been met.

A large proportion of the early settlers of this country came here from Europe to escape the bondage of laws which compelled them to support and attend government-favored churches. The centuries immediately before and contemporaneous with the colonization of America had been filled with turmoil, civil strife, and persecutions, generated in large part by established sects determined to maintain their absolute political and religious supremacy.

> Although far distant in time from our new millennium mindset, I ask you to please spend some time with what you have just read. "A large proportion of the early settlers of this country came here from Europe to escape the bondage of laws which compelled them to support and attend government-favored churches." They experienced "centuries" of "turmoil, civil strife, and persecution" generated by sects seeking to gain political and religious supremacy in a government system where religion and government were intertwined.

With the power of government supporting them, at various times and places, Catholics had persecuted Protestants, Protestants had persecuted Catholics, Protestant sects had persecuted other Protestant sects, Catholics of one shade of belief had persecuted Catholics of another shade of belief, and all of these had from time to time persecuted Jews. In efforts to force loyalty to whatever religious group happened to be on top and in league with the government of a particular time and place, men and women had been fined, cast in jail, cruelly tortured, and killed. Among the offenses for which these punishments had been inflicted were such things as speaking disrespectfully of the views of ministers of government-established churches, non-attendance at those churches, expressions of non-belief in their doctrines, and failure to pay taxes and tithes to support them.

> We should not lose sight of the historical background underlying the rationale for these clauses. When is the last time an American citizen was "fined, imprisoned, tortured or killed" because of his faith? Maybe there is something to this "separation thing," after all.

These practices of the Old World were transplanted to and began to thrive in the soil of the new America. The very charters granted by the English Crown to the individuals...designated to make the laws [for the colonies] ... authorized [them] ... to erect religious establishments which all, whether believers or non-believers, would be required to support and attend. An exercise of this authority was accompanied by a repetition of many of the Old World practices and persecutions. Catholics found themselves hounded and proscribed because of their faith; Quakers who followed their conscience went to jail; Baptists were peculiarly obnoxious to certain dominant Protestant sects; men and women of varied faiths who happened to be in a minority in a particular locality were persecuted because they steadfastly persisted in worshiping God only as their own consciences dictated. And all of these dissenters were compelled to pay tithes and taxes to support government-sponsored churches whose ministers preached inflammatory sermons designed to strengthen and consolidate the established faith by generating a burning hatred against dissenters.

> That is where we were without the "free exercise" and "establishment" clauses. Does anyone wish to return to those days?

These practices became so commonplace as to shock the freedom-loving colonials into a feeling of abhorrence. The imposition of taxes to pay ministers' salaries and to build and maintain churches and church property aroused their indignation. It was these feelings which found expression in the First Amendment...**The people [of Virginia], as elsewhere, reached**

the conviction that individual religious liberty could be achieved best under a government which was stripped of all power to tax, to support, or otherwise to assist any or all religions, or to interfere with the beliefs of any religious individual or group.

The movement toward this end reached its dramatic climax in Virginia in 1785-86 when the Virginia legislative body was about to renew Virginia's tax levy for the support of the established church. Thomas Jefferson and James Madison led the fight against this tax. **Madison wrote his great Memorial and Remonstrance against the law. In it, he eloquently argued that a true religion did not need the support of law; that no person, either believer or non-believer, should be taxed to support a religious institution of any kind; that the best interest of a society required that the minds of men always be wholly free; and that cruel persecutions were the inevitable result of government-established religions.** Madison's Remonstrance [resulted in the Virginia Assembly]... enacting the famous "Virginia Bill for Religious Liberty" originally written by Thomas Jefferson. The preamble to that Bill [and the statute itself] stated...:

> Almighty God hath created the mind free; that all attempts to influence it by temporal punishments or burthens, or by civil incapacitations, tend only to beget habits of hypocrisy and meanness, and are a departure from the plan of the Holy author of our religion, who being Lord both of body and mind, yet chose not to propagate it by coercions on either...; that to compel a man to furnish contributions of money for the propagation of opinions which he disbelieves, is sinful and tyrannical; that even the forcing him to support this or that teacher of his own religious persuasion, is depriving him of the comfortable liberty of giving his contributions to the particular pastor, whose morals he would make his pattern...That no man shall be compelled to frequent or support any religious worship, place, or ministry whatsoever, nor shall be enforced, restrained, molested, or burthened in his body or goods, nor shall otherwise suffer on account of his religious opinions or belief...

This Court has previously recognized that the provisions of the First Amendment, in the drafting and adoption of which Madison and Jefferson played such leading roles, had the same objective and were intended to provide the same protection against governmental intrusion on religious liberty as the Virginia statute. *Reynolds v. United States*...Prior to the adoption of the Fourteenth Amendment, the First Amendment did not apply as a restraint against the states. Most of them did soon provide similar constitutional protections for religious liberty. But some states persisted for about half a century in imposing restraints upon the free exercise of religion and in discriminating against particular religious groups.

Surprised?

In recent years,...the question has most frequently arisen in connection with proposed state aid to church schools and efforts to carry on religious teachings in the public schools in accordance with the tenets of a particular sect...[Numerous state court decisions]...show the difficulty in drawing the line between tax legislation which provides funds for the welfare of the general public and that which is designed to support institutions which teach religion...

This was the first case to hold that the "establishment clause" of the First Amendment, applicable to Congress, is also applicable to the states and other governmental bodies through the "incorporation" of the First & Fourteenth Amendments. In simple terms, all that means is that state and local government, as well as Congress, are forbidden from making "laws respecting an establishment of religion."

The "establishment of religion" clause...means at least this:

Neither a state nor the Federal Government can set up a church.

Neither can pass laws which aid one religion, aid all religions, or prefer one religion over another.

Neither can force nor influence a person to go to or to remain away from church against his will or force him to profess a belief or disbelief in any religion.

No person can be punished for entertaining or professing religious beliefs or disbeliefs, for church attendance or non-attendance.

No tax in any amount, large or small, can be levied to support any religious activities or institutions, whatever they may be called, or whatever form they may adopt to teach or practice religion.

Neither a state nor the Federal Government can, openly or secretly, participate in the affairs of any religious organizations or groups and *vice versa*.

In the words of Jefferson, the clause against establishment of religion by law was intended to erect "a wall of separation between church and State." *Reynolds v. United States.*

...New Jersey cannot consistently with the "establishment of religion" clause...contribute tax-raised funds to the support of an institution which teaches the tenets and faith of any church. On the other hand, other language of the amendment commands that New Jersey cannot hamper its citizens in the free exercise of their own religion. Consequently, it cannot exclude individual Catholics, Lutherans, Mohammedans, Baptists, Jews, Methodists, Non-believers, Presbyterians, or the members of any other faith, because of their faith, or lack of it, from receiving the benefits of public welfare legislation.

Do you see the dilemma? Government cannot support religion (establishment is forbidden), but neither can it discriminate against religion (free exercise is guaranteed). What happens when these principles clash?

While we do not mean to intimate that a state could not provide transportation only to children attending public schools, we must be careful, in protecting the citizens of New Jersey against state-established churches, to be sure that we do not inadvertently prohibit New Jersey from extending its general state law benefits to all its citizens without regard to their religious belief.

Measured by these standards, we cannot say that the First Amendment prohibits New Jersey from spending tax-raised funds to pay the bus fares of parochial school pupils as a part of a general program under which it pays the fares of pupils attending public and other schools. It is undoubtedly true that children are helped to get to church schools. There is even a possibility that some of the children might not be sent to the church schools if the parents were compelled to pay their children's bus fares out of their own pockets when transportation to a public school would have been paid for by the State...Moreover, state-paid policemen, detailed to protect children going to and from church schools from the very real hazards of traffic, would serve much the same purpose and accomplish much the same result as state provisions intended to guarantee free transportation of a kind which the state deems to be best for the school children's welfare. And parents might refuse to risk their children to the serious danger of traffic accidents going to and from parochial schools, the approaches to which were not protected by policemen. Similarly, parents might be reluctant to permit their children to attend schools which the state had cut off from such general government services as ordinary police and fire protection, connections for sewage disposal, public highways and sidewalks. Of course, cutting off church schools from these services, so separate and so indisputably marked off from the religious function, would make it far more difficult for the schools to operate. But such is obviously not the purpose of the First Amendment. That Amendment requires the state to be a neutral in its relations with groups of religious believers and non-believers; it does not require the state to be their adversary. State power is no more to be used so as to handicap religions than it is to favor them.

There you go. The Constitution does not require government to be the adversary of religion. Looks less like a "wall" and more like a "short fence," doesn't it?

This Court has said that parents may, in the discharge of their duty under state compulsory education laws, send their children to a religious rather than a public school if the school meets the secular educational requirements which the state has power to impose. *Pierce v. Society of Sisters.* It appears that these parochial schools meet New Jersey's requirements. The State contributes no money to the schools. It does not support them. Its legislation, as applied, does no more than provide a general program to help parents get their children, regardless of their religion, safely and expeditiously to and from accredited schools. The First Amendment has erected a wall between church and state. That wall must be kept high and impregnable. We could not approve the slightest breach. New Jersey has not breached it here. [These laws are constitutional.]

The Court, after so eloquently stating the principle of neutrality, overstates the metaphor, for a wall that is "high and impregnable" sounds like an unfriendly wall to me. Indeed, it sounds like the wall of an enemy – an "adversary" the court just said religion was not meant to be. And, an unforgiving "slightest breach" does not allow for neighborly kindnesses "over" a lower wall or the loan of a cup of sugar "through" a window in a wall, does it? It is disingenuous for this Court to expect us to believe that providing tax dollars to get students to religious schools "is not even the slightest breach" of a wall they have themselves described as a barrier more difficult to breach than the Great Wall of China.

DISSENT: Justice Jackson…I have a sympathy…with Catholic citizens who are compelled by law to pay taxes for public schools…, but…the undertones of the opinion, advocating complete and uncompromising separation of Church from State, seem utterly discordant with its conclusion yielding support to their commingling in educational matters…

The Court concludes that this "legislation, as applied, does no more than provide a general program to help parents get their children, regardless of their religion, safely and expeditiously to and from accredited schools," and it draws a [faulty] comparison between "state provisions intended to guarantee free transportation" for school children with services such as police and fire protection…

The Township of Ewing is not furnishing transportation to the children in any form; it is not operating school busses itself or contracting for their operation; and it is not performing any public service of any kind with this taxpayer's money. All school children are left to ride as ordinary paying passengers on the regular busses operated by the public transportation system. What the Township does, and what the taxpayer complains of, is at stated intervals to reimburse parents for the fares paid, provided the children attend either public schools or Catholic Church schools. This expenditure of tax funds has no possible effect on the child's safety or expedition in transit. As passengers on the public busses they travel as fast and no faster, and are as safe and no safer, since their parents are reimbursed as before…

Under the Act and resolution brought to us by this case, children are classified according to the schools they attend and are to be aided if they attend the public schools or private Catholic schools, and they are not allowed to be aided if they attend private secular schools or private religious schools of other faiths…

> We should seriously question the suggestion that the majority has upheld a system that reimburses Catholic parents, but not Baptist parents. There is nothing in the record to indicate that is true. The likelihood is that this school district does not have any non-Catholic religious schools within its boundaries.

Whether the taxpayer constitutionally can be made to contribute aid to parents of students because of their attendance at parochial schools depends upon the nature of those schools and their relation to the Church. The Constitution says nothing of education. It lays no obligation on the states to provide schools and does not undertake to regulate state systems of education if they see fit to maintain them. But they cannot…invade rights secured to citizens by the Constitution of the United States. One of our basic rights is to be free of taxation to support a transgression of the constitutional command that the authorities "shall make no law respecting an establishment of religion, or prohibiting the free exercise thereof…"

It is no exaggeration to say that the whole historic conflict in temporal policy between the Catholic Church and non-Catholics comes to a focus in their respective school policies. The Roman Catholic Church…does not leave the individual to pick up religion by chance. It relies on early and indelible indoctrination in the faith and order of the Church by the word and example of persons consecrated to the task.

Our public school, if not a product of Protestantism, at least is more consistent with it than with the Catholic culture and scheme of values. It is a relatively recent development dating from about 1840. It is organized on the premise that secular education can be isolated from all religious teaching so that the school can inculcate all needed temporal knowledge and also maintain a strict and lofty neutrality as to religion. The assumption is that after the individual has been instructed in worldly wisdom he will be better fitted to choose his religion. Whether such a disjunction is possible, and if possible whether it is wise, are questions I need not try to answer.

I should be surprised if any Catholic would deny that the parochial school is a vital, if not the most vital, part of the Roman Catholic Church…Its growth and cohesion, discipline and loyalty, spring from its schools… To render tax aid to its Church school is indistinguishable to me from rendering the same aid to the Church itself…

The state cannot maintain a Church and it can no more tax its citizens to furnish free carriage to those who attend a Church. The prohibition against establishment of religion cannot be circumvented by a subsidy, bonus or reimbursement of expense to individuals for receiving religious instruction and indoctrination…

It seems to me that the basic fallacy in the Court's reasoning, which accounts for its failure to apply the principles it avows, is in ignoring the essentially religious test by which beneficiaries of this expenditure are selected. A policeman protects a Catholic, of course -- but not because he is a Catholic; it is because he is a man and a member of our society. The fireman protects the Church school – but not because it is a Church school; it is because it is property, part of the assets of our society. Neither the fireman nor the policeman has to ask before he renders aid, "Is this man or building identified with the Catholic Church?" But before these school authorities draw a check to reimburse for a student's fare they must ask just that question, and if the school is a Catholic one they may render aid because it is such, while if it is of any other faith or is run for profit, the help must be withheld...

> As stated, because it is likely that the only religious schools in this district are Catholic, the dissent is disingenuous in suggesting that the question which must be asked is, "Are these kids going to a Catholic school?" In fact, the question that must be asked is, "Are these kids going to an accredited not-for-profit school?" That is because the statute permits reimbursement to parents of all school children (including those whose children attend religious schools) unless the schools are operating "for profit."

[The majority does not answer] the proposition...that the effect of the [First Amendment] was to take every form of propagation of religion out of the realm of things which could directly or indirectly be made public business and thereby be supported in whole or in part at taxpayers' expense. That is a difference which the Constitution sets up between religion and almost every other subject matter of legislation, a difference which goes to the very root of religious freedom and which the Court is overlooking today. **This freedom...was intended not only to keep the states' hands out of religion, but to keep religion's hands off the state, and, above all, to keep bitter religious controversy out of public life by denying to every denomination any advantage from getting control of public policy or the public purse. Those great ends I cannot but think are immeasurably compromised by today's decision...**

Religious groups are quick to invoke constitutional protections but are irked when they feel its restraints. This Court has gone a long way... to hold that public business of such paramount importance as maintenance of public order (*Cantwell v. Connecticut*), protection of the privacy of the home (*Martin v. Struthers*) and taxation (*Walz v. Tax Commission*) may not be pursued by a state in a way that even indirectly will interfere with religious proselyting.

But we cannot have it both ways. Religious teaching cannot be a private affair when the state seeks to impose regulations which infringe on it indirectly, and a public affair when it comes to taxing citizens of one faith to aid another, or those of no faith to aid all. If these principles seem harsh in prohibiting aid to Catholic education, it must not be forgotten that it is the same Constitution that alone assures Catholics the right to maintain these schools at all when predominant local sentiment would forbid them. *Pierce v. Society of Sisters.*

Nor should I think that those who have done so well without this aid would want to see this separation between Church and State broken down. **If the state may aid these religious schools, it may therefore regulate them**...I cannot read the history of the struggle to separate political from ecclesiastical affairs...without a conviction that the Court today is unconsciously giving the clock's hands a backward turn.

DISSENT: Justice Rutledge...**Not simply an established church, but any law respecting an establishment of religion is forbidden**...Madison could not have confused "church" and "religion," or "an established church" and "an establishment of religion."

> In other words, if Madison had intended to only forbid a government-run church, he would have clearly limited the clause to that point. When he expands it to "religion" in general, something broader than the foregoing was likely intended.

The Amendment's purpose was not to strike merely at the official establishment of a single sect, creed or religion, outlawing only a formal relation such as had prevailed in England and some of the colonies. Necessarily it was to uproot all such relationships. But the object was broader than separating church and state in this narrow sense. It was to create a complete and permanent separation of the spheres of religious activity and civil authority by comprehensively forbidding every form of public aid or support for religion...

[The First Amendment]...secures all forms of religious expression, creedal, sectarian or nonsectarian, wherever and however taking place, except conduct which trenches upon the like freedoms of others or clearly and presently endangers the community's good order and security. For the protective purposes of this phase of the basic freedom, street preaching, oral or by distribution of literature, has been given "the same high estate under the First Amendment as…worship in the churches and preaching from the pulpits." And on this basis parents have been held entitled to send their children to private, religious schools. Accordingly, daily religious education commingled with secular is "religion" within the guaranty's comprehensive scope. So are religious training and teaching in whatever form…"Religion" has the same broad significance in the twin prohibition concerning "an establishment." The Amendment was not duplicitous. "Religion" and "establishment" were not used in any formal or technical sense. The prohibition broadly forbids state support, financial or other, of religion in any guise, form or degree. It outlaws all use of public funds for religious purposes…

Madison was certain in his own mind that under the Constitution "there is not a shadow of right in the general government to intermeddle with religion" and that "this subject is, for the honor of America, perfectly free and unshackled. The government has no jurisdiction over it…" Nevertheless he pledged that he would work for a Bill of Rights, including a specific guaranty of religious freedom, and Virginia, with other states, ratified the Constitution on this assurance…

Madison did not believe a Bill of Rights was necessary to ensure religious freedom. He believed the original Constitution was adequate in this regard. Nevertheless, it was promised and, thus, the Bill of Rights followed.

Madison opposed every form and degree of official relation between religion and civil authority. For him religion was a wholly private matter beyond the scope of civil power either to restrain or to support. Denial or abridgment of religious freedom was a violation of rights both of conscience and of natural equality. State aid was no less obnoxious or destructive to freedom and to religion itself than other forms of state interference. "Establishment" and "free exercise" were correlative and coextensive ideas, representing only different facets of the single great and fundamental freedom. The Remonstrance, following the Virginia statute's example, referred to the history of religious conflicts and the effects of all sorts of establishments, current and historical, to suppress religion's free exercise. With Jefferson, Madison believed that to tolerate any fragment of establishment would be by so much to perpetuate restraint upon that freedom...

Many Christians bemoan Jefferson's "wall of separation" because, in my estimation, they do not understand it. Are you now convinced that "separation," properly understood and applied, is the best assurance of religious freedom – the best assurance any faith has to spread its principles? Of course, the key phrase is "properly understood and applied," right? That is what we will be exploring.

In no phase was he more unrelentingly absolute than in opposing state support or aid by taxation. Not even "three pence" contribution was thus to be exacted from any citizen for such a purpose. Remonstrance, Par. 3... The principle was as much to prevent "the interference of law in religion" as to restrain religious intervention in political matters...

Compulsory attendance upon religious exercises went out early in the process of separating church and state, together with forced observance of religious forms and ceremonies. Test oaths and religious qualification for office followed later. These things none devoted to our great tradition of religious liberty would think of bringing back. Hence today, apart from efforts to inject religious training or exercises and sectarian issues into the public schools, the only serious surviving threat to maintaining that complete and permanent separation of religion and civil power which the First Amendment commands is through use of the taxing power to support religion, religious establishments, or establishments having a religious foundation whatever their form or special religious function.

Does New Jersey's action furnish support for religion by use of the taxing power? Certainly it does, if the test remains undiluted as Jefferson and Madison made it, that money taken by taxation from one is not to be used or given to support another's religious training or belief, or indeed one's own. Today as then the furnishing of "contributions of money for the propagation of opinions which he disbelieves" is the forbidden exaction; and the prohibition is absolute for whatever measure brings that consequence and whatever amount may be sought or given to that end...

> If Justice Rutledge had prevailed, Mr. Elliot would not be forced to pay taxes that fund transportation of children to private religious schools in Berkley that "propagate opinions which he disbelieves."

An appropriation from the public treasury to pay the cost of transportation to Sunday school [or] to weekday special classes at the church or parish house...could not withstand...constitutional attack. This would be true, whether or not secular activities were mixed with the religious. If such an appropriation could not stand, then it is hard to see how one becomes valid for the same thing upon the more extended scale of daily instruction...

> This seems to make sense, doesn't it? No one would agree that your tax dollars could be used to bus Methodist children (or children of any faith) to Sunday school, even if the kids learned how to cook on the side while in attendance.

Payment of transportation is no more, nor is it any the less essential to education, whether religious or secular, than payment for tuitions, for teachers' salaries, for buildings, equipment and necessary materials. Nor is it any the less directly related, in a school giving religious instruction, to the primary religious objective all those essential items of cost are intended to achieve...Now, as in Madison's time, not the amount but the principle of assessment is wrong.

But we are told that the New Jersey statute is valid in its present application because the appropriation is for a public, not a private purpose, namely, the promotion of education, and the majority accept this idea in the conclusion that all we have here is "public welfare legislation."

...To say that New Jersey's appropriation and her use of the power of taxation for raising the funds appropriated are not for public purposes but are for private ends, is to say that they are for the support of religion and religious teaching. Conversely, to say that they are for public purposes is to say that they are not for religious ones.

This is precisely for the reason that education which includes religious training and teaching, and its support, have been made matters of private right and function, not public, by the very terms of the First Amendment. That is the effect not only in its guaranty of religion's free exercise, but also in the prohibition of establishments. It was on this basis of the private character of the function of religious education that this Court held parents entitled to send their children to private, religious schools. *Pierce v. Society of Sisters.* Now it declares in effect that the appropriation of public funds to defray part of the cost of attending those schools is for a public purpose. If so, I do not understand why the state cannot go farther or why this case approaches the verge of its power...

Our constitutional policy...does not deny the value or the necessity for religious training, teaching or observance. Rather it secures their free exercise. But to that end it does deny that the state can undertake or sustain them in any form or degree...

The reasons underlying the Amendment's policy have not vanished with time or diminished in force. Now as when it was adopted the price of religious freedom is double. It is that the church and religion shall live both within and upon that freedom. There cannot be freedom of religion, safeguarded by the state, and intervention by the church or its agencies in the state's domain or dependency on its largesse. **The great condition of religious liberty is that it be maintained free from sustenance, as also from other interferences, by the state. For when it comes to rest upon that secular foundation it vanishes with the resting.** Public money devoted to payment of religious costs, educational or other, brings the quest for more [as well as] the struggle of sect against sect for the larger share or for any...That is precisely the history of societies which have had an established religion and dissident groups [and is] the very thing Jefferson and Madison experienced and sought to guard against...**The end**

of such strife cannot be other than to destroy the cherished liberty. The dominating group will achieve the dominant benefit; or all will embroil the state in their dissensions…

The Court concludes that the aid so given is not "support" of religion. It is rather only support of education as such, without reference to its religious content, and thus becomes public welfare legislation. To this elision of the religious element from the case is added gloss in two respects, one that the aid extended partakes of the nature of a safety measure, the other that failure to provide it would make the state unneutral in religious matters, discriminating against or hampering such children concerning public benefits all others receive…

> However, that argument has no end. Bricks and mortar cannot preach, so why not build Lutheran schools with tax dollars?

This approach, if valid, supplies a ready method for nullifying the Amendment's guaranty, not only for this case and others involving small grants in aid for religious education, but equally for larger ones…

No more unjust or discriminatory in fact is it to deny attendants at religious schools the cost of their transportation than it is to deny them tuitions, sustenance for their teachers, or any other educational expense which others receive at public cost. Hardship in fact there is which none can blink. But, for assuring to those who undergo it the greater, the most comprehensive freedom, it is one written by design and firm intent into our basic law.

Of course discrimination in the legal sense does not exist. The child attending the religious school has the same right as any other to attend the public school. But he foregoes exercising it because the same guaranty which assures this freedom forbids the public school or any agency of the state to give or aid him in securing the religious instruction he seeks. Were he to accept the common school, he would be the first to protest the teaching there of any creed or faith not his own. And it is precisely for the reason that their atmosphere is wholly secular that children are not sent to public schools under the *Pierce* doctrine. But that is a constitutional necessity, because **we have staked the very existence of our country on the faith that complete separation between the state and religion is best for the state and best for religion**. Remonstrance, Par. 8, 12.

...Nor is the case comparable to one of furnishing fire or police protection, or access to public highways. These things are matters of common right, part of the general need for safety. Certainly the fire department must not stand idly by while the church burns. Nor is this reason why the state should pay the expense of transportation...of the cost of religious education...Two great drives are constantly in motion to abridge, in the name of education, the complete division of religion and civil authority which our forefathers made. One is to introduce religious education and observances into the public schools. The other, to obtain public funds for the aid and support of various private religious schools. In my opinion both avenues were closed by the Constitution...We should not be less strict to keep strong and untarnished the one side of the shield of religious freedom than we have been of the other. The judgment should be reversed.

Well, I have to agree with the dissents on this one, but religion won, so put one more in the "for" column.

First Amendment Scoreboard

Rulings "for" Religion: 12 --- Rulings "against" Religion: 1

Note that all justices agree on the "wall of separation" principle, but disagree as to how "high and impregnable" it should be. The Court searches for original intent of the Framers. This case shows how tough it is to distinguish between public welfare legislation to provide benefits intended for all and benefits tending to establish religion.

For Mr. Elliot, fighting the bus transportation tax in Berkley is, most likely, a lost cause. Although *Everson* was a five-to-four ruling and may have been wrongly decided, it has been the law since 1947 and would appear to be well settled. So, in spite of his inability to afford private school for his kids and in spite of his disagreement with the teachings of some religions being aided by the bussing, it looks like he will have to pay this tax. This case, however, lends support for the "separation" concept of Madison and Jefferson. After all, if the Court had taken Madison seriously, Jackson Elliot would not have to support William Cult's "faith" by paying taxes to get the Cult children to school. Perhaps the "wall of separation" concept is more palatable, depending upon *which side of the wall* you are on. See what I mean?

Let me introduce you to the concept of "dicta." When the justices write about principles or make statements that are not directly required for the purpose of the decision before them, that is what we call "dicta." Although it can be used to persuade in future cases, it does not rise to the level of law. For example, suppose the issue is whether prayer is allowed in public school. If, in ruling upon that issue, a justice said there is no reason why the Bible cannot be taught as part of a history lesson, that would be dicta. Teaching the Bible as history was not the issue in the case, so the comment is not necessary to the decision. However, it is a positive indication that this justice would not have a problem using the Bible in that type of program.

Coming on the heels of *Everson*, this next case presents a new twist on government aid to religion. We travel to Champaign, Illinois.

McCOLLUM v. BOARD OF EDUCATION
SUPREME COURT OF THE UNITED STATES
333 U.S. 203
March 8, 1948
[8 – 1]

OPINION: Justice Black…[Vashti McCollum was a resident and taxpayer of Champaign and a parent whose child was then enrolled in the Champaign public schools.] In 1940 interested members of the Jewish, Roman Catholic, and a few of the Protestant faiths formed a voluntary association called the Champaign Council on Religious Education. They obtained permission from the Board of Education to offer [weekly] classes in religious instruction to public school pupils in grades four to nine...Classes were made up of pupils whose parents signed printed cards requesting that their children be permitted to attend...The council employed the religious teachers at no expense to the school authorities, but **the instructors were subject to the approval and supervision of the superintendent of schools.**

> Although not discussed here, doesn't this "approval" idea sound a lot like the *Cantwell* case where a law permitting local government to approve of "religion" before soliciting was struck down?

The classes were taught in three separate religious groups by Protestant teachers, Catholic priests, and a Jewish rabbi...Classes were conducted in the regular classrooms of the school building. Students who did not choose to take the religious instruction were...required to leave their classrooms and go to some other place in the school building for pursuit of their secular studies...Students who were released from secular study for the religious instructions were required to be present at the religious classes. Reports of their presence or absence were to be made to their secular teachers.

The foregoing facts...show the use of tax-supported property for religious instruction and the close cooperation between the school authorities and the religious council in promoting religious education. The operation of the State's compulsory education system thus assists and is integrated with the program of religious instruction carried on by separate religious sects. Pupils compelled by law to go to school for secular education are released in part from their legal duty upon the condition that they attend the religious classes. This is beyond all question a utilization of the tax-established and tax-supported public school system to aid religious groups to spread their faith. And it falls squarely under the ban of the First Amendment...

[This ruling does not] manifest a governmental hostility to religion or religious teachings. A manifestation of such hostility would be at war with our national tradition as embodied in the First Amendment's guaranty of the free exercise of religion. For the First Amendment rests upon the premise that both religion and government can best work to achieve their lofty aims if each is left free from the other within its respective sphere...

Here not only are the State's tax-supported public school buildings used for the dissemination of religious doctrines. The State also affords sectarian groups an invaluable aid in that it helps to provide pupils for their religious classes through use of the State's compulsory public school machinery. This is not separation of Church and State...[Judgment Reversed.]

CONCURRENCE: Justice Frankfurter...Traditionally, organized education in the Western world was Church education. It could hardly be otherwise when the education of children was primarily study of the Word and the ways of God. Even in the Protestant countries, where there was a less close identification of Church and State, the basis of education was largely the Bible, and its chief purpose inculcation of piety. To the extent that the State intervened, it used its authority to further aims of the church. The emigrants who came to these shores brought this view of education with them. Colonial schools certainly started with a religious orientation...

The evolution of colonial education, largely in the service of religion, into the public school system of today is the story of changing conceptions regarding the American democratic society, of the functions of State-maintained education in such a society, and of the role therein of the free exercise of religion by the people. The modern public school derived from a philosophy of freedom reflected in the First Amendment. It is appropriate to recall that the Remonstrance of James Madison...was called forth by a proposal which involved support to religious education...As the momentum for popular education increased and in turn evoked strong claims for State support of religious education, contests not unlike that which in Virginia had produced Madison's Remonstrance appeared in various forms in other States...In New York, the rise of the common schools led...to the barring of tax funds to church schools, and later to any school in which sectarian doctrine was taught. **In Massachusetts, largely through the efforts of Horace Mann, all sectarian teachings were barred from the common school to save it from being rent by denominational conflict.** The upshot of these controversies...is fairly summarized by saying that long before the Fourteenth Amendment subjected the States to new limitations, the prohibition of furtherance by the State of religious instruction became the guiding principle, in law and feeling, of the American people…

It is pertinent to remind that the establishment of this principle of Separation in the field of education was not due to any decline in the religious beliefs of the people. Horace Mann was a devout Christian, and the deep religious feeling of James Madison is stamped upon the Remonstrance…The sharp confinement of the public schools to secular education was a recognition of the need of a democratic society to educate its children, insofar as the State undertook to do so, in an atmosphere free from pressures in a realm in which pressures are most resisted and where conflicts are most easily and most bitterly engendered. Designed to serve as perhaps the most powerful agency for promoting cohesion among a heterogeneous democratic people, the public school must keep scrupulously free from entanglement in the strife of sects. The preservation of the community from divisive conflicts, of Government from irreconcilable pressures by religious groups, of religion from censorship and coercion however subtly exercised, requires strict confinement of the State to instruction other than religious, **leaving to the individual's church and home, indoctrination in the faith of his choice…**

By 1875 the separation of public education from Church entanglements, of the State from the teaching of religion, was firmly established in the consciousness of the nation. In that year President Grant made his famous remarks to the Convention of the Army of the Tennessee:

> Encourage free schools, and resolve that not one dollar appropriated for their support shall be appropriated to the support of any sectarian schools. Resolve that neither the State nor nation, nor both combined, shall support institutions of learning other than those sufficient to afford every child growing up in the land the opportunity of a good common school education, unmixed with sectarian, pagan, or atheistical dogmas. Leave the matter of religion to the family altar, the church, and the private school, supported entirely by private contributions. Keep the church and the state forever separate.

…The extent to which this principle was deemed a presupposition of our constitutional system is strikingly illustrated by the fact that every State admitted into the Union since 1876 was compelled by Congress to write into its Constitution a requirement that it maintain a school system "free from sectarian control."

If any of you believe the "separation" idea is something new or that Jefferson was solely responsible for the concept, think again.

...[But,] a religious people was naturally concerned about the part of the child's education entrusted "to the family altar, the church, and the private school." The promotion of religious education took many forms. Laboring under financial difficulties and exercising only persuasive authority, various denominations felt handicapped in their task of religious education. Abortive attempts were therefore frequently made to obtain public funds for religious schools. But the major efforts of religious inculcation were a recognition of the principle of Separation by the establishment of church schools privately supported. Parochial schools were maintained by various denominations. These, however, were often beset by serious handicaps, financial and otherwise, so that the religious aims which they represented found other directions. There were experiments with vacation schools, with Saturday as well as Sunday schools. They all fell short of their purpose. It was urged that by appearing to make religion a one-day-a-week matter, the Sunday school, which acquired national acceptance, tended to relegate the child's religious education, and thereby his religion, to a minor role not unlike the enforced piano lesson.

Out of these inadequate efforts evolved the week-day church school, held on one or more afternoons a week after the close of the public school. But children continued to be children; they wanted to play when school was out, particularly when other children were free to do so. Church leaders decided that if the week-day church school was to succeed, a way had to be found to give the child his religious education during what the child conceived to be his "business hours."

...The Champaign arrangement...presents powerful elements of inherent pressure by the school system in the interest of religious sects...That a child is offered an alternative may reduce the constraint; it does not eliminate the operation of influence by the school in matters sacred to conscience and outside the school's domain. The law of imitation operates, and non-conformity is not an outstanding characteristic of children. The result is an obvious pressure upon children to attend. Again, while the Champaign school population represents only a fraction of the more than two hundred and fifty sects of the nation, not even all the practicing sects in Champaign are willing or able to provide religious instruction. The children belonging to these non-participating sects will thus have inculcated in them a feeling of separatism when the school should be the training ground for habits of community, or they will have religious instruction in a faith which is not that of their parents. As a result, the public school system of Champaign actively furthers inculcation in the religious tenets of some faiths, and in the process sharpens the consciousness of religious differences at least among some of the children committed to its care. These are… the consequences against which the Constitution was directed when it prohibited the Government common to all from becoming embroiled, however innocently, in the destructive religious conflicts of which the history of even this country records some dark pages…

It is easy to forget that "separation" helps parents get their children the religious education they deem to be important. When government gets involved, the primary role of the parent is diminished.

If it were merely a question of enabling a child to obtain religious instruction with a receptive mind, the thirty or forty-five minutes could readily be found on Saturday or Sunday. If that were all, Champaign might have drawn upon the French system, known in its American manifestation as "dismissed time," whereby one school day is shortened to allow all children to go where they please, leaving those who so desire to go to a religious school. The momentum of the whole school atmosphere and school planning is presumably put behind religious instruction, as given in Champaign, precisely in order to secure for the religious instruction such momentum and planning…

In no activity of the State is it more vital to keep out divisive forces than in its schools, to avoid confusing, not to say fusing, what the Constitution sought to keep strictly apart. "The great American principle of eternal separation" – Elihu Root's phrase bears repetition – is one of the vital reliances of our constitutional system for assuring unities among our people stronger than our diversities. It is the Court's duty to enforce this principle in its full integrity.

We renew our conviction that "**we have staked the very existence of our country on the faith that complete separation between the state and religion is best for the state and best for religion.**" *Everson v. Board of Education.* **If nowhere else, in the relation between Church and State, "good fences make good neighbors."**

That is much better – the "short <u>fence</u> of separation." All Christians should be encouraged by the dicta in the following concurring opinion of Justice Jackson.

CONCURRENCE: Justice Jackson…[We should end the Champaign plan, but] I think it remains to be demonstrated whether it is possible, even if desirable, to…completely…isolate and cast out of secular education all that some people may reasonably regard as religious instruction. Perhaps subjects such as mathematics, physics or chemistry…can be completely secularized. But it would not seem practical to teach…the arts if we are to forbid exposure of youth to any religious influences. Music without sacred music, architecture minus the cathedral, or painting without the scriptural themes would be eccentric and incomplete, even from a secular point of view. Yet the inspirational appeal of religion in these guises is often stronger than in forthright sermon. Even such a "science" as biology raises the issue between evolution and creation as an explanation of our presence on this planet. Certainly a course in English literature that omitted the Bible and other powerful uses of our mother tongue for religious ends would be pretty barren. And I should suppose it is a proper, if not an indispensable, part of preparation for a worldly life to know the roles that religion and religions have played in the tragic story of mankind. The fact is that, for good or for ill, nearly everything in our culture worth transmitting, everything which gives meaning to life, is saturated with religious influences, derived from paganism, Judaism, Christianity – both Catholic and Protestant – and other faiths accepted by a large part of the world's peoples. One can hardly respect a system of education that would leave the student wholly ignorant of the currents of religious thought that move the world society for a part in which he is being prepared. But how one can teach, with satisfaction or even with justice to all faiths, such subjects as the story of the Reformation [or] the Inquisition…is more than I know. It is too much to expect that mortals will teach subjects about which their contemporaries have passionate controversies with the detachment they may summon to teaching about remote subjects such as Confucius or Mohammed. **When instruction turns to proselyting and imparting knowledge becomes evangelism is, except in the crudest cases, a subtle inquiry…**

DISSENT: Justice Reed…[Not provided.]

Although correctly decided, religion lost.

> ### First Amendment Scoreboard
> Rulings "for" Religion: 12 --- Rulings "against" Religion: 2

Please note that our Supreme Court has never said that "God" could not be uttered in school or that the Bible or the Koran could not be studied. The same is true with religious art, music, and literature. On many occasions, the general public seems quick to criticize the Supreme Court for doing what it has never done. Now that you are "in the know," please correct your fellow citizens when they get it wrong!!! As Justice Jackson said, the problem lies when "instruction turns to proselyting – when imparting knowledge becomes evangelism."

The Champaign plan did not work, but organized religion would not give up. How about the following attempt in the Big Apple?

ZORACH v. CLAUSON
SUPREME COURT OF THE UNITED STATES
343 U.S. 306
April 8, 1952
[6 – 3]

OPINION: Justice Douglas…[In this released-time program, students who wish to have religious instruction are permitted to leave the school premises to attend. The others stay in classrooms. The Court held the program to be constitutional.] Unlike *McCollum*, this program involves neither religious instruction in public classrooms nor expenditure of public funds. "Church and State must be separated." The separation must be complete and unequivocal. **The First Amendment does not say, however, that in every and all respects there shall be a separation of Church and State**…Otherwise the state and religion would be aliens to each other – hostile, suspicious and even unfriendly. Municipalities would not be permitted to render police and fire protection to religious groups. Policemen who helped parishioners into their places of worship would violate the Constitution. Prayers in our legislative halls; the appeals of the Almighty in the messages of the Chief Executive; the proclamations making Thanksgiving Day a holiday; "so help me God" in our courtroom oaths – these and all other references to the Almighty that run through our laws, our public rituals, our ceremonies would be flouting the First Amendment. A fastidious atheist or agnostic could even object to the supplication with which the Court opens each session: "God save the United States and this Honorable Court." We would have to press the concept of separation of Church and State to these extremes to condemn the present law on constitutional grounds.

Take a close look at Douglas's list. Do any items stand out as matters that should be handled differently from the others?

The nullification of this law would have wide and profound effects. A Catholic student applies to his teacher for permission to leave the school during hours on a Holy Day of Obligation to attend a mass. A Jewish student asks his teacher for permission to be excused for Yom Kippur. A Protestant wants the afternoon off for a family baptismal ceremony. In each case the teacher requires parental consent in writing. In each case the teacher, in order to make sure the student is not a truant, goes further and requires a report from the priest, the rabbi, or the minister. The teacher in other words cooperates in a religious program to the extent of making it possible for her students to participate in it. Whether she does it occasionally for a few students, regularly for one, or pursuant to a systematized program designed to further the religious needs of all the students does not alter the character of the act. **We are a religious people whose institutions presuppose a Supreme Being.** We guarantee the freedom to worship as one chooses. We make room for as wide a variety of beliefs and creeds as the spiritual needs of man deem necessary. We sponsor an attitude on the part of government that shows no partiality to any one group and that lets each flourish according to the zeal of its adherents and the appeal of its dogma. When the state encourages religious instruction or cooperates with religious authorities by adjusting the schedule of public events to sectarian needs, it follows the best of our traditions. For it then respects the religious nature of our people and accommodates the public service to their spiritual needs. To hold that it may not would be to find in the Constitution a requirement that the government show a callous indifference to religious groups. That would be preferring those who believe in no religion over those who do believe. Government may not finance religious groups nor undertake religious instruction nor blend secular and sectarian education nor use secular institutions to force one or some religion on any person. But we find no constitutional requirement which makes it necessary for government to be hostile to religion and to throw its weight against efforts to widen the effective scope of religious influence. The government must be neutral when it comes to competition between sects. It may not thrust any sect on any person. It may not make a religious observance compulsory. It may not coerce anyone to attend church, to observe a religious holiday, or to take religious instruction. But it can close its doors or suspend its operations as to those who want to repair to their religious sanctuary for worship or instruction. No more than that is undertaken here. The problem, like many problems in constitutional law, is one of degree. Here, the public schools do no more than accommodate schedules to a program of outside religious instruction.

DISSENT: Justice Black…I see no difference between the invalid *McCollum* system and this one. Here the sole question is whether New York can use its compulsory education laws to help religious sects get attendants presumably too unenthusiastic to go unless moved to do so by the pressure of this state machinery…The state thus makes religious sects beneficiaries of its power to compel children to attend secular schools. Any use of such coercive power by the state to help or hinder some religious sects or to prefer all religious sects over nonbelievers or vice versa is just what I think the First Amendment forbids…**Under our system of religious freedom, people have gone to their religious sanctuaries not because they feared the law but because they loved their God…State help to religion injects political and party prejudices into a holy field. It too often substitutes force for prayer, hate for love, and persecution for persuasion. Government should not be allowed, under cover of the soft euphemism of "co-operation," to steal into the sacred area of religious choice.**

DISSENT: Justice Frankfurter…The Court tells us that in the maintenance of its public schools, "[The State government] can close its doors or suspend its operations" so that its citizens may be free for religious devotions or instruction. If that were the issue, it would not rise to the dignity of a constitutional controversy. Of course, a State may provide that the classes in its schools shall be dismissed, for any reason, or no reason, on fixed days, or for special occasions. The essence of this case is that the school system did not "close its doors" and did not "suspend its operations." There is all the difference in the world between letting the children out of school and letting some of them out of school into religious classes. If every one is free to make what use he will of time wholly unconnected from schooling required by law – those who wish sectarian instruction devoting it to that purpose, those who have ethical instruction at home, to that, those who study music, to that – then of course there is no conflict with the Fourteenth Amendment. The pith of the case is that formalized religious instruction is substituted for other school activity which those who do not participate in the released-time program are compelled to attend. The school system is very much in operation during this kind of released time. If its doors are closed, they are closed upon those students who do not attend the religious instruction, in order to keep them within the school. That is the very thing which raises the constitutional issue. The deeply divisive controversy aroused by the attempts to secure public school pupils for sectarian instruction would promptly end if the advocates of such instruction would content to have the school "close its doors or suspend its operations" – that is, dismiss classes in their entirety, without discrimination – instead of seeking to use the public schools as the instrument for securing attendance at denominational classes. **The unwillingness of the promoters of this movement to dispense with such use of the public schools betrays a surprising want of confidence in the inherent power of the various faiths to draw children to outside sectarian classes – an attitude that hardly reflects the faith of the greatest religious spirits.**

DISSENT: Justice Jackson…This released-time program is founded upon a use of the State's power of coercion, which, for me, determines its unconstitutionality. My evangelistic brethren confuse an objection to compulsion with an objection to religion. **It is possible to hold a faith with enough confidence to believe that what should be rendered to God does not need to be decided and collected by Caesar.** The day that this country ceases to be free for irreligion it will cease to be free for religion – except for the sect that can win political power…Today's judgment will be more interesting to students of psychology and of the judicial processes than to students of constitutional law.

Although I believe the dissents are persuasive, nevertheless, religion wins again! What do you know?

First Amendment Scoreboard
Rulings "for" Religion: 13 --- Rulings "against" Religion: 2

Justice Douglas makes a very good point that, in effect, this "released-time" program is nothing more than allowing a teacher to dismiss a student to attend a religious function. And, surely, our Constitution does not forbid a public school teacher from letting a child out of school for a family religious function. Yet, the dissents make good points, as well. Sometimes these questions are not as easy as they seem.

There are a number of important points made in the dissents that should serve as a wake-up call for Christians:

> Justice Black (in dissent)...**Under our system of religious freedom, people have gone to their religious sanctuaries not because they feared the law but because they loved their God... State help to religion injects political and party prejudices into a holy field. It too often substitutes force for prayer, hate for love, and persecution for persuasion. Government should not be allowed, under cover of the soft euphemism of "co-operation," to steal into the sacred area of religious choice.**

Why would the Christian faith or any faith need the support of government to survive in a free country? Are we truly that weak that we cannot get our children to a religious class unless we have the strong arm of government in place to threaten truancy? Folks, we do not want any part of this and, truly, both government and religion get soiled when they play together.

> Justice Frankfurter (in dissent)...**The unwillingness of the promoters of this movement to dispense with such use of the public schools betrays a surprising want of confidence in the inherent power of the various faiths to draw children to outside sectarian classes – an attitude that hardly reflects the faith of the greatest religious spirits.**

> Justice Jackson (in dissent)...**It is possible to hold a faith with enough confidence to believe that what should be rendered to God does not need to be decided and collected by Caesar.**

These statements are embarrassing to our Christian faith. So much so that our attention should turn away from seeking the helping hand of government and in, toward ourselves. We can do better. We can do much better.

Stay put – we are still in New York for the time being.

Board of Education v. Allen (1968): [6 – 3]…Justice White…[New York law requires local public school boards to <u>lend</u> secular textbooks free of charge to all students, whether attending public or private schools. Does this violate the Establishment Clause?]

[No. This law is constitutional and merely makes available to all children the benefits of a general program to lend school books free of charge. No funds or books are furnished to parochial schools and the financial benefit is to parents and children, not to schools. Perhaps free books make it more likely that some children choose to attend a sectarian school, but that was true of the state-paid bus fares in *Everson*. This does not alone demonstrate an unconstitutional degree of support for a religious institution. Of course, books are different from busses. However, the statute does *not* authorize the loan of *religious* books.]

CONCURRENCE: Justice Harlan…[Not provided.]

DISSENT: Justice Black…The majority links state and churches together in controlling the lives and destinies of our citizenship – a citizenship composed of people of myriad religious faiths, some of them bitterly hostile to and completely intolerant of the others. The same powerful sectarian religious propagandists who have succeeded in securing passage of the present law to help religious schools carry out their sectarian religious purposes can and doubtless will continue their propaganda, looking toward complete domination and supremacy of their particular brand of religion. Bus fares cannot support the validity of school books for a religious school. It requires no prophet to foresee that the majority argument will be used to provide public funds to buy real estate for religious schools or to erect buildings, to pay teachers' salaries and, finally, wind up fully supporting the religious schools. The Court's ruling bodes nothing but evil to religious peace in this country.

DISSENT: Justice Douglas…[Under this system, the parochial schools select the books they want, then the public schools either approve of them for non-religious content or not.] If the board supinely submits by approving and supplying sectarian oriented books, the struggle to keep church and state separate has been lost. If the board resists, then the battle line between church and state will have been drawn and the contest will be on to keep the school board independent or to put it under church domination and control. Whatever may be said about *Everson*, there is nothing ideological about a bus. For example, is the slaughter of the Aztecs by Cortes to be lamented for its destruction of a New World culture…or forgiven because the Spaniards carried the true Faith to a barbaric people who practiced human sacrifice?

I believe this case was wrongly decided and that Justice Douglas is persuasive in dissent. However, religion won…I suppose.

> ## First Amendment Scoreboard
> Rulings "for" Religion: 14 --- Rulings "against" Religion: 2

Guess who the plaintiff was in this case? It was the School Board. Apparently, they did not want to spend the money on books to loan to Catholics or they did not want to make tough decisions over which textbooks qualified. They asked the law to be declared unconstitutional so that the Commissioner of Education (Allen) would not remove them from their jobs if they failed to supply the books. Although Justice Black's forebodings of evil and political divisiveness have apparently not come true and, with this case, the Court has seemed to reach the limits of public expenditure involving religion, it seems Justice Douglas does have a point. Perhaps he could have said it just a bit more clearly. If this School Board finds even one word in a history book that they claim to be "evangelistic" and disapprove of textbooks submitted for approval by Catholic authorities, is the fight on for state vs. religion superiority? Will school board elections now be fought between various sects for the right to determine what books are loaned to the private schools? This is the climate one can expect when the "fence" of separation gets too low – when religion becomes too "entangled" with government. We now journey to Rhode Island and Pennsylvania in a companion case that, once again, explores how to get tax dollars to religious schools.

***Lemon v. Kurtzman* (1971):** [8 – 1] Chief Justice Burger…[Rhode Island adopted a statute that pays teachers in nonpublic schools a supplement of 15% of their annual salary. Pennsylvania adopted a statute that provides financial support to nonpublic schools via reimbursement of teachers' salaries, textbooks, and instructional material in secular subjects. Held: Both statutes are unconstitutional.]

[In Rhode Island the teachers in the religious schools applying for the supplement must only use teaching materials used in public schools and must agree in writing not to teach a course in religion while receiving the salary supplement. In Pennsylvania, a school seeking reimbursement must maintain accounting procedures to identify the separate cost of secular educational materials and cannot get reimbursement for any subject matter that contains religious teaching. To withstand constitutional muster, the statute must (1) have a secular legislative purpose, (2) its primary effect must be one that neither advances religion nor inhibits religion, and (3) it must not foster excessive government entanglement with religion. Both statutes had a viable secular purpose; i.e., to enhance the quality of secular education for all schools covered by the compulsory education laws. But, the cumulative impact of both statutes involves excessive entanglement. Unlike the *Allen* case, teachers have a substantially different ideological character than books. A continued comprehensive State surveillance will inevitably be required to ensure the restrictions are obeyed. This kind of State inspection is fraught with the sort of entanglement the Constitution forbids. Also, the potential for divisive political issues is high.] **Parochial schools came into existence because Protestant groups with political power were using the public schools to propagate their faith. The Catholics naturally rebelled. In the early 19th century, the contests between Protestants and Catholics often erupted into violence including the burning of Catholic churches. We would be blind to reality if we let "sophisticated bookkeeping" sanction "almost total subsidy of a religious institution by assigning the bulk of the institution's expenses to 'secular' activities." Sophisticated attempts to avoid the Constitution are just as invalid as simple-minded ones. Additionally,**

when a sectarian institution accepts state aid it becomes obligated under the Equal Protection Clause of the Fourteenth Amendment not to discriminate in admissions policies and faculty selection.

So, Justice Black's prediction of the slippery slope (in *Board v. Allen*) did not come true. There are limits to state aid to religion. Religion lost this round.

> ### First Amendment Scoreboard
> Rulings "for" Religion: 14 --- Rulings "against" Religion: 3

The Berkley tax for the purchase of textbooks (even secular textbooks) to be given (not loaned) to private religious schools is an invalid tax that breaches the establishment clause irrespective of whether the books are historically accurate. But, alas, the school board can remedy that problem by loaning, instead of giving, the textbooks to the schools. If that occurs, Jackson Elliot cannot likely prevail.

These five cases are very representative of "religious subsidy" jurisprudence. For sure, we know we can still say "God" and religion is winning 14 to 3.

It's time for a summary.

1947: In *Everson v. Board of Education* we learned that a tax to reimburse parents for their costs of bussing their children to public schools and private religious schools was not an establishment of religion and was upheld by the Court as a general welfare measure.

Principles: Justice Jackson makes a very strong argument in dissent that this bus subsidy is no different than taxing folks to transport children to Sunday school, which would clearly be a violation of the establishment clause. Perhaps the "wall of separation" is better described as a "short fence of separation."

History Lessons: I suggest this case is far more important for the historical background provided – the reasons why the Framers both guaranteed the freedom to exercise religion and prohibited its establishment. It is easy to forget the centuries of evils, fears, turmoil, and political unrest that accompanied a closer partnership of government and religion because our system has worked so well.

1948: In *McCollum v. Board of Education* we learned that government-owned school buildings could not be used by religious groups for proselytizing during the school day.

History Lessons: As we experimented with public schools, Massachusetts barred religious teachings precisely because of denominational conflict that was tearing the schools apart.

Dicta: This case is potentially far more important for its dicta than anything else. I speak specifically of Justice Jackson's concurring opinion and will address it below.

1952: In *Zorach v. Clauson* we learned that moving the religious classes off campus solved the *McCollum* problem. I will discuss the religious list of Justice Douglas below.

History Lessons: Christians should be encouraged by the conclusion of Justice Douglas that "we are a religious people whose institutions presuppose a Supreme Being." Of course, that should be obvious if you know anything about our history. However, it is mentioned for emphasis because I know that many of you came into this study "presupposing" that the Supreme Court would not likely acknowledge that heritage. Right?

1968: In *Board of Education v. Allen* we learned, somewhat surprisingly, that public school boards may lend secular books to private religious schools without running afoul of the establishment clause.

1971: In *Lemon v. Kurtzman* we learned that in order to withstand a constitutional challenge, statutes must have a secular purpose, their primary effect must be one that neither advances religion nor inhibits religion and they must not foster excessive government entanglement with religion. Subsidizing religious teachers' salaries and giving secular books and instructional materials to religious schools did not meet these tests.

THE SUGGESTED CHRISTIAN RESPONSE

Lost Causes:

Challenges to taxes designed to promote the general welfare are not likely to succeed even if the proceeds go, in part, to religion. Although defining "general welfare" can be difficult, challenging a bus transportation reimbursement program is a lost cause.

All faiths should resist asking for government financial support for any reason. When religion seeks the political support of government because it does not believe it can otherwise survive, the cause is lost before the request is made.

Causes to Champion:

I think it highly unlikely that any public school district in this country would financially support transportation for one faith to the exclusion of other faiths. However, if so, a challenge would be in order for those sects left out and they should prevail.

If government goes beyond transportation and a textbook loan program – if they begin taxing for bricks and mortar to build parochial elementary schools or to compensate teachers in religious institutions, then government has gone too far.

I see the issues of which textbooks to include or omit as being best resolved in the political arena at the local level. I just do not believe the judiciary should get into the education curriculum business. However, I do strongly believe that parents should be on top of this from the beginning to ensure that history is not rewritten and includes our Christian heritage. This is not a constitutional question; rather, it is a political one. Parents should get involved in their school district's operations. Hard work, I know, but necessary.

I ask you to please embrace the concurring opinion and dicta of Justice Jackson in *McCollum v. Board of Education*. **He posits it is impossible to** completely isolate secular education from a religious influence without eliminating much of the history of the world. The Constitution does not demand it, the Supreme Court does not demand it, and Christians agree! Please explain to your neighbors that the "wall of separation" was not ever meant to be that high. If Christians continue to act defeated and walk away when misguided folks tell us the Supreme Court would not favor *any* religious influence in our public schools, we play into the hands of the enemy. Knowledge is power. Let them know they are wrong. Invite them to read these cases if they need evidence.

The study of art without its religious influence is absurd. The same is true for music and sacred music. Gospel music had a major influence on all American music. Our children should never study architecture without studying the cathedrals of Rome or study English literature without studying references to the Bible.

As I have said, dicta does not set precedent, but it is persuasive. The Supreme Court of the United States has never come close to indicating that any of the foregoing is prohibited from being taught in public school and, as you can see, these topics have received their blessing. I also take great encouragement from the list Justice Douglas mentions in the *Zorach* opinion. It is also dicta. Douglas is making the point that the establishment clause does not mean that in every respect separation must be absolute. He mentions "appeals to the Almighty in Presidential messages." All of these are matters of free speech and are perfectly permissible.

The greatest lesson to be learned from this chapter is that the cause of Christianity should shun the financial support of government. Seeking the aid of Caesar will bring on the control of Caesar. Ultimately, the cause for Christ will be far more successful for the right reasons without even the slightest financial push or pull from government.

Show your Christian friends how friendly the High Court has been to religion and what we avoid with at least a "short fence of separation." No need to pout. This is America. If Christianity or any religion cannot thrive in the land of the free, on its own, and without government's financial support (and controlling hand), then where? Introduce someone to Jesus Christ, for "It's still OK to say 'God.'"

Chapter Eight

ESTABLISHMENT:
REMEMBER THE SABBATH DAY,
TO KEEP IT HOLY

Jackson Elliot's work is in sales. Mondays were historically slow sales days. So, in Texas, he worked Tuesday through Saturday. His family had always honored Sunday as the Christian Sabbath and, in fact, Lubbock had a Sunday Blue Law in effect, meaning that it was illegal to work in his type of employment on Sunday.

Berkley has a **Saturday** Blue Law. What? Welcome to California. Apparently, a majority of those on the city council are of a faith that honors Saturday as their day of Sabbath. That makes working on Saturday illegal. If Jackson honors his own day of rest on Sunday and wishes to avoid jail or a fine, he will be forced to work on Monday, the slowest sales day in the week. Of course, he could maintain his income if he works on Sunday in violation of his faith.

Jackson wondered, "Is it possible I could be criminally punished for doing something perfectly legal on every other day of the week but Saturday? What happened to the free exercise of religion? How about the establishment clause? How about just plain old freedom?" To him, it sure looked like these non-mainstream religions were being favored over Christianity. Is this law constitutional? The Supreme Court has answered this question.

Although still the law in many parts of the nation, Sunday Blue Laws are not as popular as they once were, for many states and cities have repealed them. Greed is the rule of the day. However, what did the Court do with this when Blue Laws were in vogue? Let's go to Maryland.

══

McGOWAN v. MARYLAND
SUPREME COURT OF THE UNITED STATES
366 U.S. 420
May 29, 1961
[8 – 1]

OPINION: Chief Justice Warren...The issues in this case concern the constitutional validity of Maryland criminal statutes, commonly known as Sunday Closing Laws or Sunday Blue Laws...

Seven employees of a large discount department store...in Anne Arundel County, Maryland...were indicted for the Sunday sale of a three-ring loose-leaf binder, a can of floor wax, a stapler and staples, and toy submarine in violation of [Maryland statutes]. Generally, [they prohibit], throughout the State, the Sunday sale of all merchandise except the retail sale of tobacco products, confectioneries, milk, bread, fruits, gasoline, oils, greases, drugs and medicines, and newspapers and periodicals. [Recent amendments except]...the retail sale in Anne Arundel County of all foodstuffs, automobile and boating accessories, flowers, toilet goods, hospital supplies and souvenirs. It now further provides that any retail establishment in Anne Arundel County which does not employ more than one person other than the owner may operate on Sunday...

§492...forbids all persons from doing any work or bodily labor on Sunday and forbids permitting children or servants to work on that day or to engage in fishing, hunting and unlawful pastimes or recreations. The section excepts all works of necessity and charity.

§522...disallows the opening or use of any dancing saloon, opera house, bowling alley or barber shop on Sunday. However, in addition to the exceptions noted above, §509 exempts, for Anne Arundel County, the Sunday operation of any bathing beach, bathhouse, dancing saloon and amusement park, and activities incident thereto and retail sales of merchandise customarily sold at, or incidental to, the operation of the aforesaid occupations and businesses. §90...makes generally unlawful the sale of alcoholic beverages on Sunday. However, this section, and immediately succeeding ones, provide various immunities for the Sunday sale of different kinds of alcoholic beverages, at different hours during the day, by vendors holding different types of licenses, in different political divisions of the State – particularly in Anne Arundel County...

[These employees] were convicted and each was fined five dollars and costs. The Maryland Court of Appeals affirmed...

The essence of appellants' "establishment" argument is that Sunday is the Sabbath day of the predominant Christian sects; that the purpose of the enforced stoppage of labor on that day is to facilitate and encourage church attendance; that the purpose of setting Sunday as a day of universal rest is to induce people with no religion or people with marginal religious beliefs to join the predominant Christian sects; that the purpose of the atmosphere of tranquility created by Sunday closing is to aid the conduct of church services and religious observances of the sacred day...There is no dispute that the original laws which dealt with Sunday labor were motivated by religious forces. But what we must decide is whether present Sunday legislation, having undergone extensive changes from the earliest forms, still retains its religious character.

Sunday Closing Laws go far back into American history, having been brought to the colonies with a background of English legislation dating to the thirteenth century...The law of the colonies to the time of the Revolution and the basis of the Sunday laws in the States was [a 1677 English statute that provided, in part]:

> For the better observation and keeping holy the Lord's day, commonly called Sunday: be it enacted...that all the laws enacted and in force concerning the observation of the day, and repairing to the church thereon, be carefully put in execution; and that all and every person and persons whatsoever shall upon every Lord's day apply themselves to the observation of the same, by exercising themselves thereon in the duties of piety and true religion, publicly and privately; and that no tradesman, artificer, workman, laborer,

or other person whatsoever, shall do or exercise any worldly labor or business or work of their ordinary callings upon the Lord's day, or any part thereof (works of necessity and charity only excepted);… and that no person or persons whatsoever shall publicly cry, show forth, or expose for sale any wares, merchandise, fruit, herbs, goods, or chattels, whatsoever, upon the Lord's day, or any part thereof…

Clearly,…the English Sunday legislation was in aid of the established church.

The American colonial Sunday restrictions arose soon after settlement. Starting in 1650, the Plymouth Colony proscribed servile work, unnecessary traveling, sports, and the sale of alcoholic beverages on the Lord's day and enacted laws concerning church attendance. The Massachusetts Bay Colony and the Connecticut and New Haven Colonies enacted similar prohibitions…The religious orientation of the colonial statutes was equally apparent. For example, a 1629 Massachusetts Bay instruction began, "And to the end the Sabbath may be celebrated in a religious manner…" A 1653 enactment spoke of Sunday activities "which things tend much to the dishonor of God, the reproach of religion, and the profanation of his holy Sabbath, the sanctification whereof is sometimes put for all duties immediately respecting the service of God…" These laws persevered after the Revolution and, at about the time of the First Amendment's adoption, each of the colonies had laws of some sort restricting Sunday labor.

But…nonreligious arguments for Sunday closing began to be heard more distinctively and the statutes began to lose some of their totally religious flavor. In the middle 1700s, Blackstone wrote, "The keeping one day in the seven holy, as a time of relaxation and refreshment as well as for public worship, is of admirable service to a state considered merely as a civil institution. It humanizes, by the help of conversation and society, the manners of the lower classes; which would otherwise degenerate into a sordid ferocity and savage selfishness of spirit; it enables the industrious workman to pursue his occupation in the ensuing week with health and cheerfulness."…The New York law of 1788 omitted the term "Lord's day" and substituted "the first day of the week commonly called Sunday."

Similar changes marked the Maryland statutes...With the advent of the First Amendment, the colonial provisions requiring church attendance were soon repealed.

More recently, further secular justifications have been advanced for making Sunday a day of rest, a day when people may recover from the labors of the week just passed and may physically and mentally prepare for the week's work to come. In England, during the First World War, a committee investigating the health conditions of munitions workers reported that "if the maximum output is to be secured and maintained for any length of time, a weekly period of rest must be allowed...On economic and social grounds alike this weekly period of rest is best provided on Sunday."

The proponents of Sunday closing legislation are no longer exclusively representatives of religious interests. Recent New Jersey Sunday legislation was supported by labor groups and trade associations...

Almost every State in our country presently has some type of Sunday regulation and over forty possess a relatively comprehensive system... Thus have Sunday laws evolved from the wholly religious sanctions that originally were enacted...

In 1776,...Madison co-authored Virginia's Declaration of Rights which provided that "all men are equally entitled to the free exercise of religion, according to the dictates of conscience..." Virginia had had Sunday legislation since early in the seventeenth century: in 1776, the laws penalizing "maintaining any opinions in matters of religion, forbearing to repair to the church, or the exercising any mode of worship whatsoever" were repealed, and all dissenters were freed from the taxes levied for the support of the established church. The Sunday labor prohibitions remained; apparently, they were not believed to be inconsistent with the newly enacted Declaration of rights. Madison had sought also to have the Declaration expressly condemn the existing Virginia establishment. This hope was finally realized when "A Bill for Establishing Religious Freedom" was passed in 1785. In this same year, Madison presented to Virginia legislators "A Bill for Punishing...Sabbath Breakers" which provided, in part:

If any person on Sunday shall himself be found labouring at his own or any other trade or calling, or shall employ his apprentices, servants or slaves in labour, or other business, except it be in the ordinary household offices of daily necessity, or other work of necessity or charity, he shall forfeit the sum of ten shillings for every such offence, deeming every apprentice, servant, or slave so employed, and every day he shall be so employed as constituting a distinct offence.

This became the law the following year and remained during the time that Madison fought for the First Amendment in the Congress…In 1799, Virginia pronounced "An act for establishing religious freedom" as "a true exposition of the principles of the Bill of Rights and Constitution" and repealed all subsequently enacted legislation deemed inconsistent with it. Virginia's statute banning Sunday labor stood…

We find the place of Sunday Closing Laws in the First Amendment's history both enlightening and persuasive…An early commentator opined that the "real object of the amendment was…to prevent any national ecclesiastical establishment, which should give to a hierarchy the exclusive patronage of the national government." **But, the First Amendment, in its final form, did not simply bar a congressional enactment *establishing a church*; it forbade all laws respecting an *establishment of religion*.** Thus, this Court has given the Amendment a "broad interpretation…in the light of its history and the evils it was designed forever to suppress…"

However, it is equally true that the "Establishment" Clause does not ban federal and state regulation of conduct whose reason or effect merely happens to coincide or harmonize with the tenets of some or all religions. In many instances, the Congress or state legislatures conclude that the general welfare of society, wholly apart from any religious considerations, demands such regulation. Thus, for temporal purposes, murder is illegal. And the fact that this agrees with the dictates of the Judeo-Christian religions while it may disagree with others does not invalidate the regulation. So too with the questions of adultery and polygamy. *Reynolds v. United States.* The same could be said of theft, fraud, etc., because those offenses were also proscribed in the Decalogue…

> The Decalogue is a reference to the Ten Commandments.

In light of the evolution of our Sunday Closing Laws through the centuries, and of their more or less recent emphasis upon secular considerations, it is not difficult to discern that as presently written and administered, most of them, at least, are of a secular rather than of a religious character, and that presently they bear no relationship to the establishment of religion as those words are used in the Constitution of the United States.

Throughout this century and longer, both the federal and state governments have oriented their activities very largely toward improvement of the health, safety, recreation and general well-being of our citizens…Sunday Closing Laws…have become part and parcel of this great governmental concern wholly apart from their original purposes…The present purpose and effect of most of them is to provide a uniform day of rest for all citizens; the fact that this day is Sunday, a day of particular significance for the dominant Christian sects, does not bar the State from achieving its secular goals. To say that the States cannot prescribe Sunday as a day of rest for these purposes solely because centuries ago such laws had their genesis in religion would give a constitutional interpretation of hostility to the public welfare rather than one of mere separation of church and State.

We now reach the Maryland statutes under review. The title of the major series of sections…is "Sabbath Breaking"; §492 proscribes work or bodily labor on the "Lord's day," and forbids persons to "profane the Lord's day" by gaming, fishing, et cetera…[M]any of the exempted Sunday activities in the various localities of the State may only be conducted during the afternoon and late evening; most Christian church services, of course, are held on Sunday morning and early Sunday evening. Finally, as previously noted, certain localities do not permit the allowed Sunday activities to be carried on within one hundred yards of any church where religious services are being held. This is the totality of the evidence of religious purpose which may be gleaned from the face of the present statute and from its operative effect.

The predecessors of the existing Maryland Sunday laws are undeniably religious in origin...[But], considering the language and operative effect of the current statutes, we no longer find the blanket prohibition against Sunday work or bodily labor. To the contrary, [the statute]...permits the Sunday sale of tobaccos and sweets and a long list of sundry articles which we have enumerated above; [another section] permits the Sunday sale of alcoholic beverages, products strictly forbidden by predecessor statutes; we are told that Anne Arundel County allows Sunday bingo and the Sunday playing of pinball machines and slot machines, activities generally condemned by prior Maryland Sunday legislation. Certainly, these are not works of charity or necessity. [The] current stipulation that shops with only one employee may remain open on Sunday does not coincide with a religious purpose. These provisions, along with those which permit various sports and entertainments on Sunday, seem clearly to be fashioned for the purpose of providing a Sunday atmosphere of recreation, cheerfulness, repose and enjoyment...We believe that the air of the day is one of relaxation rather than one of religion...

We accept the State Supreme Court's determination that the statute's present purposes and effect is not to aid religion but to set aside a day of rest and recreation. But this does not answer all of appellant's contentions. We are told that the State has other means at its disposal to accomplish its secular purpose...that would not even remotely or incidentally give state aid to religion. On this basis, we are asked to hold these statutes invalid on the ground that the State's power to regulate conduct in the public interest may only be executed in a way that does not unduly or unnecessarily infringe upon the religious provisions of the First Amendment. *Cantwell v. Connecticut.* However relevant this argument may be, we believe that the factual basis on which it rests is not supportable. It is true that if the State's interest were simply to provide for its citizens a periodic respite from work, a regulation demanding that everyone rest one day in seven, leaving the choice of the day to the individual, would suffice.

However, the State's purpose is not merely to provide a one-day-in-seven work stoppage. In addition to this, the State seeks to set one day apart from all others as a day of rest, repose, recreation and tranquility – a day which all members of the family and community have the opportunity

to spend and enjoy together, a day on which there
and disassociation from the everyday intensity of cc
day on which people may visit friends and relatives
during working days.

Obviously, a State is empowered to determine that a rest-one
statute would not accomplish this purpose; that it would not provide for a
general cessation of activity, a special atmosphere of tranquility, a day which
all members of the family or friends and relatives might spend together.
Furthermore, it seems plain that the problems involved in enforcing such
a provision would be exceedingly more difficult than those in enforcing a
common-day-of-rest provision.

Moreover, it is common knowledge that the first day of the week has
come to have special significance as a rest day in this country. People of all
religions and people with no religion regard Sunday as a time for family
activity, for visiting friends and relatives, for late sleeping, for passive and
active entertainments, for dining out, and the like…Sunday is a day apart
from all others. The cause is irrelevant; the fact exists. **It would seem
unrealistic for enforcement purposes and perhaps detrimental to the
general welfare to require a State to choose a common day of rest other
than that which most persons would select of their own accord.** For
these reasons, we hold that the Maryland statutes are **not** laws respecting
an establishment of religion…[Convictions affirmed.]

Logic cannot possibly support this opinion. I shall repeat the next to the
last sentence, substituting only the phrase "the majoritarian Christians"
for the phrase "most persons." To wit: "It would seem unrealistic for
enforcement purposes and perhaps detrimental to the general welfare
to require a State to choose a common day of rest other than that
which the majoritarian Christians would select of their own accord."
Isn't this the reality?

DISSENT: Justice Douglas…**The question is not whether one day out
of seven can be imposed by a State as a day of rest. The question is
not whether Sunday can by force of custom and habit be retained as**

of rest. The question is whether a State can impose criminal sanctions on those who, unlike the Christian majority that makes up our society, worship on a different day or do not share the religious scruples of the majority…I do not see how a State can make protesting citizens refrain from doing innocent acts on Sunday because the doing of those acts offends sentiments of their Christian neighbors.

The institutions of our society are founded on the belief that there is an authority higher than the authority of the State; that there is a moral law which the State is powerless to alter; that the individual possesses rights, conferred by the Creator [in the Declaration of Independence], which government must respect…For these reasons we stated in *Zorach v. Clauson*, "We are a religious people whose institutions presuppose a Supreme Being."

But those who fashioned the First Amendment decided that if and when God is to be served, His service will not be motivated by coercive measures of government. [The Establishment Clause means], as I understand it, that if a religious leaven is to be worked into the affairs of our people, it is to be done by individuals and groups, not by the Government. This necessarily means, first, that the dogma, creed, scruples, or practices of no religious group or sect are to be preferred over those of any others; second, that no one shall be interfered with by government for practicing the religion of his choice; third, that the State may not require anyone to practice a religion or even any religion; and fourth, that the State cannot compel one so to conduct himself as not to offend the religious scruples of another. The idea, as I understand it, was to limit the power of government to act in religious matters, not to limit the freedom of religious men to act religiously nor to restrict the freedom of atheists or agnostics.

The First Amendment commands government to have no interest in theology or ritual; it admonishes government to be interested in allowing religious freedom to flourish – whether the result is to produce Catholics, Jews, or Protestants, or to turn the people toward the path of Buddha, or to end in a predominantly Moslem nation, or to produce in the long run atheists or agnostics. On matters of this kind government must be neutral.

This freedom plainly includes freedom from religion with the right to believe, speak, publish and advocate anti-religious programs. Certainly the "free exercise" clause does not require that everyone embrace the theology of some church or of some faith, or observe the religious practices of any majority or minority sect. The First Amendment...prevents, of course, the selection by government of an "official" church. Yet the ban plainly extends farther than that. We said in *Everson v. Board of Education* that it would be an "establishment" of a religion if the Government financed one church or several churches. For what better way to "establish" an institution than to find the fund that will support it? The "establishment" clause protects citizens also against any law which selects any religious custom, practice, or ritual, puts the force of government behind it, and fines, imprisons, or otherwise penalizes a person for not observing it. The Government plainly could not join forces with one religious group and decree a universal and symbolic circumcision. Nor could it require all children to be baptized or give tax exemptions only to those whose children were baptized.

Could it require a fast from sunrise to sunset throughout the Moslem month of Ramadan? I should think not. Yet why then can it make criminal the doing of other acts, as innocent as eating, during the day that Christians revere?

...The issue of these cases would...be in better focus if we imagined that a state legislature, controlled by orthodox Jews and Seventh-Day Adventists, passed a law making it a crime to keep a shop open on <u>Saturdays</u>. Would a Baptist, Catholic, Methodist, or Presbyterian be compelled to obey that law or go to jail or pay a fine? Or suppose Moslems grew in political strength here and got a law through a state legislature making it a crime to keep a shop open on Fridays. Would the rest of us have to submit under the fear of criminal sanctions?

...We have then...Sunday laws that find their source in Exodus, that were brought here by the Virginians and by the Puritans, and that are today maintained, construed, and justified because they respect the views of our dominant religious groups and provide a needed day of rest...**No matter how much is written, no matter what is said, the parentage of these laws is the Fourth Commandment...**

It seems to me plain that by these laws the States compel one, under sanction of law, to refrain from work or recreation on Sunday because of the majority's religious views about that day. The State by law makes Sunday a symbol of respect or adherence. Refraining from work or recreation in deference to the majority's religious feelings about Sunday is within every person's choice. By what authority can government compel it?...The conduct held constitutionally criminal today embraces the selling of pure, not impure, food; wholesome, not obnoxious, articles. Adults, not minors, are involved. The innocent acts, now constitutionally classified as criminal, emphasize the drastic break we make with tradition.

These laws are sustained because, it is said, the First Amendment is concerned with religious convictions or opinion, not with conduct. But it is a strange Bill of Rights that makes it possible for the dominant religious group to bring the minority to heel because the minority, in the doing of acts which intrinsically are wholesome and not antisocial, does not defer to the majority's religious beliefs. Some have religious scruples against eating pork. Those scruples, no matter how bizarre they might seem to some, are within the ambit of the First Amendment. Is it possible that a majority of a state legislature having those religious scruples could make it criminal for the nonbeliever to sell pork? Some have religious scruples against slaughtering cattle. Could a state legislature, dominated by that group, make it criminal to run [a slaughter house]?

The Court balances the need of the people for rest, recreation, late sleeping, family visiting and the like against the command of the First Amendment that no one need bow to the religious beliefs of another. There is in this realm no room for balancing. I see no place for it in the constitutional scheme. A legislature of Christians can no more make minorities conform to their weekly regime than a legislature of Moslems, or a legislature of Hindus. The religious regime of every group must be respected – unless it crosses the line of criminal conduct. But no one can be forced to come to a halt before it, or refrain from doing things that would offend it. That is my reading of the Establishment Clause and the Free Exercise Clause...

The State can, of course, require one day of rest a week: one day when every shop or factory is closed…Then the "day of rest" becomes purely and simply a health measure. But the Sunday laws operate differently. They force minorities to obey the majority's religious feelings of what is due and proper for a Christian community; they provide a coercive spur to the "weaker brethren," to those who are indifferent to the claims of a Sabbath through apathy or scruple. **Can there be any doubt that Christians, now aligned vigorously in favor of these laws, would be as strongly opposed if they were prosecuted under a Moslem law that forbade them from engaging in secular activities on days that violated Moslem scruples?**

…When these laws are applied to Orthodox Jews…or to Sabbatarians their vice is accentuated. If the Sunday laws are constitutional, kosher markets are on a five-day week. Thus those laws put an economic penalty on those who observe Saturday rather than Sunday as the Sabbath. For the economic pressures on these minorities, created by the fact that our communities are predominantly Sunday-minded, there is no recourse. When, however, the State uses its coercive powers – here the criminal law – to compel minorities to observe a second Sabbath, not their own, the State undertakes to aid and "prefer one religion over another" – contrary to the command of the Constitution…

I dissent from applying criminal sanctions against any of these complainants since to do so implicates the States in religious matters contrary to the constitutional mandate. Reverend Allan C. Parker, Jr., Pastor of the South Park Presbyterian Church, Seattle, Washington, has stated my views:

> We forget that, though Sunday-worshiping Christians are in the majority in this country among religious people, we do not have the right to force our practice upon the minority. Only a Church which deems itself without error and intolerant of error can justify its intolerance of the minority.

> A Jewish friend of mine runs a small business establishment. Because my friend is a Jew his business is closed each Saturday. He respects my right to worship on Sunday and I respect his right to worship on Saturday. But there is a difference. As a

Jew he closes his store **voluntarily** so that **he will be able to worship his God in his fashion**. Fine! But, as a Jew living under Christian inspired Sunday closing laws, he is **required** to close his store on Sunday so that **I will be able to worship my God in my fashion.**

Around the corner from my church there is a small Seventh Day Baptist church. I disagree with the Seventh Day Baptists on many points of doctrine. Among the tenets of their faith with which I disagree is the 'seventh day worship.' But they are good neighbors and fellow Christians, and while we disagree we respect one another. The good people of my congregation set aside their jobs on the first of the week and gather in God's house for worship. Of course, it is easy for them to set aside their jobs since Sunday closing laws – inspired by the Church – keep them from their work. At the Seventh Day Baptist church the people set aside their jobs on Saturday to worship God. This takes real sacrifice because Saturday is a good day for business. But that is not all – they are required by law to set aside their jobs on Sunday while more orthodox Christians worship...

I do not believe that because I have set aside Sunday as a holy day I have the right to force all men to set aside that day also. Why should my faith be favored by the State over any other man's faith?

With all deference, none of the opinions filed today in support of the Sunday laws has answered that question.

I must say I think the dissent has the better argument. Once again, however, religion wins. Well, at least the Christian religion.

> ### First Amendment Scoreboard
> Rulings "for" Religion: 15 --- Rulings "against" Religion: 3

THE SUGGESTED CHRISTIAN RESPONSE

<u>Lost Causes</u>:

Challenges to Blue Laws are a dead issue because Christians won the right to be the bully on the block. This is most unfortunate. It supports my position that Christians are choosing the wrong battles. Mr. Jackson Elliot now has these choices in Berkley, California. He can honor his faith and his pocket book and commit a crime by working on Saturday, or honor his pocket book and dishonor his faith by working on Sunday, or honor his faith and take a financial loss to the competition by working on Monday. I repeat, his choices are to take a financial loss, become a criminal, or violate his faith. The same principles that caused his fellow Christians to win the battle for Sunday as "the" government-preferred day of closing in Maryland will ensure he loses to the majoritarian non-Christian faith in Berkley.

<u>Causes to Champion</u>:

The 4th Commandment is mentioned 137 times in the Bible. What does it require of Christians today? Take a look:

> **Remember to observe the Sabbath day by keeping it holy. Six days a week are set apart for your daily duties and regular work, but the seventh day is a day of rest dedicated to the Lord your God. On that day no one in your household may do any kind of work. This includes you, your sons and daughters, your male and female servants, your livestock, and any foreigners living among you. For in six days the Lord made the heavens, the earth, the sea, and everything in them; then he rested on the seventh day. That is why the Lord blessed the Sabbath day and set it apart as holy.**
>
> **Exodus 20:8-11**

Although these words of the Bible appear far easier to interpret than the words of the First Amendment, this book does not seek the meaning of this commandment for Christians today. Ask your pastor. See what he or she says.

The 1981 movie, "Chariots of Fire," won four Oscars. It was the true story of a Scottish Christian missionary, Eric Liddell, and a Jewish friend of his who competed in the 1924 Olympics. The faith of Liddell was put to the test when he learned that his heat in a race was scheduled to be run on a Sunday. Few of us know the commitment it takes to prepare for and compete in the Olympics. This young man had worked a good deal of his life to prepare for his big day, yet he refused to run the race of his temporal life, choosing instead to run the race of his eternal life. He chose to honor his God's day of Sabbath.

I do not ask whether the Fourth Commandment required these heroic measures of Mr. Liddell. After you determine what this commandment requires of you, I *do ask* you to consider the following:

➢ Would you follow this commandment if your local government cooperated with your religion and, therefore, with your livelihood?

➢ If your community did not have any closing laws, would your answers be different? Would your business still be closed on your Sabbath?

I suggest your answers to these questions are far more important than whether the Supreme Court of the United States correctly ruled in the case of *McGowan v. Maryland.* We will be discussing the Ten Commandments cases in chapter thirteen and I will have some very important questions for you to ponder at that time.

Well, it looks like we can still say "God" – especially on Sundays!

Chapter Nine

Establishment:
Prayer

Alyssa Elliot came home from her first day of school with great news to share at the family table that night. "Guess what, Mom! We started our school day with a prayer read by my teacher."

"Well, that *is* news," said Ava. "The schools in Lubbock didn't allow any kind of official prayer, did they, Jackson?"

"No. As I recall, our Board lawyer told us it was unconstitutional to mix religion with public school education, so we caved. I don't think it's right, though. It's just a shame we don't allow a brief moment in our public schools to honor God. Alyssa, honey, can you remember the prayer?"

"Not really. I do recall the word 'universe' mentioned, but I really wasn't paying attention."

Later that evening, Jackson and Ava had second thoughts. It didn't take long for the Elliots to be introduced to the Berkley School Board. Jackson wrote the Board to request a copy of their prayer policy, the frequency of official prayer, and a copy of the prayer if, indeed, the prayer was the same every time it was recited. He received the following letter response:

Dear Mr. and Mrs. Elliot:

Pursuant to Berkley City Ordinance, our District instructs each teacher to recite the following prayer on the first Monday of every month. Then, when something of major importance occurs in our world that deserves a special prayer, our Superintendent prepares a customized prayer which is also read by the teacher. These prayers are always about goodness and joy, so parents have no cause to be concerned about any fear of proselytizing your children. We hope you agree.

The following is our monthly prayer, at least for now:

> May the author of the universe enable all men to reach an understanding of their spiritual nature.

> May awareness and understanding of life expand, so that all may come to know the author of the universe.

> And may others also reach this understanding which brings Total Freedom.

Very truly yours,

BSB President

The Elliots agreed the standard prayer seemed rather innocuous, but they were concerned about the "customized prayers." What was the rule of the day in determining which events get a customized prayer? Did these events depend upon the political flavor of the School Board? They were not so sure this brand of prayer was a good idea, so Ava did some digging at the local library. She discovered that the standard prayer was a portion of an official prayer of the Church of Scientology. She had heard that this movement was popular in California, but she didn't know much about it. It didn't take her long to reach the conclusion that she did not want her kids exposed to anything dealing with the organization, for Scientologists do not believe in the divinity of Jesus Christ and one principle named in their creed is that "Man's survival depends upon himself and his attainment of brotherhood with the universe."

Jackson thought, "Maybe the Supreme Court got this one right, after all. However, how is it possible for Berkley schools to be doing this if Lubbock schools could not? What happened to the free exercise of religion? And, how about the establishment clause?" He knew he did not want his kids exposed to the culture of Scientology even if the prayer was acceptable in a vacuum. What could he do, if anything? The Supreme Court has answered this question, as well. Let's go to New York.

**Always be joyful. Keep on praying.
No matter what happens, always be thankful, for this
is God's will for you who belong to Jesus Christ.**

1 Thessalonians 5:16-18

ENGEL v. VITALE
SUPREME COURT OF THE UNITED STATES
370 U.S. 421
June 25, 1962
[8 – 1]

OPINION: Justice Black…[The Board of Education in] New Hyde Park, New York,…directed the School District's principal to cause the following prayer to be said aloud by each class in the presence of a teacher at the beginning of each school day:

> Almighty God, we acknowledge our dependence upon Thee, and we beg Thy blessings upon us, our parents, our teachers and our Country.

This daily procedure was adopted on the recommendation of the State Board of Regents, a governmental agency created by the State Constitution to which the New York Legislature has granted broad…powers over the State's public school system. These state officials composed the prayer… The parents of ten pupils brought this action in a New York State Court insisting that use of this official prayer in the public schools was contrary to the beliefs, religions, or religious practices of both themselves and their children…**The New York Court of Appeals [approved of the prayer] so long as schools did not compel any pupil to join in the prayer over his or his parents' objection…**

The petitioners contend...[these laws]...must be struck down... because [the] prayer was composed by governmental officials as a part of a governmental program to further religious beliefs...We agree...**The constitutional prohibition against laws respecting an establishment of religion must at least mean that in this country it is no part of the business of government to compose official prayers for any group of the American people to recite as a part of a religious program carried on by government.**

It is a matter of history that this very practice of establishing governmentally composed prayers for religious services was one of the reasons which caused many of our early colonists to leave England and seek religious freedom in America. The Book of Common Prayer, which was created under governmental direction and which was approved by Acts of Parliament in 1548 and 1549, set out in minute detail the accepted form and content of prayer and other religious ceremonies to be used in the established, tax-supported Church of England. **The controversies over the book and what should be its content repeatedly threatened to disrupt the peace of that country as the accepted forms of prayer in the established church changed with the views of the particular ruler that happened to be in control at the time.** Powerful groups representing some of the varying religious views of the people struggled among themselves to impress their particular views upon the Government and obtain amendments of the Book more suitable to their respective notions of how religious services should be conducted in order that the official religious establishment would advance their particular religious beliefs. Other groups, lacking the necessary political power to influence the Government on the matter, decided to leave England and its established church and seek freedom in America from England's governmentally ordained and supported religion.

It is an unfortunate fact of history that when some of the very groups which had most strenuously opposed the established Church of England found themselves sufficiently in control of colonial governments in this country to write their own prayers into law, they passed laws making their own religions the official religion of their respective colonies. Indeed, as late as the time of the Revolutionary War, there were established churches in at least eight of the thirteen former colonies and established religions in at least four of the other five. But the successful Revolution against English political domination was shortly followed by intense opposition to the practice of establishing religion by law. This opposition crystallized rapidly into an effective political force in Virginia where the minority religious groups such as Presbyterians, Lutherans, Quakers and Baptists had gained such strength that the adherents to the established Episcopal Church were actually a minority themselves. In 1785-1786, those opposed to the established Church, led by James Madison and Thomas Jefferson, who, though themselves not members of any of these dissenting religious groups, opposed all religious establishments by law on grounds of principle, obtained the enactment of the famous "Virginia Bill for Religious Liberty" by which all religious groups were placed on an equal footing so far as the State was concerned...

By the time of the adoption of the Constitution, our history shows that there was a widespread awareness among many Americans of the dangers of a union of Church and State. These people knew, some of them from bitter personal experience, that **one of the greatest dangers to the freedom of the individual to worship in his own way lay in the Government's placing its official stamp of approval upon one particular kind of prayer or one particular form of religious services.** They knew the anguish, hardship and bitter strife that could come when zealous religious groups struggled with one another to obtain the Government's stamp of approval from each King, Queen, or Protector that came to temporary power. The Constitution was intended to avert a part of this danger by leaving the government of this country in the hands of the people rather than in the hands of any monarch. But this safeguard was not enough. **Our Founders were no more willing to let the content of their prayers and their privilege of praying whenever they pleased be influenced by the ballot box than they were to let these vital matters of personal conscience depend upon the succession of monarchs. The First Amendment was added to the Constitution to stand as a guarantee that neither the power nor the prestige of the Federal Government would be used to control, support or influence the kinds of prayer the American people can say – that the people's religions must not be**

subjected to the pressures of government for change each time a new political administration is elected to office. Under that Amendment's prohibition against governmental establishment of religion, as reinforced by the provisions of the Fourteenth Amendment, government in this country, be it state or federal, is without power to prescribe by law any particular form of prayer which is to be used as an official prayer in carrying on any program of governmentally sponsored religious activity.

There can be no doubt that New York's state prayer program officially establishes the religious beliefs embodied in the Regent's prayer. The respondents' argument to the contrary, which is largely based upon the contention that the Regent's prayer is "non-denominational" and the fact that the program, as modified and approved by state courts, does not require all pupils to recite the prayer but permits those who wish to do so to remain silent or be excused from the room, ignores the essential nature of the program's constitutional defects. Neither the fact that the prayer may be denominationally neutral nor the fact that its observance on the part of the students is voluntary can serve to free it from the limitations of the Establishment Clause, as it might from the Free Exercise Clause … Although these two clauses may in certain instances overlap, they forbid two quite different kinds of governmental encroachment upon religious freedom. The Establishment Clause, unlike the Free Exercise Clause, does not depend upon any showing of direct governmental compulsion and is violated by the enactment of laws which establish an official religion whether those laws operate directly to coerce non-observing individuals or not. This is not to say, of course, that laws officially prescribing a particular form of religious worship do not involve coercion of such individuals. When the power, prestige and financial support of government is placed behind a particular religious belief, the indirect coercive pressure upon religious minorities to conform to the prevailing officially approved religion is plain. But the purposes underlying the Establishment Clause go much further than that. Its first and most immediate purpose rested on the belief that a **union of government and religion tends to destroy government and to degrade religion.** The history of governmentally established religion, both in England and in this country, showed that whenever government had allied itself with one particular form of religion, the inevitable result had been that it had incurred the hatred, disrespect and even contempt of those who held contrary beliefs. **That same history showed that many people had lost their respect for any religion that had relied upon the support of government to spread its faith.** The Establishment Clause thus stands as an expression of principle on the part of the Founders of our Constitution that religion is too personal, too sacred, too holy, to permit its "unhallowed perversion" by a civil magistrate. Another purpose of the Establishment Clause rested upon an awareness of the historical fact that governmentally established religions and religious persecutions go hand in hand. The Founders knew that only a few years after the Book of Common Prayer became the only accepted form of religious services in the established Church of England, an Act of Uniformity was passed to compel all Englishmen to attend those services and to make it a criminal offense to conduct or attend religious gatherings of any other kind – a law which was consistently flouted by dissenting religious groups in England and which contributed to widespread persecutions of people like John Bunyan who persisted in holding "unlawful religious meetings...to the great disturbance and distraction of the good subjects of this kingdom..." And they knew that similar persecutions had received the sanction of law in several of the colonies in this country soon after the establishment of official religions in those colonies. **It was in large part to get completely away from this sort of systematic religious persecution that the Founders brought into being our nation, our Constitution, and our Bill of Rights with its prohibition against any governmental establishment of religion.** The New York laws officially prescribing the Regents' prayer are inconsistent with the purposes of the Establishment Clause and with the Establishment Clause itself.

It has been argued that to apply the Constitution in such a way as to prohibit state laws respecting an establishment of religious services in public schools is to indicate a hostility toward religion or toward prayer. Nothing, of course, could be more wrong. The history of man is inseparable from the history of religion. And perhaps it is not too much to say that since the beginning of that history many people have devoutly believed that "More things are wrought by prayer than this world dreams of." It was doubtless largely due to men who believed this that there grew up a sentiment that caused men to leave the cross-currents of officially established state religions and religious persecution in Europe and come to this country filled with the hope that they could find a place in which they could pray when they pleased to the God of their faith in the language they chose. And there were men of this same faith in the power of prayer who led the fight for adoption of our Constitution and also for our Bill of Rights with the very guarantees of religious freedom that forbid the sort of governmental activity which New York has attempted here. These men knew that the First Amendment, which tried to put an end to governmental control of religion and of prayer, was not written to destroy either. They knew rather that it was written to quiet well-justified fears which nearly all of them felt arising out of an awareness that governments of the past had shackled men's tongues to make them speak only the religious thoughts that government wanted them to speak and to pray only to the God that government wanted them to pray to. It is neither sacrilegious nor antireligious to say that each separate government in this country should stay out of the business of writing or sanctioning official prayers and leave that purely religious function to the people themselves and to those the people choose to look to for religious guidance…

To those who may subscribe to the view that because the Regents' prayer is so brief and general there can be no danger to religious freedom in its governmental establishment, however, it may be appropriate to say in the words of James Madison, the author of the First Amendment:

> **It is proper to take alarm at the first experiment on our liberties…Who does not see that the same authority which can establish Christianity, in exclusion of all other Religions, may establish with the same ease any particular sect of Christians, in exclusion of all other Sects? That the same authority which can force a citizen to contribute three pence only of his property for the support of any one establishment, may force him to conform to any other establishment in all cases whatsoever?**

The judgment of the Court of Appeals of New York is reversed…

> In other words, the prayer was not approved by the Court.

CONCURRENCE: Justice Douglas…[In my estimation, the question presented by this case is much narrower than the majority indicates.] It is whether New York oversteps the bounds when it finances a religious exercise…Once government finances a religious exercise it inserts a divisive influence into our communities…

DISSENT: Justice Stewart…The Court does not hold, nor could it, that New York has interfered with the free exercise of anybody's religion. For the state courts have made clear that those who object to reciting the prayer must be entirely free of any compulsion to do so, including any "embarrassments and pressures." But the Court says that in permitting school children to say this simple prayer, the New York authorities have established "an official religion."

…I cannot see how an "official religion" is established by letting those who want to say a prayer say it. On the contrary, I think that to deny the wish of these school children to join in reciting this prayer is to deny them the opportunity of sharing in the spiritual heritage of our nation.

> Do you recall my admonition for accuracy in chapter two? I believe Justice Stewart was a good man and a fine justice, but his facts are nowhere close to correct. The Board of Education directed the school district's principal to instruct his teachers to read a prayer prepared by state officials. The reading of this prayer did not come about because of the "wish" of these school children. In truth, neither their wish nor the wish of their parents is known; that is, except for the opposite wish of the plaintiff-parents in this case.

The Court's historical review of the quarrels over the Book of Common Prayer in England throws no light for me on the issue before us in this case. England had then and has now an established church. Equally unenlightening, I think, is the history of the early establishment and later rejection of an official church in our own States. For we deal here not with the establishment of a state church, which would, of course, be constitutionally impermissible, but with whether school children who want to begin their day by joining in prayer must be prohibited from doing so.

> There simply is no evidence that these children wanted to begin their day by joining in prayer. Justice Stewart is letting his heart control his head. While his conclusion may well have been true, we simply do not know what "they" wanted. Opening the Supreme Court in prayer attended by adults not compelled by law to be present is a far cry from public elementary school. The same is true with Congress. And, a president's prayers are welcome, protected by free speech, and of his own making. Government certainly does not make a president say a prayer.

Moreover, I think that the Court's task...is not responsibly aided by the uncritical invocation of metaphors like the "wall of separation," a phrase nowhere to be found in the Constitution. What is relevant to the issue here is not the history of an established church in sixteenth century England or in eighteenth century America, but the history of the religious traditions of our people...

At the opening of each day's Session of this Court we stand, while one of our officials invokes the protection of God. Since the days of John Marshall our Crier has said, "God save the United States and this Honorable Court." Both the Senate and the House of Representatives open their daily Sessions with prayer. Each of our Presidents, from George Washington to John F. Kennedy, has upon assuming his Office asked the protection and help of God...

On April 30, 1789, **President George Washington said:**

> ...it would be peculiarly improper to omit in this first official act my fervent supplications to that Almighty Being who rules over the universe, who presides in the councils of nations, and whose providential aids can supply every human defect, that

His benediction may consecrate to the liberties and happiness of the people of the United States a Government instituted by themselves for these essential purposes, and may enable every instrument employed in its administration to execute with success the functions allotted to his charge. In tendering this homage to the Great Author of every public and private good, I assure myself that it expresses your sentiments not less than my own, nor those of my fellow-citizens at large less than either. No people can be bound to acknowledge and adore the Invisible Hand which conducts the affairs of men more than those of the United States...

On March 4, 1797, **President John Adams said:**

And may that Being who is supreme over all, the Patron of Order, the Fountain of Justice, and the Protector in all ages of the world of virtuous liberty, continue His blessing upon this nation and its Government and give it all possible success and duration consistent with the ends of His providence.

On March 4, 1805, **President Thomas Jefferson said:**

...I shall need, too, the favor of that Being in whose hands we are, who led our fathers, as Israel of old, from their native land and planted them in a country flowing with all the necessaries and comforts of life; who has covered our infancy with His providence and our riper years with His wisdom and power, and to whose goodness I ask you to join in supplications with me that He will so enlighten the minds of your servants, guide their councils, and prosper their measures that whatsoever they do shall result in your good, and shall secure to you the peace, friendship, and approbation of all nations.

On March 4, 1809, **President James Madison said:**

But the source to which I look...is in...my fellow citizens, and in the counsels of those representing them in the other departments associated in the care of the national interests. In these my confidence will under every difficulty be best placed, next to that which we have all been encouraged to feel in the guardianship and guidance of that Almighty Being whose power regulates the destiny of nations, whose blessings have been so conspicuously dispensed to this rising Republic, and to whom we are bound to address our devout gratitude for the past, as well as our fervent supplications and best hopes for the future.

On March 4, 1865, **President Abraham Lincoln said:**

...Fondly do we hope, fervently do we pray, that this mighty scourge of war may speedily pass away. Yet, if God wills that it continue until all the wealth piled by the bondsman's two hundred and fifty years of unrequited toil shall be sunk, and until every drop of blood drawn with the lash shall be paid by another drawn with the sword, as was said three thousand years ago, so still it must be said "the judgments of the Lord are true and righteous altogether."

With malice toward none, with charity for all, with firmness in the right as God gives us to see the right, let us strive on to finish the work we are in, to bind up the nation's wounds, to care for him who shall have borne the battle and for his widow and his orphan, to do all which may achieve and cherish a just and lasting peace among ourselves and with all nations.

On March 4, 1885, **President Grover Cleveland said:**

...And let us not trust to human effort alone, but humbly acknowledging the power and goodness of Almighty God, who presides over the destiny of nations, and who has at all times been revealed in our country's history, let us invoke His aid and His blessing upon our labors.

On March 5, 1917, **President Woodrow Wilson said:**

...I pray God I may be given the wisdom and the prudence to do my duty in the true spirit of this great people.

On March 4, 1933, **President Franklin D. Roosevelt said:**

In this dedication of a Nation we humbly ask the blessing of God. May He protect each and every one of us. May He guide me in the days to come.

On January 21, 1957, **President Dwight D. Eisenhower said:**

Before all else, we seek, upon our common labor as a nation, the blessings of Almighty God. And the hopes in our hearts fashion the deepest prayers of our whole people.

On January 20, 1961, **President John F. Kennedy said:**

The world is very different now...And yet the same revolutionary beliefs for which our forbears fought are still at issue around the globe – the belief that the rights of many come not from the generosity of the state but from the hand of God. With a good conscience our only sure reward, with history the final judge of our deeds, let us go forth to lead the land we love, asking His blessings and His help, but knowing that here on earth God's work must truly be our own.

Are Presidential prayers in the same category as government-sponsored prayers for minors to recite? Did any "law" require any president to say a prayer?

The Court today says that the state and federal governments are without constitutional power to prescribe any particular form of words to be recited by any group of the American people on any subject touching religion. One of the stanzas of "The Star-Spangled Banner," made our National Anthem by Act of Congress in 1931, contains these verses:

Blest with victory and peace, may the heav'n rescued land Praise the Pow'r that hath made and preserved us as a nation! Then conquer we must, when our cause it is just, And this be our motto "In God is our Trust."

In 1954 Congress added a phrase to the Pledge of Allegiance to the Flag so that it now contains the words "one Nation under God, indivisible, with liberty and justice for all." In 1952 Congress enacted legislation calling upon the President each year to proclaim a National Day of Prayer. Since 1865 the words "IN GOD WE TRUST" have been impressed on our coins. Countless similar examples could be listed, but there is no need to belabor the obvious. It was all summed up by this Court just ten years ago in a single sentence: "We are a religious people whose institutions presuppose a Supreme Being."

If you did not read the majority opinion carefully, you might be tempted to say "It's _not_ OK for our children to say 'God' in school." Of course, the only thing the justices said was that "government-sponsored official prayer" is prohibited. I wonder, after this case, is it OK for your children to say "God" in the cafeteria, in the hallways, on the playground, in class? Is it OK for teachers in public school to refer to the Creator in the Declaration of Independence? Have you yet seen any evidence whatsoever that the law prohibits such discussion? I have not. Using our same principles for "scoring," this time we have to put one in the "against" column because "government-sponsored official prayer" was denied in the public schoolhouse.

> ### First Amendment Scoreboard
> Rulings "for" Religion: 15 --- Rulings "against" Religion: 4

If you are over 60, you probably know the name of Madalyn Murray O'Hair. An atheist, many believe she was the first to challenge prayer in public school. Actually, since she had nothing to do with the *Engel* case, that is not true. She was the plaintiff in a case decided along with the next case, but she had little, if anything, to do with any of these prayer decisions.

Is the prohibition of official government-sponsored mandatory prayer in public schools necessarily a bad thing for Christians? I beg you to further explore this entire chapter before you reach a decision.

Justice Stewart's presidential quotes and other illustrations show three things: (1) we have a rich Christian heritage, (2) presidents and many others speak of God all the time, freely and openly, and (3) none of his examples have a thing to do with official prayer in public elementary school. As to point (2), apparently none of these presidents and others listed got the message that we cannot speak of the things of God. I have never found the name of the person that started that rumor. Have you?

Right out of the box, we can tell Mr. Elliot that Lubbock's school board attorney was right. He *can* do something about this brand of Berkley religious indoctrination of his children. The Supreme Court's interpretation of the religion clauses is clear. Berkley Schools may not participate in official prayers even if they are innocuous. Jackson would win a lawsuit if he wishes to put an end to this activity and, therefore, to the Church of Scientology prayer in his child's school.

How do you feel about this? Is it a question of which prayer you prefer? Or, is it a question of which religion you prefer? Would it be OK with you if prayers read to your children were based on teachings of a cult, as long as the words of the prayer themselves were reasonable? If Alyssa had not mentioned the prayer, the Elliots may never have heard a thing about it. Webster didn't mention it. Why not? Because his friends at Berkley High turned him on to Scientology and he knew his folks would protest, so he chose not to bring it home to them. Should official prayer be permitted in public grade schools only if the majoritarian board members are Christian? And, even then, should it be permitted only if the prayer is so watered down, so as to appease as many sects as possible, that it loses much of its spiritual meaning? I have a lot of suggestions regarding this subject, but will hold off until we complete the prayer cases.

Sometimes the Court consolidates two or more cases if the issues are the same. We are off to Abington, Pennsylvania, and Baltimore, Maryland, for another look at prayer, not just anywhere, but, once again, in public schools.

***Abington School Dist. v. Schempp* (1963)**: [8-1] Justice Clark...[A Pennsylvania statute requires the reading of 10 verses from the Holy Bible daily without commentary. A Baltimore statute is similar except the Lord's Prayer is also read. Participation for both is voluntary...a dissenter may be excused. Held: Both programs are unconstitutional...]

It is insisted that unless these religious exercises are permitted, a "religion of secularism is established" in our schools. **We agree the State may not "establish a religion of secularism" in the sense of affirmatively opposing religion, thus preferring those who believe in no religion to those who do.** We do not agree this decision has that effect. It might well be said that one's education is not complete without a study of comparative religion...**The Bible is worthy of study for its literary and historic qualities. Nothing we say here prevents the foregoing.** But, these readings are "religious exercises," in violation of the command of the First Amendment that government must maintain neutrality, neither aiding nor opposing religion. We do not accept that this holding collides with the majority's right to free exercise. **While the Free Exercise clause prohibits the State from denying rights of free exercise to anyone, it has never meant that a majority could use the machinery of the state to practice its beliefs.**

> I want to pause a moment for that to sink in. Do we Christians need the "machinery of the state" in order to practice our beliefs? Doesn't that just sound wrong to you? Perhaps even dangerous?

CONCURRENCE: Justice Douglas...[Public funds are being used to fund a religious exercise.]

CONCURRENCE: Justice Brennan...**Not every involvement of religion in public life is unconstitutional**, but the exercises are a form of involvement that clearly violates the Establishment Clause...I do not agree that the invalidation of these exercises permits this Court no alternative but to declare unconstitutional every vestige of cooperation or accommodation between religion and government. What is forbidden are those involvements which serve the essentially religious activities of religious institutions, employ the organs of government for essentially religious purposes or use essentially religious means to serve governmental ends where secular means would suffice. On the other hand, there may be myriad forms of involvements of government with religion which do not import such dangers and should not be deemed to violate the Establishment Clause.

A brief survey of these forms of accommodation will reveal that the First Amendment commands no official hostility toward religion, but only a strict neutrality in matters of religion.

➢ **Provisions for churches and chaplains at military establishments or for chaplains in penal institutions.** Since government has deprived such persons of opportunities to practice their faith where they choose, in order to avoid infringing on free exercise, the government may provide the foregoing. Such a principle would support excusing children from school on their religious holiday. Government may allow temporary use of public buildings by religious organizations when their churches are unavailable because of disaster or emergency.

> Government funds churches on military bases and in prisons!
> **GIs and felons *can* say "God."**

➢ **Legislative prayer...**Legislators are mature adults who may presumably absent themselves.
➢ **Non-devotional use of the Bible in public schools.** Today's holding does not foreclose teaching about the Holy Scriptures or about comparative religion in literature or history. **Any attempt to use rigid limits upon the mere mention of God or references to the Bible would be fraught with dangers.**

> Maybe you should read that again! Then, tell your neighbors that "God" *does* have a place in government and in school, even in *public* school. The rumor is FALSE! Stop repeating it!

> **Activities which, although religious in origin, have ceased to have religious meaning.** Blue Laws. "In God We Trust." The reference to divinity in the pledge of allegiance may simply recognize the historical fact that our nation was believed to have been founded "under God." The pledge may be no more of a religious exercise than the reading of Lincoln's Gettysburg Address which contains illusion to the same historic fact.

I am not sure I find Justice Brennan's conclusion that these concepts and phrases have "lost their religious meaning" to be very comforting. It sounds like a reason "to put up with God," instead of a reason "to worship God," does it not? More on this later.

DISSENT: Justice Stewart…There is a substantial free exercise claim for those who affirmatively desire to have their children's school day open with the reading of the Bible. Yes, under *Pierce*, parents are free to send their kids to a religious school. But, under *Murdock* we learn that "freedom of speech, freedom of the press and freedom of religion are available to all, not merely to those who can pay their own way." The majority places religion in an artificial and state-created disadvantage. Permission for such exercises is necessary if schools are to be truly neutral in matters of religion. What our Constitution protects is the freedom of each of us (Jew, Catholic, Baptist, Buddhist) to believe or disbelieve, worship or not, pray or keep silent, according to his own conscience. It is conceivable these school boards would find it impossible to administer a system of religious exercises that are completely free of official coercion for dissenters. But I think we must not assume that school boards so lack the qualities of inventiveness and good will as to make impossible the achievement of that goal.

Look at the religious activities Justice Brennan approves of in his concurrence. All of this is *dicta*, but please correct your fellow citizens when they have the misguided concept that our Supreme Court is "anti-everything-religious." Nevertheless, score one in the "against" column.

```
┌─────────────────────────────────────────────────────┐
│  ┌────────────────────────────────────────────────┐ │
│  │            First Amendment Scoreboard           │ │
│  │  Rulings "for" Religion: 15 --- Rulings "against" Religion: 5  │ │
│  └────────────────────────────────────────────────┘ │
└─────────────────────────────────────────────────────┘
```

This next case will throw you off a bit, but if you think about its deeper meaning, you will likely better understand its outcome. Let's look at prayer among adults at the heart of government in the Nebraska legislature. We are off to Omaha.

═══

MARSH v. CHAMBERS
SUPREME COURT OF THE UNITED STATES
463 U.S. 783
July 5, 1983
[6 – 3]

OPINION: Chief Justice Burger...The question presented is whether the Nebraska Legislature's practice of opening each legislative day with a prayer by a chaplain paid by the State violates the Establishment Clause of the First Amendment...The opening of sessions of legislative and other... public bodies with prayer is deeply embedded in the history and tradition of this country...

Although prayers were not offered during the Constitutional Convention, the First Congress, as one of its early items of business, adopted the policy of selecting a chaplain to open each session with prayer. Thus, on April 7, 1789, the Senate appointed a committee "to take under consideration the manner of electing Chaplains." On April 9, 1789, a similar committee was appointed by the House of Representatives. On April 25, 1789, the Senate elected its first chaplain; the House followed suit on May 1, 1789. A statute providing for the payment of these chaplains was enacted into law on September 22, 1789.

On September 25, 1789, three days after Congress authorized the appointment of paid chaplains, final agreement was reached on the language of the Bill of Rights. Clearly the men who wrote the First

Amendment Religion Clauses did not view paid legislative chaplains and opening prayers as a violation of that Amendment, for the practice of opening sessions with prayer has continued without interruption ever since that early session of Congress...

It can hardly be thought that...[the Framers] intended the Establishment Clause of the Amendment to forbid what they had just declared acceptable...

This unique history leads us to accept the interpretation of the First Amendment draftsmen who saw no real threat to the Establishment Clause arising from a practice of prayer similar to that now challenged. We conclude that legislative prayer presents no more potential for establishment than the provision of school transportation (*Everson v. Board of Education*)...or tax exemptions for religious organizations (*Walz*)...

The Establishment Clause does not always bar a state from regulating conduct simply because it "harmonizes with religious canons." Here, the individual claiming injury by the practice is an adult, presumably not readily susceptible to "religious indoctrination." In light of the unambiguous and unbroken history of more than 200 years, there can be no doubt that the practice of opening legislative sessions with prayer has become part of the fabric of our society.

To invoke Divine guidance on a public body entrusted with making the laws is not, in these circumstances, an establishment of religion or a step toward establishment; it is simply a tolerable acknowledgment of beliefs widely held among the people of this country...

We turn then to the question of whether any features of the Nebraska practice violate the Establishment Clause. Beyond the bare fact that a prayer is offered, three points have been made: first, that a clergyman of only one denomination – Presbyterian – has been selected for 16 years; second, that the chaplain is paid at public expense; and third, that the prayers are in the Judeo-Christian tradition. Weighted against the historical background, these factors do not serve to invalidate Nebraska's practice...

The Court of Appeals was concerned that [the Chaplain's] long tenure has the effect of giving preference to his religious views. We cannot, any more than Members of the Congresses of this century, perceive any suggestion that choosing a clergyman of one denomination advances the beliefs of a particular church. To the contrary, the evidence indicates that [the Chaplain] was reappointed because his performance and personal qualities were acceptable to the body appointing him. [He] was not the only clergyman heard by the legislature; guest chaplains have officiated at the request of various legislators and as substitutes during [his] absences...We conclude that his long tenure does not in itself conflict with the Establishment Clause.

Nor is the compensation of the chaplain from public funds a reason to invalidate the Nebraska Legislature's chaplaincy; remuneration is grounded in historic practice initiated, as we noted earlier, by the same Congress that drafted the Establishment Clause of the First Amendment...The content of the prayer is not of concern to judges where, as here, there is no indication that the prayer opportunity has been exploited to proselytize or advance any one, or to disparage any other, faith or belief. That being so, it is not for us to embark on a sensitive evaluation or to parse the content of a particular prayer. [Nebraska's prayer policy does not violate the Constitution.]

DISSENT: Justice Brennan...That the "purpose" of legislative prayer is pre-eminently religious rather than secular seems to me self-evident. "To invoke Divine guidance on a public body entrusted with making the laws" is nothing but a religious act. Moreover, whatever secular functions legislative prayer might play – formally opening the legislative session, getting the members of the body to quiet down, and imbuing them with a sense of seriousness and high purpose – could so plainly be performed in a purely nonreligious fashion that to claim a secular purpose for the prayer is an insult to the perfectly honorable individuals who instituted and continue the practice.

The "primary effect" of legislative prayer is also clearly religious. As we said in the context of officially sponsored prayers in the public schools, "prescribing a particular form of religious worship," even if the individuals involved have the choice not to participate, places "indirect coercive pressure upon religious minorities to conform to the prevailing officially approved religion..." *Engel v. Vitale.* More importantly, invocations in Nebraska's legislative halls explicitly link religious belief and observance to the power and prestige of the State. "The mere appearance of a joint exercise of legislative authority by Church and State provides a significant symbolic benefit to religion in the minds of some by reason of the power conferred." *Abington v. Schempp.*

Finally, there can be no doubt that the practice of legislative prayer leads to excessive "entanglement" between the State and religion. *Lemon* pointed out that "entanglement" can take two forms: First, a state statute or program might involve the state impermissibly in monitoring and overseeing religious affairs. In the case of legislative prayer, the process of choosing a "suitable" chaplain, whether on a permanent or rotating basis, and insuring that the chaplain limits himself or herself to suitable prayers, involves precisely the sort of supervision that agencies of government should if at all possible avoid. Second, excessive entanglement might arise out of the divisive political potential of a state statute or program. Ordinarily political debate and division, however vigorous or even partisan, are normal and healthy manifestations of our democratic system of government, but political division along religious lines was one of the principal evils against which the First Amendment was intended to protect. The potential divisiveness of such conflict is a threat to the normal political process.

In this case, this second aspect of entanglement is also clear. The controversy between Senator Chambers and his colleagues, which had reached the stage of difficulty and rancor long before this lawsuit was brought, has split the Nebraska Legislature precisely on issues of religion and religious conformity. The record in this case also reports a series of instances, involving legislators other than Senator Chambers, in which invocations by Reverend Palmer and others led to controversy along religious lines. And in general, the history of legislative prayer has been far more eventful – and divisive – than a hasty reading of the Court's opinion might indicate.

...The principles of separation and neutrality implicit in the Establishment Clause serve many purposes. Four of these are particularly relevant here.

[1] To guarantee the individual right to conscience...

[2] To keep the state from interfering in the essential autonomy of religious life, either by taking upon itself the decision of religious issues, or by

unduly involving itself in the supervision of religious institutions or officials.

[3] To prevent the trivialization and degradation of religion by too close an attachment to the organs of government...

[4] To help assure that essentially religious issues, precisely because of their importance and sensitivity, not become the occasion for battle in the political arena. With regard to most issues, the government may be influenced by partisan argument and may act as a partisan itself. In each case, there will be winners and losers in the political battle, and the losers' most common recourse is the right to dissent and the right to fight the battle again another day. With regard to matters that are essentially religious, however, the Establishment Clause seeks that there should be no political battles, and that no American should at any point feel alienated from his government because that government has declared or acted upon some "official" or "authorized" point of view on a matter of religion.

...Even before the First Amendment was written, the Framers of the Constitution broke with the practice of the Articles of Confederation and many state constitutions, and did not invoke the name of God in the document. This omission of a reference to the Deity was not inadvertent; nor did it remain unnoticed. Moreover, Thomas Jefferson and Andrew Jackson, during their respective terms as president, both refused on Establishment Clause grounds to declare national days of thanksgiving or fasting. And James Madison, writing subsequent to his own presidency on essentially the very issue we face today, stated:

> Is the appointment of Chaplains to the two Houses of Congress consistent with the Constitution, and with the pure principle of religious freedom?

> In strictness, the answer on both points must be in the negative. The Constitution of the U.S. forbids everything like an establishment or a national religion. The law appointing Chaplains establishes a religious worship for the national representatives, to be performed by Ministers of religion, elected by a majority of them; and these are to be paid out of the national taxes. Does not this involve the

principle of a national establishment, applicable to a provision for a religious worship for the Constituent as well as the representative Body, approved by the majority, and conducted by Ministers of religion paid by the entire nation.

Legislative prayer clearly violates the principles of neutrality and separation that are embedded within the Establishment Clause...It has the potential for degrading religion by allowing a religious call to worship to be intermeshed with a secular call to order. And it injects religion into the political sphere by creating the potential that each and every selection of a chaplain, or consideration of a particular prayer, or even reconsideration of the practice itself, will provoke a political battle along religious lines and ultimately alienate some religiously identified group of citizens...**Certainly, bona fide classes in comparative religion can be offered in the public schools. And certainly, the text of Abraham Lincoln's Second Inaugural Address which is inscribed on a wall of the Lincoln Memorial need not be purged of its profound theological content.** The practice of offering invocations at legislative sessions cannot, however, simply be dismissed as a tolerable acknowledgment of beliefs widely held among the people of this country. "Prayer is religion in act.".... Reverend Palmer and other members of the clergy...are engaged by the legislature to lead it – as a body – in an act of religious worship...We are not faced here with the right of the legislature to allow its members to offer prayers during the course of general legislative debate. We are certainly not faced with the right of legislators to form voluntary groups for prayer or worship...

> Yet another clear example of the numerous ways we *can* say "God." Legislators may offer prayers of their own volition and may form voluntary groups for prayer or worship.

Rather, we are faced here with the regularized practice of conducting official prayers, on behalf of the entire legislature, as part of the order of business constituting the formal opening of every single session of the legislative term. If this is free exercise, the Establishment Clause has no meaning whatsoever…The argument is made occasionally that a strict separation of religion and state robs the nation of its spiritual identity. I believe quite the contrary. It may be true that individuals cannot be "neutral" on the question of religion. But the judgment of the Establishment Clause is that neutrality by the organs of government on questions of religion is both possible and imperative. **Alexis de Tocqueville** wrote the following concerning his travels through this land in the early 1830s:

> The religious atmosphere of the country was the first thing that struck me on arrival in the United States…In France I had seen the spirits of religion and of freedom almost always marching in opposite directions. In America I found them intimately linked together in joint reign over the same land. My longing to understand the reason for this phenomenon increased daily. To find this out, I questioned the faithful of all communions; I particularly sought the society of clergymen, who are the depositories of the various creeds and have a personal interest in their survival…; **all thought that the main reason for the quiet sway of religion over their country was the complete separation of church and state.** I have no hesitation in stating that throughout my stay in America I met nobody, lay or cleric, who did not agree about that.

…If the Court had struck down legislative prayer today, it would likely have stimulated a furious reaction. But it would also, I am convinced, have invigorated both the "spirit of religion" and the "spirit of freedom." I respectfully dissent.

DISSENT: Justice Stevens…In a democratically elected legislature, the religious beliefs of the chaplain tend to reflect the faith of the majority of the lawmakers' constituents. Prayers may be said by a Catholic priest in the Massachusetts Legislature and by a Presbyterian minister in the Nebraska Legislature, but I would not expect to find a Jehovah's Witness or a disciple of Mary Baker Eddy or the Reverend Moon serving as the official chaplain in any state legislature. Regardless of the motivation of the majority that exercises the power to appoint the chaplain, it seems to me that the designation of a member of one religious faith to serve as the sole official chaplain of a state legislature for a period of 16 years constitutes the preference of one faith over another in violation of the Establishment Clause of the First Amendment…

As has often been stated by the Court, "Constitutional rights are not subject to a vote." In other words, they are not subjugated to the will of the majority. Yet, this Court in this case gives great weight to a "tolerable acknowledgment of widely held beliefs." Although I am hard pressed to criticize the outcome of this case, I feel its foundation in logic is lacking. Saying a prayer to adults who are not compelled to be present for the first few seconds of the day, in itself does not appear to be a problem. The problem lies in spending the tax money of constituents of all faiths to hire a chaplain of one faith. Something doesn't feel right about the outcome, though. I suppose we have to score this one "for" religion, but I predict problems ahead. (See chapter sixteen.)

> ### First Amendment Scoreboard
> Rulings "for" Religion: 16 --- Rulings "against" Religion: 5

Have we been to Alabama yet? Here we go!

WALLACE v. JAFFREE
SUPREME COURT OF THE UNITED STATES
472 U.S. 38
June 4, 1985
[6 – 3]

OPINION: Justice Stevens…[Whether an Alabama statute that authorizes a period of silence "for meditation or voluntary prayer" in public schools is an impermissible establishment of religion? Held: The statute is unconstitutional.] The statute was not motivated by a clearly secular purpose – indeed, it had no secular purpose. A legislative attempt to return prayer to public schools is quite different from merely protecting every student's right to engage in voluntary prayer during an appropriate moment of silence during the school day. **Nothing in the Constitution as interpreted by this Court prohibits public school students from voluntarily praying at any time before, during or after the school day.**

> Now we're talkin'. School kids can pray "all day." Of course, that means they can say "God" in public schools and it's OK! Who knew?

The moment of silence statute for the purpose of "meditation" is not invalid. But, the addition of "voluntary prayer" to the statute indicates the State's intention to characterize prayer as a favored practice. Such a course is not consistent with complete government neutrality toward religion.

DISSENT: [Justice Rehnquist takes a new look at the Framers' intent.] "The Establishment Clause has been unfortunately...freighted with Jefferson's misleading "wall" metaphor for nearly 40 years. His letter to the Danbury Baptists was written 14 years after the Bill of Rights was adopted. Madison's writings make it clear that the clause was meant to prohibit a 'national religion' and perhaps to prevent discrimination between sects. **He did not see it as requiring neutrality on the part of government between religion and irreligion.** He was definitely not concerned about whether government might aid all religions evenhandedly." [Rehnquist refers to the First Congress statute that retained a legislative chaplain and the Northwest Ordinance adopted by the First Congress that stated, "religion, morality and knowledge, being necessary to good government and the happiness of mankind, schools and the means of education shall forever be encouraged." He suggests we might want to look at an Eighteenth Century dictionary for the definition of "establishment": "The first American dictionary defined 'establishment' as 'the act of establishing...or ordaining, such as the episcopal form of religion in England.' Our recent opinions have with embarrassing candor conceded that the 'wall of separation' is merely a 'blurred...barrier which is not wholly accurate and can only be dimly perceived.'"] History must judge whether it was the Father of his country (President Washington) in 1789 or a majority of the Court today, which has strayed from the meaning of the Establishment Clause.

If the establishment clause was only intended to prohibit a national church (or, with the Fourteenth Amendment, a state-run church) and to prohibit discrimination between sects, Justice Rehnquist argues that it was not intended to prefer irreligion over religion nor to prohibit non-discriminatory aid to all religion. Of course, all that does is alter the "line drawing," heretofore known as "wall erecting." For, even if the Court eventually goes along with the Rehnquist principle, it will still be faced with drawing a line in the sand. In other words, when does a government "establish" a state-run church? When does government action discriminate between sects? Answer: Wherever you draw the "line" or "build the wall" or construct the "short fence." Would Justice Rehnquist permit the Lord's Prayer in schools, a clearly Christian-based prayer? Perhaps he would permit rotating prayers representing children of all represented faiths. It is fairly clear, however, that he would have no problem discriminating against atheists. Nevertheless, we are still left with determining when "some religions are aided as opposed to all religion," are we not? Score one "against."

First Amendment Scoreboard

Rulings "for" Religion: 16 --- Rulings "against" Religion: 6

It is time to graduate in Providence, Rhode Island. All aboard!

LEE v. WEISMAN
SUPREME COURT OF THE UNITED STATES
505 U.S. 577
June 24, 1992
[5 – 4]

OPINION: Justice Kennedy...School principals in the public school system of the city of Providence, Rhode Island, are permitted to invite members of the clergy to offer invocation and benediction prayers as part of the formal graduation ceremonies for middle schools and for high schools. The question before us is whether [this practice] is consistent with the Religion Clauses of the First [and Fourteenth] Amendments. [Deborah Weisman, then age 14, graduated from Nathan Bishop Middle School, a public school in Providence, at a formal ceremony in June, 1989. For many years it has been the policy of the Providence School Committee and the Superintendent of Schools to permit principals to invite members of the clergy to give invocations and benedictions at middle school and high school graduations...Daniel Weisman, Deborah's father, objected; however,...the school principal, Robert E. Lee, nevertheless invited a rabbi to deliver prayers at the graduation exercises for Deborah's class. Rabbi Leslie Gutterman, of the Temple Beth El in Providence, accepted. Deborah's father also objected to high school graduation ceremonies as Deborah would likely graduate from high school in this District in a few years.]

It has been the custom of Providence school officials to provide invited clergy with a pamphlet entitled "Guidelines for Civic Occasions," prepared by the National Conference of Christians and Jews. The Guidelines recommend that public prayers at nonsectarian civic ceremonies be composed with "inclusiveness and sensitivity," though they acknowledge that "prayer of any kind may be inappropriate on some civic occasions." The principal gave Rabbi Gutterman the pamphlet before the graduation and advised [that his prayers]...should be nonsectarian. Rabbi Gutterman's prayers were as follows:

--- INVOCATION ---

God of the Free, Hope of the Brave:
For the legacy of America where diversity is celebrated and the rights of minorities are protected, we thank You.
May these young men and women grow up to enrich it.
For the liberty of America, we thank You.
May these new graduates grow up to guard it.
For the political process of America in which all its citizens may participate, for its court system where all may seek justice, we thank You.
May those we honor this morning always turn to it in trust.

For the destiny of America, we thank You.

May the graduates of Nathan Bishop Middle School so live that they might help to share it.

May our aspirations for our country and for these young people, who are our hope for the future, be richly fulfilled. AMEN.

--- BENEDICTION ---

O God, we are grateful to You for having endowed us with the capacity for learning which we have celebrated on this joyous commencement.

Happy families give thanks for seeing their children achieve an important milestone.

Send Your blessings upon the teachers and administrators who helped prepare them.

The graduates now need strength and guidance for the future.

Help them to understand that we are not complete with academic knowledge alone.

We must each strive to fulfill what You require of us all: To do justly, to love mercy, to walk humbly.

We give thanks to You, Lord, for keeping us alive, sustaining us and allowing us to reach this special, happy occasion. AMEN.

...Attendance at graduation ceremonies is voluntary.

The school board...argued that these short prayers and others like them at graduation exercises are of profound meaning to many students and parents throughout this country who consider that due respect and acknowledgment for divine guidance and for the deepest spiritual aspirations of our people ought to be expressed at an event as important in life as a graduation...

The District Court held that [the] practice of including invocations and benedictions in public school graduations violated the Establishment Clause...and it [ordered the school to cease] the practice. The court applied the three-part...test set forth in *Lemon v. Kurtzman*. [That is,] to satisfy the Establishment Clause a governmental practice must (1) reflect a clearly secular purpose; (2) have a primary effect that neither advances nor inhibits religion; and (3) avoid excessive government entanglement with religion.

The District Court held that [the school] violated the second part of the test, and so did not address either the first or the third. The court decided…that the effects test of *Lemon* is violated whenever government action "creates an identification of the state with a religion, or with religion in general" or when "the effect of the governmental action is to endorse one religion over another, or to endorse religion in general." The court determined that the practice of including invocations and benedictions, even so-called nonsectarian ones, in public school graduations creates an identification of governmental power with religious practice, endorses religion, and violates the Establishment Clause…[The Court of Appeals affirmed. So do we. The practice violates all 3 parts of the *Lemon* test.]

DISSENT: Justice Scalia…Our interpretation of the Establishment Clause should "comport with what history reveals was the contemporaneous understanding of its guarantees."…Thus, "the existence from the beginning of the nation's life of a practice, while not conclusive of its constitutionality…, is a fact of considerable import in the interpretation" of the Establishment Clause…From our nation's origin, prayer has been a prominent part of governmental ceremonies and proclamations [and presidential inaugurations and Thanksgiving]…

In addition to this general tradition of prayer at public ceremonies, there exists a more specific tradition of invocations and benedictions at public school graduation exercises. By one account, the first public high school graduation ceremony took place in Connecticut in July 1868…when "15 seniors from the Norwich Free Academy marched in their best Sunday suits and dresses into a church hall and waited through majestic music and long prayers."…The invocation and benediction have long been recognized to be "as traditional as any other parts of the school graduation program and are widely established."

The Court presumably would separate graduation invocations and benedictions from other instances of public "preservation and transmission of religious beliefs" on the ground that they involve **psychological coercion.**" I find it a sufficient embarrassment that our Establishment Clause jurisprudence regarding holiday displays…has come to require scrutiny more commonly associated with interior decorators than with the judiciary.

When you get to chapter twelve (the "symbols" cases), you will see what Justice Scalia means by suggesting that experience as an interior decorator would be a valuable addition to an application for Supreme Court Justice!

But interior decorating is a rock-hard science compared to psychology practiced by amateurs...The Court has gone beyond the realm where judges know what they are doing.

The Court's argument that state officials have "coerced" students to take part in the invocation and benediction at graduation ceremonies...is incoherent...

The Court declares that students' "attendance and participation in the invocation and benediction are in a fair and real sense obligatory."... According to the Court, students at graduation who want "to avoid the fact or appearance of participation" in the invocation and benediction are psychologically obligated by "public pressure, as well as peer pressure,... to stand as a group or, at least, maintain respectful silence" during those prayers. This assertion – the very linchpin of the Court's opinion – is almost as intriguing for what it does not say as for what it says. It does not say, for example, that students are psychologically coerced to bow their heads, [fold their hands in prayer], pay attention to the prayers, utter "Amen," or in fact pray...It claims only that students are psychologically coerced "to stand...or, at least, to maintain respectful silence."

...The Court's notion that a student who simply sits in respectful silence during the invocation and benediction (when all others are standing) has somehow joined – or would somehow be perceived as having joined – in the prayers is nothing short of ludicrous. We indeed live in a vulgar age. But surely our social conventions have not coarsened to the point that anyone who does not stand on his chair and shout obscenities can reasonably be deemed to have assented to everything said in his presence. Since the Court does not dispute that students exposed to prayer at graduation ceremonies retain (despite "subtle coercive pressures") the free will to sit, there is absolutely no basis for the Court's decision. It is fanciful enough to say that "a reasonable dissenter, 'standing head erect in a class of bowed heads,' could believe that the group exercise signified her own participation or approval of it." It is beyond the absurd to say that she could entertain such a belief while pointedly declining to rise.

But let us assume the very worst, that the nonparticipating graduate is "subtly coerced"…to stand! Even that half of the disjunctive does not remotely establish a "participation" (or an "appearance of participation") in a religious exercise. The Court acknowledges that "in our culture standing…can signify adherence to a view or simple respect for the views of others."…But if it is a permissible inference that one who is standing is doing so simply out of respect for the prayers of others that are in progress, then how can it possibly be said that a "reasonable dissenter…could believe that the group exercise signified her own participation or approval?" Quite obviously, it cannot. I may add, moreover, that maintaining respect for the religious observances of others is a fundamental civic virtue that government (including the public schools) can and should cultivate – so that even if it were the case that the displaying of such respect might be mistaken for taking part in the prayer, I would deny that the dissenter's interest in avoiding even the false appearance of participation constitutionally trumps the government's interest in fostering respect for religion generally.

The opinion manifests that the Court itself has not given careful consideration to its test of psychological coercion. For if it had, how could it observe, with no hint of concern or disapproval, that students stood for the Pledge of Allegiance, which immediately preceded Rabbi Gutterman's invocation? The government can, of course, no more coerce political orthodoxy than religious orthodoxy. Moreover, since the Pledge…has been revised…to include the phrase "under God," recital of the Pledge would appear to raise the same Establishment Clause issue as the invocation and benediction…Must the Pledge therefore be barred from the public schools (both from graduation ceremonies and from the classroom)? In *Barnette* we held that a public school student could not be compelled to recite the Pledge; we did not even hint that she could not be compelled to observe respectful silence – indeed, even to stand in respectful silence – when those who wished to recite it did so…

I also find it odd that the Court concludes that the high school graduates may not be subjected to this supposed psychological coercion, yet refrains from addressing whether "mature adults" may. I had thought that the reason graduation from high school is regarded as so significant an event is that it is generally associated with transition from adolescence to young adulthood. Many graduating seniors, of course, are old enough to vote. Why, then, does the Court treat them as though they were first-graders? Will we soon have a jurisprudence that distinguishes between mature and immature adults?

The other "dominant fact" identified by the Court is that "state officials direct the performance of a formal religious exercise" at school graduation ceremonies. "Directing the performance of a formal religious exercise" has a sound of liturgy to it, summoning up images of the principal directing acolytes where to carry the cross, or showing the rabbi where to unroll the Torah…All the record shows is that principals…have invited clergy to deliver invocations and benedictions at graduations; and that Principal Lee invited Rabbi Gutterman, provided him a two-page pamphlet, prepared by the National Conference of Christians and Jews, giving general advice on inclusive prayer for civic occasions, and advised him that his prayers at graduation should be nonsectarian. How these facts can fairly be transformed into the charges that Principal Lee "directed and controlled the content of Rabbi Gutterman's prayer," that school officials "monitor prayer" and attempted to "compose official prayers" and that the "government involvement with religious activity in this case is persuasive," is difficult to fathom. The Court identifies nothing in the record remotely suggesting that school officials have ever drafted, edited, screened, or censored graduation prayers, or that Rabbi Gutterman was a mouthpiece of the school officials…

The deeper flaw in the Court's opinion…lies…in the Court's making violation of the Establishment Clause hinge on such a precious question. The coercion that was a hallmark of historical establishments of religion was coercion of religious orthodoxy and of financial support **by force of law and threat of penalty**. Typically, attendance at the state church was required; only clergy of the official church could lawfully perform sacraments; and dissenters…faced an array of civil disabilities…

The Establishment Clause was adopted to prohibit such an establishment of religion at the federal level (and to protect state establishments of religion from federal interference). I will further acknowledge for the sake of argument that, as some scholars have argued, by 1790 the term "establishment" had acquired an additional meaning – "financial support of religion generally, by public taxation" – that reflected the development of "general or multiple" establishments, not limited to a single church. But that would still be an establishment coerced by force of law. And I will further concede that our constitutional tradition, from the Declaration of Independence and the first inaugural address of Washington, quoted earlier, down to the present day, has, with a few aberrations, ruled out of order government-sponsored endorsement of religion – even when no legal coercion is present, and indeed even when no ersatz, "peer-pressure" psycho-coercion is present – where the endorsement is sectarian, in the sense of specifying details upon which men and women who believe in a benevolent, omnipotent Creator and Ruler of the world are known to differ (for example, the divinity of Christ). But there is simply no support for the proposition that the officially sponsored nondenominational invocation and benediction read by Rabbi Gutterman – with no one legally coerced to recite them – violated the Constitution of the United States. To the contrary, they are so characteristically American they could have come from the pen of George Washington or Abraham Lincoln himself.

Thus, while I have no quarrel with the Court's general proposition that the Establishment Clause "guarantees that government may not coerce anyone to support or participate in religion or its exercises," I see no warrant for expanding the concept of coercion beyond acts backed by threat of penalty – a brand of coercion that, happily, is readily discernible to those of us who have made a career of reading the disciples of Blackstone [an English legal scholar] rather than of Freud. The Framers were indeed opposed to coercion of religious worship by the national government; but, as their own sponsorship of nonsectarian prayer in public events demonstrates, they understood that "speech is not coercive; the listener may do as he likes."

...The Court relies on our school prayer cases, *Engel* and *Abington*. But..., they do not support...the Court's psycho-journey...*Engel* and *Abington* do not constitute an exception to the rule...that public ceremonies may include prayer; rather, they simply do not fall within the scope of the rule (for the obvious reason that **school instruction is not a public ceremony**)...

We have made clear our understanding that school prayer occurs within a framework in which legal coercion to attend school (i.e., coercion under threat of penalty) provides the ultimate backdrop. In *Abington*, for example, we emphasized that the prayers were "prescribed as part of the curricular activities of students who are required by law to attend school." *Engel's* suggestion that the school prayer program at issue there – which permitted students to "remain silent or be excused from the room" – involved indirect coercive pressure should be understood against this back-drop of legal coercion. The question whether the opt-out procedure in *Engel* sufficed to dispel the coercion resulting from the mandatory attendance requirement is quite different from the question whether forbidden coercion exists in an environment utterly devoid of legal compulsion. And finally, our school prayer cases turn in part on the fact that the classroom is inherently an instructional setting, and daily prayer there – where parents are not present to counter the students' emulation of teachers as role models and the children's susceptibility to peer pressure – might be thought to raise special concerns regarding state interference with the liberty of parents to direct the religious upbringing of their children: "Families entrust public schools with the education of their children, but condition their trust on the understanding that the classroom will not purposely be used to advance religious views that may conflict with the private beliefs of the student and his or her family." *Pierce v. Society of Sisters*. Voluntary prayer at graduation – a one-time ceremony at which parents, friends, and relatives are present – can hardly be thought to raise the same concerns...

Given the odd basis for the Court's decision, invocations and benedictions will be able to be given at public school graduations next June, as they have been for the past century and a half, so long as school authorities make clear that anyone who abstains from screaming in protest does not necessarily participate in the prayers. All that is seemingly needed is an announcement, or perhaps a written insertion at the beginning of the graduation program, to the effect that, while all are asked to rise for the invocation and benediction, none is compelled to join them, nor will be assumed, by rising, to have done so. That obvious fact recited, the graduates and their parents may proceed to thank God, as Americans have always done, for the blessings He has generously bestowed on them and on their country...

The Founders of our Republic knew the fearsome potential of sectarian religious belief to generate civil dissension and civil strife. And they also knew that nothing, absolutely nothing, is so inclined to foster among religious believers of various faiths a toleration – no, an affection – for one another than voluntarily joining in prayer together, to the God whom they all worship and seek. Needless to say, no one should be compelled to do that, but it is a shame to deprive our public culture of the opportunity, and indeed the encouragement, for people to do it voluntarily. The Baptist or Catholic who heard and joined in the simple and inspiring prayers of Rabbi Gutterman on this official and patriotic occasion was inoculated from religious bigotry and prejudice in a manner that cannot be replicated. **To deprive our society of that important unifying mechanism, in order to spare the non-believer what seems to me the minimal inconvenience of standing or even sitting in respectful nonparticipation, is as senseless in policy as it is unsupported in law...**

Justice Scalia has the better argument, hands down. In fact, the majority opinion in this case does fall under the category of "culture war." Score one in the "against" column, for prayer lost again.

> ### First Amendment Scoreboard
> Rulings "for" Religion: 16 --- Rulings "against" Religion: 7

Let's summarize.

1962: In *Engel v. Vitale* we learned that government-composed official prayer as part of a religious program carried on in public schools is constitutionally prohibited.

Principles: One of the greatest dangers to the freedom of the individual to worship in his own way lies in the government's placing its official stamp of approval upon one particular kind of prayer or one particular form of religious service. Our Founders were no more willing to let the content of their prayers and their privilege of praying whenever they pleased be influenced by the ballot box than they were to let these vital matters of personal conscience depend upon the succession of monarchs. A union of government and religion tends to destroy government and to degrade religion. Religion is too personal, too sacred, too holy, to permit its unhallowed perversion by a civil magistrate.

History Lessons: The practice of establishing governmentally composed prayers for religious services was one of the reasons many of our early colonists left England to seek religious freedom in America. The Book of Common Prayer created controversy that continually threatened peace in England.

1963: In *Abington School Dist. v. Schempp* we learned that government-required reading of 10 verses from the Holy Bible daily without commentary and the Lord's Prayer in public school is unconstitutional.

Principles: The majority who happens to be in office or on the school board cannot use the machinery of the state to practice its religious beliefs. What is forbidden are those involvements which (1) serve the essentially religious activities of religious institutions, (2) employ the organs of government for essentially religious purposes, or (3) use essentially religious means to serve governmental ends where secular means would suffice.

Dicta: Government may not "establish a religion of secularism" in the sense of affirmatively opposing religion, thus preferring those who believe in no religion to those who do. One's education is not complete without a study of comparative religion. The Bible is worthy of study for its literary and historic qualities. Not every involvement of religion in public life is unconstitutional. Provisions may be made by government for churches and chaplains at military establishments or for chaplains in penal institutions because folks could not otherwise practice their religion freely. Government may allow temporary use of public buildings by religious organizations when their churches are unavailable because of disaster or emergency. Any attempt to use rigid limits upon the mere mention of God or references to the Bible would be fraught with dangers.

1983: In *Marsh v. Chambers* we learned that a state may pay a chaplain to open legislative sessions with prayer without violating the Constitution.

Dicta: Legislators may say prayers on the floor or form voluntary prayer groups. Bona fide classes in comparative religion can be offered in the public schools. And, the text of Abraham Lincoln's Second Inaugural Address which is inscribed on a wall of the Lincoln Memorial need not be purged of its profound theological content.

1985: In *Wallace v. Jaffree* we learned that an official period of silence for "meditation or prayer" in public schools is not permitted.

Dicta: However, nothing in the Constitution prohibits public school students from voluntarily praying on their own at any time before, during, or after the school day.

1992: In *Lee v. Weisman* we learned that a government-sponsored prayer at a graduation ceremony in grade school is prohibited.

Principles: Such a practice creates an identification of government power with religious practice, endorses religion, and violates the establishment clause.

THE SUGGESTED CHRISTIAN RESPONSE

Lost Causes:

Official government-required or sponsored non-ceremonial prayer in public grade school is a lost cause, but this truly is a cause to champion.

Causes to Champion:

Topic: Non-Ceremonial Prayer in Public School

I believe we Christians get upset about things we do not understand which causes us to fight for reversing rulings we should be applauding and, more importantly, to overlook what is truly important in our walk with Christ.

It is very easy to exaggerate the holdings of *Engel, Abington,* and *Wallace.* These are the major Supreme Court cases on the topic of government-sponsored non-ceremonial public grade school prayer. These cases only forbid an extraordinarily narrow subset of a child's potential prayer life, wouldn't you agree?

If your child goes to public school, do you *really* want him or her to be subjected daily to the state's idea of a proper prayer? Do you trust government with any aspect of your child's religious education, even if it is limited to one prayer a day? Is the quest for the right to official prayer in public school being fought for our children or is it better described as a battle for power between Christian adults and government?

If you disagree with the Supreme Court's decisions, would you be pleased with the Berkley edition of government-sponsored non-ceremonial public grade school prayer for your child, a government-sponsored Scientology prayer? How about a Muslim prayer? And, for Scientologists and Muslims, how about a Christian prayer? If not, it would appear you are okay with government-sponsored non-ceremonial public grade school prayer as long as the school board employs prayers not only in accord with your faith, but also in accord with your customized view of how you believe prayers of your faith should be drafted. Now do you understand why we have at least a short fence of separation?

I know it's not easy sometimes to walk a mile in someone else's shoes. The Elliot family found that out the hard way when they moved to a new community and became a minority overnight. No one can deny we are a much more diverse society today on a number of fronts than we were in the 1700s. One clear difference is the number of faiths and denominations that abound.

I began first grade in 1957. That was five years prior to the *Engel* decision. *Engel* was the first case to hold government-sponsored non-ceremonial public grade school prayer unconstitutional. All of my twelve years of grade school were of the public variety and I do not remember any such prayers at any grade level, before or after *Engel*.

You might say, "Tad, you surely didn't have government-sponsored non-ceremonial public grade school prayer *after Engel* – that would have been illegal." Well, you never know. There may be some areas of the country that still do recite such prayers. You see, all government personnel take an oath to support the Constitution and, therefore, are theoretically bound to abide by Supreme Court decisions. However, that does not mean they do. So, I am betting that some school district somewhere still has government-sponsored non-ceremonial public grade school prayer because no one in that community is complaining.

Let's look at just how favorable the Court has been to religion in the rulings and *dicta* taken straight out of just these five prayer cases. Show your neighbors the following truths.

> ➤ Government may not "establish a religion of secularism" in the sense of affirmatively opposing religion, thus preferring those who believe in no religion to those who do.
> ➤ Bona fide classes in comparative religion can be offered in public schools.
> ➤ The Bible is worthy of study for its literary and historic qualities in public school.
> ➤ Provisions may be made by government for churches and chaplains at military establishments.
> ➤ Provisions may be made by government for chaplains in penal institutions.
> ➤ Government may allow temporary use of public buildings by religious organizations when their churches are unavailable because of disaster or emergency.
> ➤ **Any attempt to use rigid limits upon the mere mention of God or references to the Bible in public school is frowned upon by the Court.**
> ➤ A state may pay a chaplain who may open legislative sessions with prayer.
> ➤ Legislators may say prayers on the floor or form voluntary prayer groups.
> ➤ The religious text of quotes inscribed on memorial walls need not be purged of their profound theological content.
> ➤ **Nothing in the Constitution prohibits public school students from voluntarily praying at any time before, during, or after the school day.**

That is an impressive list. All that is missing, as it relates to minor public school children, is a 20-second government-drafted prayer which leads me to ask several questions that might serve to help you focus on what is truly important about prayer.

Do you believe prayer is important to God? Should prayer be a part of your child's life?

Do you pray with your children? When? How often?

Would you consider sending your child off to school with prayer each day? If not, why would you ever complain that the law does not permit the machinery of the state to do it for you?

Do you teach your children to pray before meals at home? In public?

I do not address whether such prayers are something you should include in your family life. That is up to you. However, I have more telling questions. If you do not instill prayer in your children, why not?

Do you bow your head and at least act like you are praying in a Bible study group? During a congregational prayer at a church service? In a public setting when a group, such as a Rotary club, prays over a meal?

Is it uncomfortable for you to pray with your family over a meal at a restaurant? If so, why do you think that is? **If you are upset about government-sponsored prayer being taken out of public school, why are you embarrassed to pray with your public school children in public?**

Remember Charley at the WWII Memorial from chapter two? In response to his wife's complaint that the inscribers failed to complete FDR's quote with "so help us God," he walked away sadly and said, *"We're not supposed to say things like that now."* Well, one thing is for sure. Included in the bullet list, above, is a statement that religious quotes inscribed in stone are not unconstitutional. **If the inscribers left FDR's words off because they believed "we can't say 'God' anymore," they were flat wrong!**

Fictional Charley is not the only one who has uttered those words. After playing a videotape of public school children chanting praises to President

Obama, Sean Hannity of Fox News said, "Isn't it a shame in this country that this kind of thing is going on in our public schools, yet these same kids cannot mention 'God' in our public schools."

I guess I have to forgive him, for I am quite sure he is just like Amanda, Charley, Helen, and all of the good folks who hit the send button on the WWII story – a story that seems to affirm we cannot say "God" anymore. However, *you* no longer have that excuse and I am reasonably sure Mr. Hannity would retract his statement if he ever reads this book. See, folks, the rumor that Charley and Sean are spreading is **false**. The Court has not come close to that kind of hostility to things of God. However, every day the lie is repeated, as Lenin said, someday that lie will, in fact, become our reality.

Before closing this chapter, I am reminded of yet another e-mail ditty going around concerning Tennessee football. In order to prove what I believe should be most important to Christians, I will present it here with my comments. And, in case it is not based 100% on accurate reporting, I will change the names and make it a hypothetical.

This is a statement that was read over the PA system at a County High School football game in Anyplace, Tennessee, by the school principal.

"It has always been the custom at County High School football games, to say a prayer and play the National Anthem, to honor God and country. Due to a recent ruling by the Supreme Court, I am told that saying a prayer is a violation of federal case law."

> Of course, that is just a false statement. Kids (and teachers, for that matter) can say prayers all over the public school facility. The only prohibition is official government-sponsored prayer. The statement is an unfair description of the Court's rulings.

"As I understand the law at this time, I can use this public facility to approve of sexual perversion and call it 'an alternative lifestyle,' and if someone is offended, that's OK. I can use it to condone sexual promiscuity, by dispensing condoms and calling it 'safe sex.' If someone is offended, that's OK. I can even use this public facility to present the merits of killing an unborn baby as a 'viable means of birth control.' If someone is offended, no problem."

> I'm not so sure the Supreme Court has addressed these other issues. Let's stick to religion. You, Ms Principal, can also teach the Bible and numerous matters touching upon religion and, if someone is offended, that is OK.

"I can designate a school day as 'Earth Day' and involve students in activities to worship religiously and praise the goddess of 'Mother Earth' and call it 'ecology.'"

> Please, if you are truly worshiping, then, no, you cannot do so.

"I can use literature, videos and presentations in the classroom that depicts people with strong, traditional Christian convictions as 'simple minded' and 'ignorant' and call it 'enlightenment.'"

> I do not know why you would want to do that, but if you do, it would likely be protected free speech because you are not proselytizing for a religion.

"However, if anyone uses this facility to honor God and to ask Him to bless this event with safety and good sportsmanship, then federal case law is violated."

> That is false! Anyone can honor God and ask Him to bless the event - anyone but you, the principal, over the loudspeaker as a government-sponsored religious act.

"This appears to be inconsistent at best, and at worst, diabolical. Apparently, we are to be tolerant of everything and anyone, except God and His Commandments."

These inaccurate conclusions are diabolical. The principal has it all wrong because she is misinformed of what the Court has said. She is part of the growing problem that helps the lie appear to be true that we just cannot say "God" anymore. Cut it out!

"Nevertheless, as a school principal, I frequently ask staff and students to abide by rules with which they do not necessarily agree. For me to do otherwise would be inconsistent at best, and at worst, hypocritical. I suffer from that affliction enough unintentionally. I certainly do not need to add an intentional transgression. For this reason, I shall render to Caesar that which is Caesar's and refrain from praying at this time."

Good. You cannot do so publicly with the loudspeaker because you are government acting in a public school where minor children are practically compelled by law to attend. There is a very good reason for that. Ask Jackson Elliot of Berkley, California. He will tell you why.

"However, if you feel inspired to honor, praise and thank God and ask Him, in the name of Jesus, to bless this event, please feel free to do so. As far as I can tell, that's not against the law – yet."

Beautiful! And, why is it they can pray on their own at a public school? Because the freedoms our Constitution protects have been preserved by our Supreme Court. Use them. Get a grip on the truth.

Oh, by the way, since this principal believes government should be able to urge public school children to follow Jesus, I presume she would have no problem if a Muslim principal urged public school children to follow Allah; because, if the High Court ever permits the former, they will be compelled to permit the latter. Just wondering.

"The only place they didn't pray was in the Supreme Court of the United States of America – the seat of 'justice' in 'one nation, under God.'"

> After having read the prayer cases issued by the Supreme Court, is there one of you that can say that is a fair statement?

"Somehow our County remembered what so many have forgotten. We are given the freedom of religion, not the freedom from religion. Praise God that His remnant remains!"

> "Many have forgotten" because "many" live by false rumor, not because the Supreme Court has forgotten these liberties.

"Jesus said, 'If you are ashamed of me before men, then I will be ashamed of you before my Father.' If you are not ashamed, pass this on."

Here we go again. Go ahead. Pass it on if you want America to wallow in ignorance. That scripture is not the least bit fair to the Supreme Court and, out of context, it has no meaning. For example, would the principal suggest that if a ten-year-old child fails to stand up in the middle of a math problem at school and shout, "Hallelujah to God," he can be fairly described as being "ashamed of Christ before men"?

Although no doubt well-intended, the integrity of this principal's message is lost in its gross inaccuracy. My only parting advice to her is that if she still does not understand just how much prayer *is* permitted by the very Court she condemns or if she must be the one holding the loudspeaker, she always has the option of teaching in a religious school where *all* the children are there because their parents want to control the prayers that are said. The Constitution also gives her that right. It's just that simple.

Anyway, when it comes to public school athletic contests, the public may organize all the prayer they want, independent of those that govern. It's their right. And, please, **"It's not OK"** to pass the former e-mail message on without this explanation. It is loaded with false rumor.

If you know your Bible, you know it teaches us to **"Keep on praying. No matter what happens…"** 1 Thessalonians 5:17-18. I ask all Christians and those of other faiths to explore the possibilities of prayer in your life and in the lives of your children. Understand that your children absolutely can say "God" at school. As long as they do not disrupt the educational process, they can speak of God with their fellow students, pray over their meal in the cafeteria, mention the importance of God in their lives at a "show and tell," and even discuss God with their teachers.

Do you think Christ is more concerned with a twenty-second prayer that can only be said (or heard) through the filter of state machinery or the unceasing prayer that can be said by your children during any of the remaining twenty-three hours, fifty-nine minutes and forty seconds of their day? And, as for that twenty seconds, please understand that if any faith is ever successful in getting government-sponsored prayer back into public school, that victor must be prepared to accept the blame for the very real possibility of having earned the right of conflicting faiths to compose the prayers your children will be subjected to.

Topic: Ceremonial Prayer/Moment of Silence in Public School

I agree with Justice Scalia that the graduation prayers in the *Lee* case should have been permitted to stand. Why? What is the difference between government-sponsored non-ceremonial public grade school prayer and government-sponsored **ceremonial** public grade school prayer, especially at high school graduation?

As we saw in *Marsh*, government prayers in legislative halls are okay because those subjected to them are adults, fully capable of joining in or respectfully awaiting their conclusion. With the exception of a few child prodigies, seventeen-year-old graduates and younger siblings of graduates, most attendees of high school graduation ceremonies are adults. This is not daily indoctrination. I do not believe exposure to one prayer in a lifetime is going to harm the psyche of any child, no matter what is said. If you do, you must not have a television in your home.

Although Justice Scalia's advice that a government disclaimer in a graduation bulletin should take care of the majority's coercion problem may have been a bit tongue in cheek, you might consider suggesting the same to your school board if you wish to pursue official prayer at graduation.

In a bit of good news, the Supreme Court recently denied an appeal from the Seventh Circuit Court of Appeals upholding an Illinois statute that requires public schools to observe a daily period for "silent prayer or reflection on the anticipated activities of the day." Kids in Illinois can pray silently together. See, God is not forbidden in public school.

And, finally, I do not believe the Supreme Court has ever ruled on the right of a high school valedictorian to tap their freedoms of speech and religion should they choose to include mention of their walk with God in their graduation speech. I certainly favor their right to do so, but please understand that a Muslim valedictorian would have the same right. Even then, surely no one believes one prayer of another faith would have devastating consequences to its audience.

In closing out the topic of prayer, please let all skeptics know that, as I said in chapter two, **It Really Is OK To Say "God"** in America "almost" anywhere "almost" anytime in "almost" any manner you or your child wishes. And, the primary reason that political strife will not accompany that right is that we cannot say "God" anywhere anytime in any manner we wish. In effect, we forego a government-coerced daily 20-second ritual for our children in return for maximum freedom of religion.

Maximize the freedom of prayer in your life and in the lives of your children and may God bless America! There you go. I said it again and, guess what? **It's still OK!**

Chapter Ten

ESTABLISHMENT:
EVOLUTION

All aboard for Arkansas.

===

Epperson v. Arkansas **(1968):** [9-0] Justice Fortas...[Arkansas adopted an anti-evolution statute in 1928 to prohibit the teaching in public schools and universities of the theory that man evolved from apes. This statute was an adaptation of the famous Tennessee "monkey law" adopted in 1925 that was upheld in the celebrated *Scopes v. State* decision of the Tennessee Supreme Court. In 1965 the Little Rock School Board, on recommendation from their biology teachers, proscribed a textbook that taught Darwin's theory of evolution. Ms Epperson faced a dilemma. If she taught this book, she risked criminal prosecution for violating the state law. If she did not, she risked being fired by the school board. She sought to void the state statute. The Arkansas Supreme Court upheld it in a two-sentence opinion as an exercise of the State's power to specify the curriculum in public schools and did not address the competing constitutional questions at all.]

[Held: The Arkansas Supreme Court is reversed. Prohibiting the teaching of evolution is unconstitutional. Government must be neutral in matters of religious theory. The overriding effect of the law is that it selects from the body of knowledge a particular segment which it proscribes for the sole reason that it is deemed to conflict with a particular religious doctrine; that is, with a particular interpretation of the Book of Genesis by a particular religious group.] The First Amendment does not permit the State to require that teaching and learning must be tailored to the principles or prohibitions of any religious sect or dogma. While study of religions and of the Bible from a literary and historic viewpoint, presented objectively as part of a secular program of education, need not collide with the First Amendment's prohibition, the State may not adopt programs or practices in its public schools or colleges which aid or oppose any religion.

Notice the *Epperson* Court does not say a state must teach evolution and it does not decide whether "creation science" could be taught. It merely says when a school board wishes to teach evolution, a state statute that prohibits its teaching is unconstitutional. How about a brain teaser? If evolution is taught and if the Biblical account of the creation of man cannot be constitutionally taught, are students' rights to "free exercise" being undermined? Is this an "establishment of non-religion"? Or, are Protestants left with the same decision Catholics had to make when Protestants had political power in our early public schools? If the foregoing turns out to be the law, what is the Protestant option? More Protestant-based schools? Are we then left with public schools attended solely by children of atheists and/or the apathetic and/or poor Protestants? Things are heating up a bit, aren't they? Score one "against" religion.

> ### First Amendment Scoreboard
> Rulings "for" Religion: 16 --- Rulings "against" Religion: 8

Louisiana, here we come!

EDWARDS v. AGUILLARD
SUPREME COURT OF THE UNITED STATES
482 U.S. 578
June 19, 1987
[7 – 2]

OPINION: Justice Brennan...The question for decision is whether Louisiana's "Balanced Treatment for Creation-Science and Evolution-Science in Public School Instruction Act" (Creationism Act) [violates the Establishment Clause of the First Amendment].

The Creationism Act forbids the teaching of the theory of evolution in public schools *unless* accompanied by instruction in "creation science." No school is required to teach evolution or creation science. If either is taught, however, the other must also be taught. The theories of evolution and creation science are statutorily defined as "the scientific evidences for creation or evolution and inferences from those scientific evidences."...The District Court...[and] the Court of Appeals...held that the Act violated the Establishment Clause...[We affirm.]

The Court has applied a three-pronged test to determine whether legislation comports with the Establishment Clause. First, the legislature must have adopted the law with a secular purpose. Second, the statute's principal or primary effect must be one that neither advances nor inhibits religion. Third, the statute must not result in an excessive entanglement of government with religion. *Lemon v. Kurtzman*. State action violates the Establishment Clause if it fails to satisfy any of these prongs...

The Court has been particularly vigilant in monitoring compliance with the Establishment Clause in elementary and secondary schools. Families entrust public schools with the education of their children, but condition their trust on the understanding that the classroom will not purposely be used to advance religious views that may conflict with the private beliefs of the student and his or her family...[Here], appellants have identified no clear secular purpose for the Louisiana Act...

> Do you see any distorted logic here? We will discuss this at the end of the chapter.

The goal of providing a more comprehensive science curriculum is not furthered either by outlawing the teaching of evolution or by requiring the teaching of creation science. While the court is normally deferential to a state's articulation of a secular purpose, it is required that the statement of such purpose be sincere and not a sham...

It is clear from the legislative history that the purpose of the legislative sponsor, Senator Bill Keith, was to narrow the science curriculum. During the legislative hearing, Senator Keith stated: "My preference would be that neither [creationism nor evolution] be taught." Such a ban on teaching does not promote – indeed, it undermines – the provision of a comprehensive scientific education.

It is equally clear that requiring schools to teach creation science with evolution does not advance academic freedom. The Act does not grant teachers a flexibility that they did not already possess to supplant the present science curriculum with the presentation of theories, besides evolution, about the origin of life. Indeed, the Court of Appeals found that no law prohibited Louisiana public school teachers from teaching any scientific theory. As the president of the Louisiana Science Teachers Association testified, "any scientific concept that's based on established fact can be included in our curriculum already, and no legislation allowing this is necessary." The Act provides Louisiana schoolteachers with no new authority. Thus the stated purpose is not furthered by it...

We agree with the Court of Appeals' conclusion that the Act does not serve to protect academic freedom, but has the distinctly different purpose of discrediting "evolution by counterbalancing its teaching at every turn with the teaching of creationism..."

> I am beginning to feel a little creepy. Has Big Brother arrived?

The preeminent purpose of the Louisiana Legislature was clearly to advance the religious viewpoint that a supernatural being created humankind... Senator Keith's leading expert on creation science, Edward Boudreaux, testified at the legislative hearings that the theory of creation science included belief in the existence of a supernatural creator...(noting that "creation scientists" point to high probability that life was "created by an intelligent mind"). Senator Keith also cited testimony from other experts to support the creation-science view that "a creator [was] responsible for the universe and everything in it." The legislative history therefore reveals that the term "creation science," as contemplated by the legislature that adopted this Act, embodies the religious belief that a supernatural creator was responsible for the creation of humankind.

Furthermore, it is not happenstance that the legislature required the teaching of a theory that coincided with this religious view. The legislative history documents that the Act's primary purpose was to change the science curriculum of public schools in order to provide persuasive advantage to a particular religious doctrine that rejects the factual basis of evolution in its entirety. The sponsor of the Creationism Act, Senator Keith, explained during the legislative hearings that his disdain for the theory of evolution resulted from the support that evolution supplied to views contrary to his own religious beliefs. According to Senator Keith, the theory of evolution was consonant with the "cardinal principles of religious humanism, secular humanism, theological liberalism [and] atheism." The state senator repeatedly stated that scientific evidence supporting his religious views should be included in the public school curriculum to redress the fact that the theory of evolution incidentally coincided with what he characterized as religious beliefs antithetical to his own. The legislation therefore sought to alter the science curriculum to reflect endorsement of a religious view that is antagonistic to the theory of evolution...

As in *Epperson*, the legislature passed the Act to give preference to those religious groups which have as one of their tenets the creation of humankind by a divine creator. The "overriding fact" that confronted the Court in *Epperson* was "that Arkansas' law selects from the body of knowledge a particular segment which it proscribes for the sole reason that it is deemed to conflict with...a particular interpretation of the Book of

Genesis by a particular religious group." Similarly, the Creationism Act is designed *either* to promote the theory of creation science which embodies a particular religious tenet by requiring that creation science be taught whenever evolution is taught *or* to prohibit the teaching of a scientific theory disfavored by certain religious sects by forbidding the teaching of evolution when creation science is not also taught. The Establishment Clause, however, "forbids *alike* the preference of a religious doctrine *or* the prohibition of theory which is deemed antagonistic to a particular dogma." Because the primary purpose of the Creationism Act is to advance a particular religious belief, the Act endorses religion in violation of the First Amendment.

We do not imply that a legislature could never require that scientific critiques of prevailing scientific theories be taught. Indeed, the Court acknowledged in *Stone* that its decision forbidding the posting of the Ten Commandments did not mean that no use could ever be made of the Ten Commandments, or that the Ten Commandments played an exclusively religious role in the history of Western Civilization. In a similar way, teaching a variety of scientific theories about the origins of humankind to schoolchildren might be validly done with the clear secular intent of enhancing the effectiveness of science instruction. But because the primary purpose of the Creationism Act is to endorse a particular religious doctrine, the Act furthers religion in violation of the Establishment Clause.

Why not teach comparative origin theory?

The Louisiana Creationism Act advances a religious doctrine by requiring either the banishment of the theory of evolution from public school classrooms or the presentation of a religious viewpoint that rejects evolution in its entirety. The Act violates the Establishment Clause of the First Amendment because it seeks to employ the symbolic and financial support of government to achieve a religious purpose. [The judgment of the Court of Appeals is Affirmed.]

DISSENT: Justice Scalia…The parties are sharply divided over what creation science consists of. Appellants insist that it is a collection of educationally valuable *scientific* data that has been censored from classrooms by an embarrassed scientific establishment. Appellees insist it is not science at all but thinly veiled religious doctrine...

At least at this stage in the litigation, it is plain to me that we must accept appellants' view of what the statute means. To begin with, the statute itself defines "creation-science" as "the *scientific evidences* for creation and inferences from those *scientific evidences*." If, however, that definition is not thought sufficiently helpful, the means by which the Louisiana Supreme Court will give the term more precise content is quite clear – and again, at this stage in the litigation, favors the appellants' view...The only evidence in the record of the "received meaning and acceptation" of "creation science" is found in five affidavits filed by appellants. In those affidavits, two scientists, a philosopher, a theologian, and an educator, all of whom claim extensive knowledge of creation science, swear that it is essentially a collection of *scientific* data supporting the theory that the physical universe and life within it appeared suddenly and have not changed substantially since appearing. These experts insist that creation science is a strictly scientific concept that can be presented without religious reference. At this point, then, we must assume that the Balanced Treatment Act does not require the presentation of religious doctrine...

For the purpose of the *Lemon* test..., if those legislators who supported the Balanced Treatment Act in fact acted with a "sincere" secular purpose, the Act survives the first component of the *Lemon* test, regardless of whether that purpose is likely to be achieved by the provisions they enacted.

Our cases have also confirmed that when the *Lemon* Court referred to "a secular...purpose," it meant "a secular purpose." The author of *Lemon*, writing for the Court, has said that invalidation under the purpose prong is appropriate when "there [is] no question that the statute or activity was motivated wholly by religious considerations." *Wallace v. Jaffree*...In all three cases in which we struck down laws under the Establishment Clause for lack of a secular purpose, we found that the legislature's sole motive was to promote religion. See *Wallace v. Jaffree; Epperson v. Arkansas*...Thus, the majority's invalidation of the Balanced Treatment Act is defensible only if the record indicates that the Louisiana Legislature had no secular purpose.

It is important to stress that the purpose forbidden by *Lemon* is the purpose "to advance religion." **Our cases in no way imply that the Establishment Clause forbids legislators merely to act upon their religious convictions.** We surely would not strike down a law providing money to feed the hungry or shelter the homeless if it could be demonstrated that, but for the religious beliefs of the legislators, the funds would not have been approved. Also, **political activism by the religiously motivated is part of our heritage.**

Notwithstanding the majority's implication to the contrary, we do not presume that the sole purpose of a law is to advance religion merely because it was supported strongly by organized religions or by adherents of particular faiths. To do so would deprive religious men and women of their right to participate in the political process. Today's religious activism may give us the Balanced Treatment Act, but yesterday's resulted in the abolition of slavery, and tomorrow's may bring relief for famine victims.

Similarly, we will not presume that a law's purpose is to advance religion merely because it "happens to coincide or harmonize with the tenets of some or all religions." *McGowan v. Maryland...*Thus, the fact that creation science coincides with the beliefs of certain religions, a fact upon which the majority relies heavily, does not itself justify invalidation of the Act. Finally, our cases indicate that even certain kinds of governmental actions undertaken with the specific intention of improving the position of religion do not "advance religion" as that term is used in *Lemon*. Rather, we have said that in at least two circumstances government *must* act to advance religion, and that in a third it *may* do so.

First, since we have consistently described the Establishment Clause as forbidding not only state action motivated by the desire to advance religion, but also that intended to "disapprove," "inhibit," or evince "hostility" toward religion...and since we have said that governmental "neutrality" toward religion is the preeminent goal of the First Amendment,...a State which discovers that its employees are inhibiting religion must take steps to prevent them from doing so, even though its purpose would clearly be to advance religion. Thus, if the Louisiana Legislature sincerely believed that the state's science teachers were being hostile to religion, our cases indicate that it could act to eliminate that hostility without running afoul of *Lemon's* purpose test...

> Now, there's something to shout about. "If a state legislature sincerely believed that the state's science teachers were being hostile to religion, it could act to eliminate that hostility without running afoul of *Lemon's* purpose test." That might be useful down the road.

I now turn to the purposes underlying adoption of the Balanced Treatment Act...There is ample evidence that the majority is wrong in holding that the Balanced Treatment Act is without secular purpose...Before summarizing the testimony of Senator Keith and his supporters, I wish to make clear that I by no means intend to endorse its accuracy. But my views (and the views of this Court) about creation science and evolution are (or should be) beside the point. Our task is not to judge the debate about teaching the origins of life, but to ascertain what the members of the Louisiana Legislature believed. The vast majority of them voted to approve a bill which explicitly stated a secular purpose; what is crucial is not their wisdom in believing that purpose would be achieved by the bill, but their sincerity in believing it would be...

The witnesses repeatedly assured committee members that "hundreds and hundreds" of highly respected, internationally renowned scientists believed in creation science and would support their testimony. Senator Keith and his witnesses testified essentially as [follows]:

[1] There are two and only two scientific explanations for the beginning of life – evolution and creation science. Both are bona fide "sciences." Both posit a theory of the origin of life and subject that theory to empirical testing. Evolution posits that life arose out of inanimate chemical compounds and has gradually evolved over millions of years. Creation science posits that all life forms now on earth appeared suddenly and relatively recently and have changed little. Since there are only two possible explanations of the origin of life, any evidence that tends to disprove the theory of evolution necessarily tends to prove the theory of creation science, and vice versa. For example, the abrupt appearance in

the fossil record of complex life, and the extreme rarity of transitional life forms in that record, are evidence for creation science.

[2] ...The evidence for evolution is far less compelling than we have been led to believe. Evolution is not a scientific "fact," since it cannot actually be observed in a laboratory. Rather, evolution is merely a scientific theory or "guess." It is a very bad guess at that. The scientific problems with evolution are so serious that it could accurately be termed a "myth."

[3] Creation science is educationally valuable. Students exposed to it better understand the current state of scientific evidence about the origin of life. Those students even have a better understanding of evolution. Creation science can and should be presented to children without any religious content.

[4] Although creation science is educationally valuable and strictly scientific, it is now being censored from or misrepresented in the public schools. Evolution, in turn, is misrepresented as an absolute truth. Teachers have been brainwashed by an entrenched scientific establishment composed almost exclusively of scientists to whom evolution is like a "religion." These scientists discriminate against creation scientists so as to prevent evolutions' weaknesses from being exposed.

[5] The censorship of creation science has at least two harmful effects. First, it deprives students of knowledge of one of the two scientific explanations for the origin of life and leads them to believe that evolution is proven fact; thus, their education suffers and they are wrongly taught that science has proved their religious beliefs false. Second, it violates the Establishment Clause. The United States Supreme Court has held that secular humanism is a religion. [In a footnote to the *Torcaso* case (see chapter five) the Court found: "Among religions in this country which do not teach what would generally be considered a belief in the existence of God are...Secular Humanism.] Belief in evolution is a central tenet of that religion. Thus, by censoring creation science and instructing students that evolution is fact, public school teachers are now advancing religion in violation of the Establishment Clause...

The Court today plainly errs in holding that the Louisiana Legislature passed the Balanced Treatment Act for exclusively religious purposes... Had the Court devoted to this central question of the meaning of the legislatively expressed purpose a small fraction of the research into legislative history that produced its quotations of religiously motivated statements by individual legislators, it would have discerned quite readily what "academic freedom" meant: Students' freedom from indoctrination. **The legislature wanted to ensure that students would be free to decide for themselves how life began, based upon a fair and balanced presentation of the scientific evidence – that is, to protect "the right of each [student] voluntarily to determine what to believe (and what not to believe) free of any coercive pressures from the State."** The legislature did not care whether the topic of origins was taught; it simply wished to ensure that when the topic was taught, students would receive "all of the evidence.".... The Act's reference to "creation" is not convincing evidence of religious purpose. The Act defines creation science as "scientific evidence" and Senator Keith and his witnesses repeatedly stressed that the subject can and should be presented without religious content. We have no basis on the record to conclude that creation science need be anything other than a collection of scientific data supporting the theory that life abruptly appeared on earth. Creation science, its proponents insist, no more must explain whence life came than evolution must explain whence came the inanimate materials from which it says life evolved. But even if that were not so, to posit a past creator is not to posit the eternal and personal God who is the object of religious veneration...Even appellees concede that a valid secular purpose is not rendered impermissible simply because its pursuit is prompted by concern for religious sensitivities.

If a history teacher <u>falsely</u> told her students that the bones of Jesus Christ had been discovered..., I cannot believe (despite the majority's implication to the contrary) that legislators or school board members would be constitutionally prohibited from taking corrective action, simply because that action was prompted by concern for the religious beliefs of the misinstructed students...**The people of Louisiana, including those who are Christian fundamentalists, are quite entitled, as a secular matter, to have whatever scientific evidence there may be against evolution** presented in their schools, just as Mr. Scopes was entitled to present whatever scientific evidence there was for it...Because I believe that the Balanced Treatment Act had a secular purpose...[I would reverse the judgment of the Court of Appeals.]

> The Court is referring to the *Tennessee v. Scopes* case, memorialized in the movie "Inherit the Wind."

I had no problem with *Epperson* in striking down a statute that prohibited the teaching of evolution. I do have a serious problem with this case. The Majority Opinion states up front: "Families entrust public schools with the education of their children, but condition their trust on the understanding that the classroom will not purposely be used to advance religious views that may conflict with the private beliefs of the student or his family." If we assume our representative form of government is, indeed, representative, then the majority of families of Louisiana apparently disagree. The majority's conclusion about what Louisiana families wanted is false; yet, we have learned that constitutional rights are not the subject of a vote – i.e., not the subject of majoritarian rule. That is why certain rights are guaranteed to all, including the minority. The question is not whether families want this Act. Paternalism seems to be the rule of the day for Justice Brennan. The difficulty with this Act and these concepts are that this is the first time we are confronted with public education that is teaching something counter to Christian beliefs, specifically as it relates to the origin of man. The right to free exercise of religion was placed at the pinnacle of constitutional protection in *Wisconsin v. Yoder*. It seems that where the mere "potential" for establishment clashes with the right to free exercise, free exercise should prevail. If we do not permit the teaching of creation science while, at the same time, require the teaching of evolution, we are submitting "impressionable children" to only one theory and censoring their right to *all* of the scientific knowledge on this subject.

In my mind, this is a prime example of "judicial activism" where the majority has taken it upon themselves to decide what is best for the children of Louisiana (and the nation) in complete rejection of what Louisiana parents had decided was best for their children. Unfortunately, we will have to score this one "against" religion.

First Amendment Scoreboard

Rulings "for" Religion: 16 --- Rulings "against" Religion: 9

These are the only two "origin of man" cases to have reached the Supreme Court, summarized as follows:

1968: In *Epperson v. Arkansas* we learned that government may not ban the teaching of evolution in public schools.

Principles: The First Amendment does not permit the State to require that teaching and learning must be tailored to the principles or prohibitions of any religious sect or dogma. While study of religions and of the Bible from a literary and historic viewpoint, presented objectively as part of a secular program of education, need not collide with the First Amendment's prohibition, the State may not adopt programs or practices in its public schools or colleges which "aid or oppose" any religion.

1987: In *Edwards v. Aguillard* we learned a state cannot condition the teaching of evolution upon the teaching of creation science.

Dicta (in dissent): Political activism by the religiously motivated is part of our heritage. We do not presume that the sole purpose of a law is to advance religion merely because it was supported strongly by organized religions or by adherents of particular faiths. To do so would deprive religious men and women of their right to participate in the political process.

THE SUGGESTED CHRISTIAN RESPONSE

Causes to Champion:

Something tells me this particular fight is not over. Who is harmed the most if we only permit one concept to be taught in public school? What harm is there in telling a student that one theory of creation involves a supreme being? The only alternative is to give them less knowledge, not more, and that, it seems to me, is unfair to them.

Normally, I would say the only way to reverse a Supreme Court ruling is to amend the Constitution and that would be a truly insurmountable task on this topic. However, innovative legislative drafting and the continued pressure of new evidence may someday impress enough of the justices into reversing the *Aguillard* case.

If you are motivated to do so, consider going to www.nwcreation.net. This web site lists several organizations on the front line of the creation science fight. Do your homework and consider donating to the cause of an organization you find to be reputable. Additionally, you might search out a good book for your elementary schoolchildren on creation science and do a bit of homeschooling yourself.

Chapter Eleven

ESTABLISHMENT:
TAXATION

We covered the "result" of the next case in chapter five. Now, let's get to the reasoning. It is 1970 in NYC!

WALZ v. TAX COMMISSION
SUPREME COURT OF THE UNITED STATES
397 U.S. 664
May 4, 1970
[8 – 1]

OPINION: Chief Justice Burger...Appellant, owner of real estate in Richmond County, New York, sought...to prevent the New York City Tax Commission from granting property tax exemptions to religious organizations for religious properties used solely for religious worship. The exemption... is authorized by...the New York Constitution, which provides...: "Real property owned by a corporation or association organized exclusively for the moral or mental improvement of men and women, or for **religious, bible, tract,** charitable, benevolent, **missionary**, hospital, infirmary, educational, public playground, scientific, literary, bar association, medical society, library, patriotic, historical or cemetery purposes...and used exclusively for carrying out thereupon one or more of such purposes...**shall be exempt** from taxation as provided in this section."

[Walz contends] that the...grant of an exemption to church property indirectly requires [him] to make a contribution to religious bodies and thereby violates provisions prohibiting establishment of religion under the First Amendment which under the Fourteenth Amendment is binding on the States...[The lower courts upheld the exemption.] We... affirm...

The Court has struggled to find a neutral course between the two Religion Clauses, both of which are cast in absolute terms...and if expanded to a logical extreme, would tend to clash with the other...

The course of constitutional neutrality in this area cannot be an absolutely straight line; rigidity could well defeat the basic purpose of these provisions, which is to insure that no religion be sponsored or favored, none commanded, and none inhibited. The general principle deducible from the First Amendment and all that has been said by this Court is this: that we will not tolerate either governmentally established religion or governmental interference with religion. Short of those expressly proscribed governmental acts there is **room for play in the joints** productive of a benevolent neutrality which will permit religious exercise to exist without sponsorship and without interference...

> "Room for play in the joints" is another way of saying the "wall" should really be more like a "short fence."

Adherents of particular faiths and individual churches frequently take strong positions on public issues...Of course, churches as much as secular bodies and private citizens have that right. **No perfect or absolute separation is really possible**; the very existence of the Religion Clauses is an involvement of sorts – one that seeks to mark boundaries to avoid excessive entanglement.

The hazards of placing too much weight on a few words or phrases of the Court is abundantly illustrated within the pages of the Court's opinion in *Everson*...The Court did not regard [bus fares] to schools teaching a particular religious faith as any more a violation of the Establishment

Clause than providing "state-paid policemen, detailed to protect children… [at the schools] from the very real hazards of traffic…"

Mr. Justice Jackson, in perplexed dissent in *Everson*, noted that "the undertones of the opinion, advocating complete and uncompromising separation…seem utterly discordant with its conclusion…"

One can sympathize with Mr. Justice Jackson's logical analysis but agree with the Court's eminently sensible and realistic application of the language of the Establishment Clause. In *Everson* the Court declined to construe the Religion Clauses with a literalness that would undermine the ultimate constitutional objective as illuminated by history. Surely, bus transportation and police protection to pupils who receive religious instruction "aid" that particular religion to maintain schools that plainly tend to assure future adherents to a particular faith by having control of their total education at an early age. No religious body that maintains schools would deny this as an affirmative if not dominant policy of church schools. But if as in *Everson* busses can be provided to carry and policemen to protect church school pupils, we fail to see how a broader range of police and fire protection given equally to all churches, along with nonprofit hospitals, art galleries, and libraries receiving the same tax exemption, is different for purposes of the Religion Clauses.

Similarly, making textbooks available to pupils in parochial schools in common with public schools was surely an "aid" to the sponsoring churches because it relieved those churches of an enormous aggregate cost for those books. Supplying of costly teaching materials was not seen either as manifesting a legislative purpose to aid or as having a primary effect of aid contravening the First Amendment. *Board v. Allen.* In so holding the Court was heeding both its own prior decisions and our religious tradition…

With all the risks inherent in programs that bring about administrative relationships between public education bodies and church-sponsored schools, we have been able to chart a course that preserved the autonomy and freedom of religious bodies while avoiding any semblance of established religion. This is a "tight rope" and one we have successfully traversed.

The legislative purpose of the property tax exemption is neither the advancement nor the inhibition of religion; it is neither sponsorship nor hostility. New York, in common with the other States, has determined that certain entities that exist in a harmonious relationship to the community at large, and that foster its "moral or mental improvement," should not be inhibited in their activities by property taxation or the hazard of loss of those properties for nonpayment of taxes. It has not singled out one particular church or religious group or even churches as such; rather, it has granted exemption to all houses of religious worship within a broad class of property owned by nonprofit, quasi-public corporations which include hospitals, libraries, playgrounds, scientific, professional, historical, and patriotic groups. The State has an affirmative policy that considers these groups as beneficial and stabilizing influences in community life and finds this classification useful, desirable, and in the public interest...

The limits of permissible state accommodation to religion are by no means co-extensive with the noninterference mandated by the Free Exercise Clause. To equate the two would be to deny a national heritage with roots in the Revolution itself. **We cannot read New York's statute as attempting to establish religion**; it is simply sparing the exercise of religion from the burden of property taxation levied on private profit institutions...

Determining that the legislative purpose of tax exemption is not aimed at establishing, sponsoring, or supporting religion does not end the inquiry, however. We must also be sure that the end result – the effect - is not an excessive government entanglement with religion. **The test is inescapably one of degree.** Either course, taxation of churches or exemption, occasions some degree of involvement with religion. Elimination of exemption would tend to expand the involvement of government by giving rise to tax valuation of church property, tax liens, tax foreclosures, and the direct confrontations and conflicts that follow in the train of those legal processes.

Granting tax exemptions to churches necessarily operates to afford an indirect economic benefit and also gives rise to some, but yet a lesser, involvement than taxing them. In analyzing either alternative the questions are whether the involvement is excessive, and whether it is a continuing one calling for official and continuing surveillance leading to an impermissible degree of entanglement…

The grant of a tax exemption is not sponsorship since the government does not transfer part of its revenue to churches but simply abstains from demanding that the church support the state. No one has ever suggested that tax exemption has converted libraries, art galleries, or hospitals into arms of the state or put employees "on the public payroll." There is no genuine nexus between tax exemption and establishment of religion… The exemption creates only a minimal and remote involvement between church and state and far less than taxation of churches. It restricts the fiscal relationship between church and state, and tends to complement and reinforce the desired separation insulating each from the other…

All of the 50 States provide for tax exemption of places of worship, most of them doing so by constitutional guarantees. For so long as federal income taxes have had any potential impact on churches – over 75 years – religious organizations have been expressly exempt from the tax. Such treatment is an "aid" to churches no more and no less in principle than the real estate tax exemption granted by States. Few concepts are more deeply embedded in the fabric of our national life, beginning with pre-Revolutionary colonial times, than for the government to exercise at the very best this kind of benevolent neutrality toward churches and religious exercise generally so long as none was favored over others and none suffered interference…

Nothing in this national attitude toward religious tolerance and two centuries of uninterrupted freedom from taxation has given the remotest sign of leading to an established church or religion and on the contrary it has operated affirmatively to help guarantee the free exercise of all forms of religious belief. Thus, it is hardly useful to suggest that tax exemption is…the "nose of the camel in the tent" leading to an established church. If tax exemption can be seen as this first step toward "establishment" of religion, as Justice Douglas fears, the second step has been long in coming…[Judgment Affirmed.]

DISSENT: Justice Douglas…[Not provided.]

We already gave this one to religion in chapter five, so our scoreboard does not change.

> ### First Amendment Scoreboard
> Rulings "for" Religion: 16 --- Rulings "against" Religion: 9

THE SUGGESTED CHRISTIAN RESPONSE

I fully agree with the outcome of *Walz*. The only lasting message for Christians is to understand that exemption from taxation is about as close as religion should ever get to government when it comes to the realm of finances.

Chapter Twelve

ESTABLISHMENT:
SYMBOLS

As Christmas neared, the Elliots noticed some very odd California traditions. For example, "Merry Christmas" was not heard much. Instead, advertisements and people on the street said "Happy Holidays." The kids noticed something being built at the Berkley City Park on their way home from school. Webster asked if they could go for a family ride after supper and check it out.

They parked in the shopping district and walked across the street to the park. It appeared carpenters employed by the city were constructing a stage. After introducing himself and saying they were new to the area, Webster asked a worker what they were doing.

"You haven't heard about our Holiday Extravaganza? Well, so as not to offend anyone, during these holidays leading up to the 25th, we put on a play in the park."

"I get it. You mean the story of Christ's birth – the nativity scene and such, right?" said Webster.

"Well, not exactly. You see, several years ago a group of Christians convinced City Hall to buy a life-size nativity scene for the park. Boy, did that ever cause a ruckus. Several other faiths complained. At least it was resolved without a lawsuit. Although not all agreed, the city came up with this idea of a play. Oh, Christ is in the play, for sure, along with Moses, Confucius,

Mohammed, Gandhi, Socrates, and others. We celebrate all of the great philosophers at this season."

Jackson stepped up. "Yes, but you do celebrate the birth of Jesus Christ during the play, surely?"

"Actually, no we don't. This play is all about world peace and beauty, not whose God is best."

"But, sir, Jesus Christ is the author of peace. And, there is nothing more beautiful than the sacrifice He made for mankind," said Ava, somewhat flustered.

"Oh, yeah?" said the laborer. "Well, I don't know anything about that, but if one of you wants to play the part of Socrates, it's still open. Gotta get to work. Happy Holidays."

Welcome to California. The Elliots returned home that evening in a melancholy mood. This surely didn't resemble anything close to a Texas Christmas.

Webster was determined to share the true Christmas spirit. He said, "Look, we all must share God's word at this time of year and say 'Merry Christmas' to everyone we meet. I don't care what their traditions are."

Jackson and Ava were saddened by it all and wondered if they had made the right decision to come out West. "You know, Ava," said Jackson, "I have this vague recollection that our Supreme Court has said city government cannot get involved with nativity scenes and such. If that is true, I wonder how Berkley can get away with a play that amounts to a slap in the face of Christianity at Christmas, of all times?"

Was Jackson's recollection correct? What could he do about it, anyway? What should he do?

Christians, Jews, Muslims, and those of other faiths, have every right to wield political influence as a group on a par with the NRA, the ACLU, the NAACP, the KKK, or any other group or individual. Example: Any religion has the absolute right to take a political stand on abortion. It's called freedom of religion and freedom of speech.

However, there is a difference between a religion that lobbies for a cause founded upon a belief and a religion that seeks the support of government in order to survive.

Christians (or any sect) should be very, very careful about deciding to seek that type of support from government. They just might get what they ask for and, in the next case, they did – in my opinion, to the long-term detriment of Christianity, religion in general, and the nation as a whole. The majority had the chutzpah (ironically, a Hebrew term meaning "unbelievable gall") to attempt a snow job on us with intellectually dishonest conclusions.

It's not difficult to read between the lines. In spite of a clear constitutional mandate to remove the nativity scene in the next case, the majority did not want to be labeled as "the Court that took Christ out of Christmas." Of course, that would not have been a fair conclusion if the case had turned out differently. Not participating in a nativity undertaking does not take Christ out of Christmas, it just takes religious strife out of government and helps maintain the holiness of religion. What they have done, however, foretells of serious harm to the victor; i.e., to Christianity. As I was initially reading the opinion, I predicted problems ahead. You will see what I mean. The majority opinion loves to cite *McGowan* (Sunday closing laws) and *Allen* (loan of textbooks) and *Marsh* (legislative prayer) in support of its position. As I have said before, I believe these three cases were incorrectly decided.

As serious as it is, I just cannot resist the temptation to have some fun with these next two cases. So, I will take some time with them and interject my personal comments in a slightly different format. There is so much to comment upon that I don't use textboxes. I simply indent under "Comment." We are off to Pawtucket, Rhode Island. Merry Christmas!

LYNCH v. DONNELLY
SUPREME COURT OF THE UNITED STATES
465 U.S. 668
March 5, 1984
[5 – 4]

The Issue:

Whether the Establishment Clause prohibits a municipality from including a crèche (nativity scene) in its annual Christmas display?

The Holding:

This particular nativity scene (incorporated into the entire Christmas display) does not violate the Constitution and may stay.

The Facts:

[Annually,] Pawtucket, Rhode Island, erects a Christmas display it paid for, owns, and maintains in a private park. The display includes a Santa Claus house, reindeer pulling Santa's sleigh, candy-striped poles, a Christmas tree, carolers, cutout figures (representing a clown, an elephant and a teddy bear), colored lights, a large banner reading "Seasons Greetings," and a nativity scene.

The crèche, which has been included in the display for 40 or more years, consists of the traditional figures, including the infant Jesus, Mary and Joseph, angels, shepherds, kings, and animals, all ranging in height from 5 inches to 5 feet. The nativity scene originally cost the city $1,365. It now has a value of $200. Annual erection and dismantling costs $20. Nominal expense is required to light it and no money has been expended on maintenance for 10 years.

The Burger Majority Opinion:

The majority opinion was written by Justice Burger and was joined by Justices O'Connor, White, Powell, and Rehnquist.

BURGER:...Pawtucket residents and ... the ACLU brought this action... challenging the city's inclusion of the crèche in the annual display. The

District Court held that the city's inclusion of the crèche in the display violates the Establishment Clause [and]...found that, by including the crèche in the Christmas display, the city has "tried to endorse and promulgate religious beliefs" and that "erection of the crèche has the real and substantial effect of affiliating the city with the Christian beliefs that the crèche represents." This "appearance of official sponsorship," it believed, "confers more than a remote and incidental benefit on Christianity." Last, although the court acknowledged the absence of administrative entanglement, it found that excessive entanglement has been fostered as a result of the political divisiveness of including the crèche in the celebration. The city was permanently enjoined from including the crèche in the display. [The Court of Appeals affirmed.] We...reverse.

> **COMMENT:** So, the United States Supreme Court winds up allowing this particular nativity scene to stand. Wait until you see why.

BURGER: This Court has explained that the purpose of the Establishment and Free Exercise Clauses of the First Amendment is "to prevent, as far as possible, the intrusion of either the church or the state into the precincts of the other." At the same time, however, the Court has recognized that "total separation is not possible in an absolute sense. Some relationship between government and religious organizations is inevitable."

> **COMMENT:** "To prevent as far as possible?" Why does Christianity need the government of all faiths to purchase, erect, light, or maintain one of its most cherished symbols? Christian sects are perfectly capable of expending their own money to erect a nativity scene on their own church property! Yet, the majority apparently says, in permitting the display, "We have gone as far as possible in preventing the intrusion of either the church or the state into the precincts of the other." Here, although I, too, do not believe that "total separation is either required or possible" or desirable, in this instance, not only is it obviously possible, it is, I contend, very desirable for reasons that follow.

BURGER: The Constitution does not require complete separation of church and state; it affirmatively mandates accommodation, not merely tolerance, of all religions, and forbids hostility toward any. Anything less would require the "callous indifference" we have said was never intended by the Establishment Clause.

> **COMMENT:** This is not "accommodation of all religions." It is hostile to all but Christianity and, if the nativity scene is shabby (as it appeared to be in this case), it is even hostile to Christianity. Forbidding city ownership, erection, and maintenance is not callous indifference. Forbidding a church to place its own nativity scene on its own property (through a zoning law, for example) would be callous indifference which would likely serve to strike down the zoning law, but denying this nativity scene clearly does not portray a callous indifference to Christianity. Now that the Court has ruled that Pawtucket's nativity scene is permitted, if Jews, Buddhists, or Satanists want the city to purchase, erect, and maintain a Menorah, a statue of Buddha, or the Devil himself at Christmas, it appears Pawtucket must either abandon its nativity scene or comply with legitimate requests of its other citizens who also contribute tax dollars to Pawtucket. City Hall got its victory precisely because its majority (likely Christians) had the political power to prevail in even purchasing the nativity scene, much less in winning Supreme Court approval. The political war is now on for Pawtucket's purse. And who are the potential combatants? Religions of every faith and denomination, as well as atheists. Congratulations to the Christians of Pawtucket. You got exactly what you asked for. Are you as willing to live with the consequences?

Government should stay out of the business of purchasing, erecting or maintaining tangible, clearly religious property. That is the business of the church and only the church. I cannot believe this opinion. It strikes at the very core of the 200+ religion clause cases the Court has correctly decided.

BURGER: The First Congress paid a chaplain to open legislative sessions with prayer and 17 of the delegates to the Constitutional Convention wound up in the First Congress, the implication being that if the delegates who were also in the First Congress thought legislative prayer was okay, they really didn't intend the "wall of separation" to be as impenetrable as the Court has made it over the years.

There is insufficient evidence to establish that the inclusion of the nativity scene is a purposeful or surreptitious effort to express some kind of subtle governmental advocacy of a particular religious message.

> **COMMENT:** What? I simply do not understand how the majority expects to sell such a concept. Would Pawtucket display a nativity scene without the Christ child in it? What reaction would the city fathers get if, instead of a nativity scene, the city displayed a Menorah or a miniature mosque?

BURGER: The nativity scene has a secular purpose in celebrating the "Holiday" and in "depicting historical origins of the Holiday." To conclude that the primary effect of including the nativity scene is to advance religion would require that we view it as more of an endorsement of religion than the Sunday Closing Laws (*McGowan*) and the off-campus released time program (*Zorach*).

> **COMMENT:** What? Note that the Court must be embarrassed by its logic, for it cannot even bring itself to refer to "Christmas" in this analysis – it refers instead to the "Holiday." There is simply no question but that this city's purchase of a purely Christian religious symbol advances the cause of religion – one religion. To state the contrary does not make it so. As for large sums of public money, hold on! As I recall, the Court found of great significance that the textbooks in *Allen* were not given to the schools or the parents – they were loaned to the students. Plus, of great significance in *Allen* was the fact that the books were secular and, therefore, not to be used for religious purposes. And, in *Everson*, I recall the Court saying the bus subsidy was relatively minimal. Please. This argument is disingenuous, for, regardless of the sum, this nativity scene is not secular in nature. Also, *Walz* was decided on "entanglement" grounds and, as I recall, it made a big deal of saying that government was, after all, not giving money to religion or sponsoring religion. It was simply not charging religion a tax.

Consistency, please! *McGowan* was wrongly decided, but at least a day of tranquility for all is far more of a secular purpose than the historical significance of a nativity scene. And, at least in theory, the *Zorach* released-time program was available to all faiths - hardly a case to cite in support of one faith's symbol.

BURGER: Here, whatever benefit there is to one faith or religion or to all religions is indirect, remote, and incidental. This is no more an endorsement of religion than…exhibition of hundreds of religious paintings in governmentally supported museums.

COMMENT: First, there clearly is no benefit to all religions – just the Christian religion. It also is absolutely direct, hardly remote, and clearly not incidental. And, please, paintings in a museum is to a nativity scene at the hub of a city's shopping district at Christmas as apples are to oranges. To my knowledge, government does not typically own paintings it displays in a museum. They are on loan for display. Also, one presumes that government-owned museums display a wide variety of religious paintings. I don't see a Buddha or a Menorah on Pawtucket's "Religious Display Inventory."

BURGER: Entanglement is a question of kind and degree. In this case, however, there [was not administrative entanglement]…There is no evidence of contact with the church authorities concerning the content or design of the exhibit prior to or since Pawtucket's purchase of the crèche.

COMMENT: The majority makes this comment to support a lack of entanglement. In other words, if there had been annual controversial debate over the design of the display, the Court would be more inclined to find entanglement and, therefore, it would be more inclined to order the display removed. However, the majority again attempts to fool us. The crèche is 40 years old. The design of the display likely occurred once with little or no record made of the discussion which likely did not come up again. The very reason why there is likely no record of the debate or entanglement is the very reason the crèche should go. That is, there is no debate or church contact because the members of city government were likely the majoritarian Christians. There is no need to contact the church when the city fathers represent the church. And, that is the problem – the very idea that city fathers represent the church in a government activity is what is forbidden by the Establishment Clause.

BURGER: No expenditure for maintenance of the crèche has been necessary; and, since the city owns the crèche, now valued at $200, the tangible material it contributes is *de minimis*.

COMMENT: Clearly, this majority places some degree of significance on the insignificance of this nativity scene. It would appear that even the majority could have a problem with Pawtucket if the nativity scene had cost $15,000 and the gifts to Jesus had been gold, frankincense, and myrrh. Once again, congratulations to the Christian political majority of Pawtucket. Apparently, because your depiction of one of the most sacred of Christian events was shabby, you won the right to keep it shabby. **Better not upgrade.** If you think I'm kidding, just wait.

BURGER: The District Court stated this display has had a calm 40-year history. And, although the District Court found that the political divisiveness engendered by this very lawsuit was evidence of excessive entanglement, a litigant cannot, by the very act of commencing a lawsuit, create the appearance of divisiveness and then exploit it as evidence of entanglement.

COMMENT: I agree with the stated principle. However, once again, Christians across the land can thank the powers that be in Pawtucket. For, now that this case has been decided in their favor, will the next 40 years or ten or one be so calm? How will city fathers around the country react to a Jewish application for a Menorah? A Buddhist application? Will this result in political divisiveness not caused by the act of commencing a lawsuit in the future, but by the result of this decision in the present?

BURGER: Justice Brennan (in dissent) describes the crèche as a "re-creation of an event that lies at the heart of Christian faith." The crèche, like a painting, is passive; admittedly it is a reminder of the origins of Christmas.

COMMENT: This opinion is so wrought with fiction that I could comment on nearly every sentence. Justice Brennan is clearly correct. Let's explore what the majority is trying to prove with the "passive" comment. Is that supposed to mean that, because it is passive, it is constitutional? Would live animals and actors playing Mary, Joseph, and Jesus make it unconstitutional? Why? Would it be because people would be more likely to actually contemplate the origins of Christmas and recognize the nativity scene for what it truly represents if it was live? Again, is it the insignificance, the poor quality, and the passivity of this particular nativity scene that the majority relies upon to "keep Christ in Christmas"? What irony! While Pawtucket likely had good intentions, the rationale for its victory is outrageously insulting to Christians. Here is a short list of so-called passive symbols: the Confederate flag; the swastika; a white-hooded robe; cartoon caricatures of Mohammed. Need I say more?

Finally, the crèche is far more than a reminder of the origins of Christmas. It is the sole reason to have Christmas, yet the only way they can justify "keeping Christ in Christmas" is to minimize Christ's importance at Christmas! Truly unbelievable. How can these obviously very intelligent folks be so blind to reality? **In order to avoid strife between various faiths or within various faiths and, therefore, in order to help religion flourish and prosper, there should be at least a "short fence of separation" between Caesar and God. If the divider falls, government will strong-arm religion.**

BURGER: The fears of political problems that gave rise to the Religion Clauses in the 18th century are of far less concern today. Any notion that these symbols pose a real danger of establishment of a state church is farfetched indeed.

COMMENT: First, with this ruling, the majority is likely inviting the fears and political problems of the past to the table of the present. Second, it is true that Pawtucket's nativity scene is not likely the precursor of "The State Church of Rhode Island."

However, time and time again, the Court has said, "This Court has given the Amendment a 'broad interpretation...in the light of its history and the evils it was designed forever to suppress...' It has found that the Constitution affords protection against religious establishment far more extensive than merely to forbid a national or state church."

BURGER: We hold that, notwithstanding the religious significance of the crèche, the city of Pawtucket has not violated the Establishment Clause... [Judgment reversed. The nativity scene stands.]

The O'Connor Concurrence:

O'CONNOR: The Establishment Clause prohibits government from making adherence to a religion relevant in any way to a person's standing in the political community. Government can run afoul of that prohibition in two ways: excessive entanglement which may give institutions access to government not fully shared by non-adherents of the religion and foster the creation of political constituencies defined along religious lines and government endorsement or disapproval of religion. Endorsement sends a message to non-adherents that they are outsiders, not full members of the political community and to adherents that they are the favored ones.

COMMENT: Then why, Justice O'Connor, did you side with the majority? Are not Jews, in this case, the politically disfavored outsiders of whom you speak?

Personally, I cannot recall a local election in which I have voted where a person's religion was an issue. However, if religion enters government, every election would be about religion. And, let me be clear. I welcome any politician to exercise his faith, even in government – especially in government. In fact, he would be a hypocrite to do otherwise. No, I object to religious issues being the subject of political votes. There is quite a difference. In other words, we ought not be voting for city aldermen based upon whether they will install a religious symbol at Christmas. We ought to be voting on how they will run the business of government.

O'CONNOR: The central issue is whether Pawtucket has endorsed Christianity. Pawtucket did not intend to convey any message of endorsement of Christianity or disapproval of non-Christian religions. The evident purpose of including the crèche was not promotion of the religious content but celebration of the public holiday through its traditional symbols. What is crucial is that a government practice not have the effect of communicating a message of government endorsement or disapproval of religion. Although the religious significance of the crèche is not neutralized by the setting, the overall holiday setting changes what viewers may fairly understand to be the purpose of the display, just as a museum setting for a painting negates any message of endorsement of content.

> **COMMENT:** Justice O'Connor seems to be saying that because the nativity scene has lost its religious significance and has become just another plastic Santa or clown or elephant, it does not convey a message of government endorsement. What a slap in the face to Christianity. Pawtucket, you got what you asked for.

The Brennan Dissent:

BRENNAN: [Justice Brennan is joined by Justices Marshall, Blackmun, and Stevens.] The majority leaves open the question of a free-standing crèche or cross. Nothing in the setting in which this crèche is displayed obscures or diminishes the plain fact that Pawtucket's action amounts to endorsement of a particular faith. Although the majority's reluctance to disturb a community's chosen method of celebrating such an agreeable holiday is understandable, that cannot justify departure from controlling precedent. Pawtucket's maintenance and display at public expense of a symbol as distinctively sectarian as a crèche simply cannot be squared with our prior cases. It is plainly contrary to the purposes and values of the Establishment Clause to pretend, as the Court does, that the otherwise secular setting of Pawtucket's nativity scene dilutes in some fashion the crèche's singular religiosity, or that the city's annual display reflects nothing more than an acknowledgment of our shared national heritage. Neither the character of the Christmas holiday itself, nor our heritage of religious expression supports this result. Indeed, our remarkable and precious religious diversity as a nation, which the Establishment Clause seeks to protect, runs directly counter to this decision.

COMMENT: Ditto!

BRENNAN: "A union of government and religion tends to destroy government and degrade religion." *Engel.* In order to support the secular purpose prong of *Lemon,* Pawtucket said it sought to attract people to the downtown area to promote Christmas retail sales and to engender a spirit of goodwill. All of Pawtucket's stated purposes can be accomplished through other means. In fact, such motives are fully served by the plastic Santa Claus, reindeer, etc., in the remainder of the display. No, the primary effect of including the crèche is to place government's imprimatur of approval on the particular religious beliefs exemplified by the crèche. Those who believe in the message of the nativity receive their unique and exclusive benefit of public recognition and approval of their views. The views of those who do not believe in such a message are apparently not worthy of the same public support. It was precisely this form of religious chauvinism that the Establishment Clause was intended to forever prohibit. Government will now have to become involved in accommodating similar requests from other religions, thus bringing on the real potential for considerable strife. To suggest, as the Court does, that such a symbol is merely "traditional" and therefore no different from Santa's house or reindeer is not only offensive to those for whom the crèche has profound significance, but insulting to those who insist for religious or personal reasons that the story of Christ is in no sense a part of "history" nor an unavoidable element of our national "heritage." For a non-Christian, to be excluded on religious grounds by one's elected government is an insult and an injury that, until today, could not be countenanced by the Establishment Clause.

COMMENT: I couldn't agree more!

The Blackmun Dissent:

BLACKMUN: The crèche has been relegated to the role of a neutral harbinger of the holiday season, useful for commercial purposes, but devoid of any inherent meaning and incapable of enhancing the religious tenor of a display of which it is an integral part. The city has its victory, albeit a

Pyrrhic one. The import of this decision is to encourage use of the crèche in a municipally sponsored display where Christians feel constrained in acknowledging its symbolic meaning and non-Christians feel alienated by its presence. This is a misuse of a sacred symbol. I cannot join the Court in denying either the force of our precedents or the sacred message that is at the core of the nativity scene.

> **COMMENT:** Can Pawtucket now erect a shabby inexpensive cross at Easter? Maybe, if it makes sure to place hundreds of plastic eggs and Easter bunnies nearby so as to diminish the significance of the Crucifixion and Resurrection. Unfortunately, although not likely intended, this Court's fear of taking Christ out of Christmas has served to degrade Christianity at Christmas. That's what happens when religion and government play together. They both get soiled.

According to our scoring rules, religion won, but I feel it lost. I predict Christians will rue the day they won the right to a shabby nativity scene in Pawtucket, Rhode Island.

> ### First Amendment Scoreboard
> Rulings "for" Religion: 17 --- Rulings "against" Religion: 9

If this opinion is not someday overruled, it will lead to chaos and strife among all religions and, indeed, even within Christian denominations. Surely, the Christians that lobbied to continue with this nativity tradition did not do so for its commercial value. Is Christianity so weak it cannot provide its message without government expenditure - on its own property – or on the property of Christian homes?

It only took five short years for *Lynch v. Donnelly* to come home to roost! If *Lynch* had been correctly decided, we would not be discussing this next case. Due to an unspoken fear of being labeled as the Court that took Christ out of Christmas and because they did not do the right thing and follow their own precedents in *Lynch*, this next ruling not only takes Christ out of Christmas – it places the Jewish religion ahead of the Christian religion at Christmas, for heaven's sake!

ALLEGHENY COUNTY v. ACLU
SUPREME COURT OF THE UNITED STATES
492 U.S. 573
July 3, 1989
[5 – 4] & [6 – 3]

The Issues:

Whether the Establishment Clause prohibits a county from including a particular crèche in a Christmas display?

Whether the Establishment Clause prohibits a county from including a particular Menorah in a Christmas display?

The Holding:

ON THESE FACTS...THE SUPREME COURT HOLDS THAT
THE NATIVITY SCENE "GOES"
AND THE MENORAH "STAYS."

Keep this in mind as we proceed through the reasoning.

TO CHRISTIANS:
HOW DOES IT FEEL TO BE IN THE MINORITY?

TO JEWS AND CHRISTIANS:
IS THIS WAR OF RELIGIONS DESIRABLE?
ISN'T THIS EXACTLY WHAT THE FRAMERS
INTENDED TO AVOID?

TO ATHEISTS:
DOES SUPREME COURT INFIGHTING HELP YOUR CAUSE?

DOES ANYONE WIN BY ENTANGLING RELIGIOUS
SYMBOLS WITH GOVERNMENT?

231

The story you are about to read is true.
The names have not been changed to protect
the innocent or to save the guilty.

There are a thousand stories in the city.
This is one of them.

My name's Friday – Joe Friday.

I'm a cop.

Just The Facts, M'am:

Investigation #1

The Scene: The Grand Staircase at the Allegheny County Courthouse (Pittsburgh), the "main, most beautiful, and most public part" of the courthouse.

The Date: Since 1981 to now (1989), the display described has been located at the Grand Staircase.

The Objects Under Investigation: A nativity scene with a wooden fence on three sides, an angel declaring "Gloria in Excelsis Deo" on a banner, a plaque stating the display was donated by a Catholic group, poinsettias around the fence "framing" the nativity scene, and two small evergreens with red bows. No plastic Santa Claus.

The Owner of the Nativity Scene: A Catholic group.

Joe Friday's Observations: "I was near the Grand Staircase. Charlie, the security man, gave me a tip. He said it had been an average day of foot traffic. He paid particular attention to anyone that might look in the direction of the nativity scene to determine whether their facial expression indicated that they just might think the County had something to do with the fact that the nativity scene was present at the "most beautiful location" in the building. He concluded that out of 500 pedestrians that day, 50 paid no attention, 400 thought the

County was somehow connected to Christianity, and 50 wondered why there was no Menorah at the Courthouse. I thanked him and told him to keep it under his hat until further notice."

Investigation #2

The Scene: The City-County Building (Pittsburgh)...one block from the County Courthouse (where the crèche is located).

The Date: Since 1982 to now (1989), the display described has been located in front of the City-County Building.

The Objects Under Investigation: A 45-foot Christmas tree with lights and ornaments; a sign at the foot of the tree declaring "Salute to Liberty" which says: "During this holiday season, the city of Pittsburgh salutes liberty. Let these festive lights remind us that we are the keepers of the flame of liberty and our legacy of freedom"; a symbolic representation of Chanukah (an annual Jewish holiday) that includes an 18-foot Menorah (celebrating a Jewish miracle and a Jewish historical event); all erected by city employees. [Although unstated, by omission it is safe to assume there was no plastic Santa Claus.]

The Owner of the Menorah: A Jewish group.

Joe Friday's Observations: "I parked the squad car near the City-County Building. This time I made my own observations, watching carefully for any indication of conclusions on the faces of those who saw the Menorah. I noted that although one could avoid viewing the nativity scene at the Grand Staircase over at the Courthouse, it was impossible to miss the Menorah, it being located in front of the only entrance to the City-County Building. Anyway, I counted 200 expressions of holiday cheer, 300 expressions of surprise that the government was somehow sponsoring a religious symbol, 150 that didn't know what it was, and 200 that very much supported its presence. It had been a long day. I vowed that I would get to the bottom of this, whatever it was. I filed my report."

The Blackmun Majority Opinion:

The majority opinion was written by Justice Blackmun and was joined by Justices Stevens, O'Connor, Brennan, and Marshall.

BLACKMUN: On May 8, 1987, the District Court denied [a request to remove the nativity scene and Menorah]. Relying on *Lynch v. Donnelly*, the court stated that "the crèche was but part of the holiday decoration of the stairwell and a foreground for the high school choirs which entertained each day at noon." Regarding the Menorah, the court concluded that "it was but an insignificant part of another holiday display." The court also found that "the displays had a secular purpose" and "did not create an excessive entanglement of government with religion."

...The Court of Appeals reversed...and determined that the crèche and the Menorah must be understood as endorsing Christianity and Judaism...This Court understands the Establishment Clause to mean that government may not promote or affiliate itself with any religious doctrine or organization and...may not involve itself too deeply in a religious institution's affairs... "Neither a state nor the Federal Government can...pass laws which aid one religion, aid all religions, or prefer one religion over another...or openly or secretly participate in the affairs of any religious organizations or groups." In recent years, we have paid particularly close attention to whether the challenged governmental practice either has the purpose or effect of endorsing religion, a concern that has long had a place in our Establishment Clause jurisprudence. Government may not promote one religion or religious theory against another or even against the militant opposite. At the very least, the Clause prohibits government from appearing to take a position on questions of religious belief or from making adherence to a religion relevant in any way to a person's standing in the political community. *Lynch v. Donnelly*.

> **COMMENT:** The majority attempts to square its undoing of the nativity scene and its approval of the Menorah with its foregoing stated principles of constitutional law. However, in reality, neither the crèche nor the Menorah are constitutionally justified.

BLACKMUN: The rationale of the majority opinion in *Lynch* is none too clear...First, the opinion states that the inclusion of the crèche in the display was "no more an advancement or endorsement of religion" than other "endorsements" this Court has approved in the past – but the opinion offers no discernible measure for distinguishing between permissible and impermissible endorsements. Second, the opinion observes that any benefit the government's display of the crèche gave to religion was no more than "indirect, remote, and incidental" – without saying how or why.

O'Connor's concurrence in *Lynch* provides a sound analytical framework for evaluating governmental use of religious symbols. Her concurrence squarely rejects the notion that this Court will tolerate some government endorsement of religion. She rejected any endorsement of religion as invalid. Her concurrence concluded that because the crèche was displayed along with purely secular symbols, its setting "changed what viewers may fairly understand to be the purpose of the display and negates any message of endorsement of Christian beliefs."

The four *Lynch* dissenters (myself [Blackmun], Stevens, Marshall and Brennan) agreed with the concurrence that the controlling question was whether Pawtucket had run afoul of the Establishment Clause by endorsing religion through the display of the crèche, but reached a different answer.

Our task is to determine whether these displays, "in their respective particular physical settings, have the effect of endorsing or disapproving religious beliefs."

There is no doubt that the crèche is capable of communicating a religious message.

> **COMMENT:** Doesn't this case already give you a creepy feeling, whether you are a Jew or a Christian?

BLACKMUN: Here, the religious meaning of the crèche is unmistakably clear. "Glory to God in the Highest," says the angel. Glory to God because of the birth of Jesus. Here, nothing in the context of the display detracts from the crèche's religious message. The *Lynch* display had a series of non-religious objects [Santa, reindeer, etc.]. Here, the crèche stands alone as the single element of the display. The floral decorations cannot be viewed as somehow equivalent to the secular symbols in the overall *Lynch* display. Indeed, the floral frame draws attention to the message inside the frame and contributes to, rather than detracts from, the endorsement of religion conveyed by the crèche.

> **COMMENT:** I get it. If the message of Christ's birth is diminished, downgraded, placed in a seldom-used hallway, or such, then the Constitution may permit its presence?!?!?!?

BLACKMUN: The county could not say that surrounding a Cross with Easter lilies would negate the endorsement of Christianity...Its contention that the traditional Christmas greens negate the endorsement effect fares no better.

> **COMMENT:** Okay. If we add goofy-looking Easter bunnies and a thousand plastic eggs, can the county erect a Cross at Easter? If not in front of the courthouse, how about in back by the dumpster? I note the majority has described the "two small evergreens with red bows" as "traditional Christmas greens." Are they trying to "spin" small Christmas trees into mere "greens"? Do you think they need to do that since they approved of the Menorah, alongside a 45-foot Christmas tree? Is it the size of the tree that matters?

BLACKMUN: The crèche is in "the most beautiful" part of the courthouse. No viewer could reasonably think that it occupied this location without the support and approval of the government. Thus, by permitting this display in this particular setting, the county sends a message that it supports and promotes the Christian praise to God that is the crèche's religious message. [The nativity scene must go.]

> **COMMENT:** Let me get this straight. Although the nativity scene is at the "most beautiful" place in the courthouse, at least it is *inside* the courthouse. The Menorah, however, is in front of the City-County Building where all who go by the building (not just those who enter the building) will view it. Do you really expect us to believe that a nativity scene does not send a message promoting praise to the Christian God if it is in the corner or is shabby looking or has a Santa Claus nearby?

BLACKMUN: [Next, the majority launches a scathing attack on Justice Kennedy's dissent.] Justice Kennedy repeatedly accuses the majority of harboring a latent hostility or callous indifference toward religion. Nothing could be further from the truth…These accusations could be said to be as offensive as they are absurd. Justice Kennedy has misperceived a respect for religious pluralism (a respect commanded by the Constitution) as hostility or indifference to religion. No misperception could be more antithetical to the values embodied in the Establishment Clause.

> **COMMENT:** The Justices do not normally make personal attacks on one another, regardless of how heated they may feel about an issue. Can anyone see what religious strife can do to otherwise perfectly rational adults? Why can't the majority see this or the monumental entanglement issues they have now brought to the fore in deciding to get involved with religious symbols?

BLACKMUN: The Menorah is a religious symbol to commemorate a "miracle," but its message is not exclusively religious. The Menorah is the primary visual symbol for a holiday that, like Christmas, has both religious and secular dimensions.

> **COMMENT:** Look out, Judaism. I'm not sure, but it looks like the High Court is about to cheapen the importance of your religious symbols, too!

BLACKMUN: The Menorah here stands next to a Christmas tree and a sign saluting liberty. Together, they create an overall holiday setting that represents both Christmas and Chanukah – two holidays, not one. The mere fact that Pittsburgh displays symbols of both Christmas and Chanukah does not end the constitutional inquiry. If the city celebrates both Christmas and Chanukah as religious holidays, then it violates the Establishment Clause. The simultaneous endorsement of Judaism and Christianity is no less constitutionally infirm than the endorsement of Christianity alone. Conversely, if the city celebrates both Christmas and Chanukah as secular holidays, then its conduct is beyond the reach of the Establishment Clause. Because government may celebrate Christmas as a secular holiday, it follows that government may also acknowledge Chanukah as a secular holiday. Simply put, it would be a form of discrimination against Jews to allow Pittsburgh to celebrate Christmas as a cultural tradition while simultaneously disallowing the city's acknowledgment of Chanukah as a contemporaneous cultural tradition.

Accordingly, the relevant question here is whether the combined display of the tree, the sign, and the Menorah has the effect of endorsing both Christian and Jewish faiths, or rather simply recognizes that both Christmas and Chanukah are part of the same winter-holiday season, which has attained a secular status in our society...The latter seems more plausible and is in line with *Lynch.*

The Christmas tree, unlike the Menorah, is not itself a religious symbol... The 45-foot tree occupies the central position...; the 18-foot Menorah is positioned to one side...It is much more sensible to interpret the meaning of the Menorah in light of the tree, rather than vice versa...Although the city has used a symbol with religious meaning as its representation of Chanukah, this is not a case in which the city has reasonable alternatives that are less religious in nature. It is difficult to imagine a predominantly secular symbol of Chanukah that the city could place next to its Christmas tree. An 18-foot dreidel (top) [which has meaning to Jews] would look out of place and might be interpreted by some as mocking the celebration of Chanukah...Where the government's secular message can be conveyed by two symbols, only one of which carries religious meaning, an observer reasonably might infer from the fact that the government has chosen to use the religious symbol that the government means to promote religious faith...But where, as here, no such choice has been made, this inference of endorsement is not present. Given all these considerations, it is not sufficiently likely that residents of Pittsburgh will perceive the combined display of the tree, the sign, and the Menorah as an endorsement or disapproval of their individual religious choices. [The Menorah stays!]

> **COMMENT:** Justice Blackmun, you do not provide much in the way of what secular message the Menorah sends. Are you speaking of a historical event as being secular? It would seem that Christ's birth is a historical event, yet you rule against the nativity scene. Apparently, if the Menorah was placed in between two Christmas trees, thus "framing" the Menorah (as poinsettias frame the crèche

over at the Courthouse), then the Menorah must go because, after all, a viewer's eyes would then be trained on the Menorah and we cannot permit government to send such a focused message. Right? And, furthermore, because you care as a parent would, you must protect the rest of us children from views that are too focused. We can handle an unframed nativity scene, but not a framed one, is that it? You would not require a traditional Jewish dreidel to be placed in the vicinity of the Menorah in order to save the Menorah because that might degrade Chanukah. That is understandable and welcome; however, those that permitted the crèche in *Lynch* on the basis that assorted junk minimizes the message of a nativity scene, would apparently like to see assorted junk around the Menorah. Government should get out of the religious symbol business altogether. In an attempt to accommodate religion, it pits Christianity against Judaism. Shame on this decision. It not only fuels the heretofore non-existent fires of religious strife, its logic is altogether wanting. First, cut the paternalism and get real. Every viewer of any religious symbol in any location, no matter how shabby or how cluttered by non-religious junk, is going to get the religious message. Second, even if the Menorah could somehow be theoretically justified in its surroundings, this decision sends an exceptionally clear message: This Court approves of Judaism, but does not approve of Christianity. While that is not the likely intent, I am appalled that this majority does not clearly see that as the practical effect of their decision. I thought we were taught by them that perception is more important than intent!

The O'Connor Concurrence:

O'CONNOR: If government is to be neutral in matters of religion, rather than showing either favoritism or disapproval towards citizens based upon their personal religious choices, government cannot endorse the religious practices and beliefs of some without sending a clear message to non-adherents that they are outsiders or less than full members of the political community. The question under the endorsement analysis is whether a reasonable observer would view such long-standing practices as a disapproval of his or her particular religious choices, in light of the fact that they serve a secular purpose rather than a sectarian one and **have largely lost their significance over time.**

COMMENT: Remember, Justice O'Connor approved of the nativity scene in *Lynch* in part because, in her mind, the nativity scene has lost its religious significance over time. Anyone care to disagree?

The Brennan Dissent:

BRENNAN: (concurring in part; dissenting in part): I continue to believe that the display of an object that retains a specifically Christian (or other) religious meaning is incompatible with the separation of church and state demanded by our Constitution. I, therefore, agree that the nativity scene here signals an endorsement of the Christian faith [and must go]. I cannot agree, however, that the Menorah display shows no such favoritism towards Christianity, Judaism, or both. I should have thought the answer as to the first display supplied the answer to the second.

COMMENT: Who wouldn't?

BRENNAN: To suggest that a nativity scene is merely traditional and therefore no different than Santa's house or reindeer is not only offensive to those who insist that the story of Christ is in no sense a part of "history" nor an unavoidable element of our national "heritage"…The Menorah is indisputably a religious symbol, used ritually in a celebration that has deep religious significance. That, in my view, is all that need be said. Whatever secular practices the holiday of Chanukah has taken on in its contemporary observance are beside the point. [Both the nativity scene and the Menorah must go!]

COMMENT: Agreed!

The Stevens Dissent:

STEVENS (concurring in part; dissenting in part): The Establishment Clause should be construed to create a strong presumption against the display of religious symbols on public property. There is always a risk that such symbols will offend nonmembers of the faith being advertised as well as adherents who consider the particular advertisement disrespectful. Some devout Christians believe the crèche should be placed only in reverential settings, not as an aid to commercialism. In this very suit, some Jews opposed the use to which the Menorah was put. Displays of this sort inevitably have a greater tendency to emphasize sincere and deeply felt differences among individuals than to achieve an ecumenical goal. The Establishment Clause does not allow public bodies to foment such disagreement. [Both the nativity scene and Menorah must go!]

> **COMMENT:** Three cheers for Justices Stevens, Brennan, and Marshall and throw in a hearty hallelujah!!! These men have been consistent, logical and very wise. There is hope, after all. They get what the others cannot see or refuse to admit.

The Kennedy Concurrence:

KENNEDY: (concurring in part; dissenting in part): [Both the nativity scene and the Menorah should stay!] The crèche and the Menorah are purely passive symbols. Passersby who disagree with the messages conveyed are free to ignore them. Few of our traditional practices recognizing the part religion plays in our society can withstand an "outsider's test" under a faithful application of that formula. Examples: American Presidents have issued Thanksgiving Day proclamations; they have established a National Day of Prayer; this Court opens its sessions with "God save the United States and this honorable Court"; the legislature employs chaplains; the Pledge of Allegiance has "under God" in it; "In God we trust" is on our currency.

> **COMMENT:** Remember Justice Rehnquist's dissent in *Wallace v. Jaffree*? His review of the Framers' intent concludes that none of them intended to prefer irreligion over religion. I said then that if that historical conclusion is accurate, then any governmental accommodation of religion (if otherwise constitutional) does not fall as unconstitutional merely because it may offend atheists. Anyway, assuming that to be true, with one exception, the litany of examples Justice Kennedy provides are easily distinguishable. Here goes:

Thanksgiving Day proclamations/National Day of Prayer: These practices do not favor one religion over another. The only potential offense is to atheists.

Legislatures employ chaplains: I continue to disagree with the *Marsh* case even on this new theory that says religion may be preferred over irreligion. Why? Because money is spent on a chaplain of one faith or denomination which could, and I am sure does, cause political infighting, etc.

"Under God" in the Pledge of Allegiance: No preference here, except as against atheists.

"In God we trust" on our currency: No preference here, except as against atheists.

On my theory, all of these can be squared with the fact that the Menorah and the nativity scene must go! The primary reason why I disagree with those who would permit them both to stand foretells of very serious consequences, for I do not see any way to then prohibit a display by a group of Satanists across from the nativity scene at the Courthouse. I rest my case. Those that would permit both the Menorah and the nativity scene place great emphasis on the fact that these symbols are merely passive. As previously stated, however, some symbols are extraordinarily rife with the most powerful of messages. Many times, cherished symbols are far more powerful than volumes of words or assembled armies.

In keeping with the Dragnet theme, this case shall end as it began with our investigator signing off.

/s/ Joe Friday
Detective Joe Friday
(I'm a Cop)

There you have it. Judaism won and Christianity lost – the very thing the Framers wanted to avoid. Or, was Judaism the ultimate loser? Did it survive only because it sent less of a serious religious message than the nativity scene? We have to score one for each side of this judicial fiasco.

First Amendment Scoreboard

Rulings "for" Religion: 18 --- Rulings "against" Religion: 10

Again, here is a summary in chronological fashion.

1984: In *Lynch v. Donnelly* we learned that government was permitted to own, maintain, and erect a nativity scene at Christmas.

Principles: This nativity scene has a secular purpose in celebrating the "Holiday" and its historical origins. This particular display is not more beneficial to or more an endorsement of religion than a loan of secular textbooks to religious schools or reimbursing bus transportation to parents of religious school students or real estate tax exemptions for churches or closing businesses on Sundays and, after all, the money expended by Pawtucket was minimal. The evident purpose of this display was not to promote any religious message – it was to celebrate a public holiday. This overall setting minimized the religious significance of Christ's birth, so it's OK?!?

Dicta (in dissent): A union of government and religion tends to destroy government and degrade religion. The crèche has been relegated to the role of a neutral harbinger of the holiday season, useful for commercial purposes, but devoid of any inherent meaning and incapable of enhancing the religious tenor of a display of which it is an integral part. The city has its victory, albeit a Pyrrhic one. The import of this decision is to encourage use of the crèche in a municipally sponsored display where Christians feel constrained in acknowledging its symbolic meaning and non-Christians feel alienated by its presence. This is a misuse of a sacred symbol.

1989: In *Allegheny County v. ACLU* we learned that because the nativity scene in Pittsburgh was in a conspicuous area of the courthouse and a significant upgrade from its shabby counterpart in Pawtucket, its religious message would resound too much with citizens and, therefore, it had to come down. The Menorah, on the other hand, was more historical than the historical fact of Christ's birth and was not quite as in-your-face as the framed nativity scene down the street. Therefore, the Menorah was favored over the nativity scene.

<u>Dicta</u>: Justice O'Connor states religious symbols have largely lost their religious significance over time.

<u>Dicta (in dissent)</u>: Per Justice Stevens: **"Some devout Christians believe the crèche should be placed only in reverential settings, not as an aid to commercialism."**

At a minimum, due to the manner in which the Supreme Court of the United States has interpreted the religious symbol cases and because the Christians in Berkley at one time fought to establish a nativity scene, the Elliots are probably going to have to live with the myriad-of-philosophers version of a California Christmas.

THE SUGGESTED CHRISTIAN RESPONSE

<u>Causes to Champion</u>:

I am hoping a majority of the High Court will someday see the folly of these religious symbol decisions, and realize the potential for religious strife over the fight for religious symbol turf is precisely what the Framers wished to avoid.

So, I am encouraging Christians to champion the cause of keeping official religious symbols as far away from government as possible. In addition to what happened in Berkley to my fictional family, I provide a true story that dramatically explains my point.

Harken back to Christmas of 2008. The scene was the State Capitol building in Olympia, Washington, where the governor okayed the annual Christmas tree and nativity scene to be displayed. After an atheist group requested their display to be erected, apparently the governor yielded and that lit Fox News' Bill O'Reilly's fuse.

The atheist display was a placard that read:

There are no gods,
no devils,
no angels,
no heaven or hell.
There is only our natural world.
Religion is but myth and superstition
that hardens hearts and enslaves minds.

For what seemed at least three weeks, O'Reilly gave the atheists some of the best free advertising they could have ever hoped for. He berated Governor Gregoire for "allowing" this to go on. It seemed like the atheist creed was displayed every night on national cable television.

I do not for a moment doubt his sincerity, but Bill, if you read this, I hate to tell you that you were wrong. Why? Because you, not unlike Amanda, Charley, and Sean Hannity, were ignorant of the law on this topic.

Although I believe the Supreme Court got it wrong in *Lynch v. Donnelly*, that made the Seattle caper perfectly legal. As I predicted, when that majority allowed the shabby nativity scene to be displayed by local government in Rhode Island, the Pandora's-religious-symbol box was opened in Washington State and around the nation.

Eventually, Washington's Republican Attorney General and Governor Gregoire put out this statement:

> The U.S. Supreme Court has been consistent and clear that, under the Constitution's First Amendment, once government admits one religious display or viewpoint onto public property, it may not discriminate against the content of other displays, including viewpoints of nonbelievers.

During the ensuing days and weeks following O'Reilly's initial tirade, I believe additional displays began appearing at the State Capitol building including a Menorah, a Kwanzaa display, and, eventually, a display celebrating Seinfeld's Festivus. Nothing wrong with a sense of humor. This parade of religious symbol displays was caused by the *Lynch v. Donnelly* decision.

God is on time every time! As I was completing this chapter, I ran across a second true story. You will never guess where it originated - the real Berkeley, California.

With Christmas 2006 only weeks away, there was trouble brewing from factions that wanted the city to display a nativity scene and those that wanted to block it and even those Christians who didn't want any part of it if the only way it would prevail would be to commingle it with plastic junk.

The display in question included three wise men, animals, an angel, a wooden manger, and scattered piles of hay. Get this! When the ACLU threatened a lawsuit, the city moved Santa's mailbox closer to the nativity scene. No doubt, the city fathers had read *Lynch* and knew they would have more success if they junked up the display that seeks to honor the birth of the Lord Jesus Christ.

Ultimately, the Berkeley City Council felt they had two choices: (1) to secularize the display enough to make it acceptable to the ACLU or (2) get it out from under City control in some fashion. In a 6-1 vote, they chose to give it to the Berkeley Clergy Association to display on church property.

This used to make me sad, but anymore it makes me angry that Christians would dishonor God by mixing our sacred symbols with government. In my opinion, this plays right into the hands of those who seek our demise.

If you seek to involve government in the nativity scene business, please understand the following:

[1] The better the quality, the less chance you will have of success.

[2] The clearer the message of Christ's birth, the less chance you will have of success.

[3] The best chance you will have of winning such a contest will be to place the nativity scene in a low travel area such as a hallway or, better yet, a basement.

[4] And, of utmost importance, please know that if you prevail, you will have earned the right of all faiths or those of no faith to put up their symbols, some of which could actually contradict the message of Christ's birth. Unless *Lynch* is reversed, **I predict that someday we will see a Satanic display at Christmas because a handful of Christians in Pawtucket sought and won the favor of government. Lest you think the Supreme Court would never honor such a display, think again and remember that "religious beliefs need not be acceptable, logical, consistent, or comprehensible to others in order to merit First Amendment protection."** *Church of the Lukumi Babalu Aye v. Hialeah.*

When it comes to celebrating Christmas, it would be hard to improve on a wonderful popular e-mail you may have seen entitled "A Letter From Jesus Christ," as follows:

It has come to my attention that many of you are upset that folks are taking My name out of the season. Maybe you've forgotten that I wasn't actually born during this time of the year and that it was some of your predecessors who decided to celebrate My birthday on what was actually a time of pagan festivals. But I do appreciate being remembered at anytime.

How I personally feel about this celebration can probably be most easily understood by those of you who have been blessed with children of your own. I don't care what you call the day. If you want to celebrate My birth just get along and love one another. Now, having said that, let Me go on.

If it bothers you that the town in which you live doesn't allow a scene depicting My birth, then just get rid of a couple of Santas and snowmen and put in a small nativity scene **on your own front lawn**. If all My followers did that there wouldn't be any need for such a scene on the town square because there would be many of them all around town.

Stop worrying about the fact that people are calling the tree a holiday tree instead of a Christmas tree. It was I who made all trees. You can and may remember Me anytime you see any tree. Decorate a grape vine if you wish. I actually spoke of that one in a teaching explaining who I am in relation to you and what each of our tasks were. If you have forgotten that one, look up John 15:1-8.

If you want to give Me a present in remembrance of My birth, here is my wish list. Choose something from it.

➢ Instead of writing protest letters objecting to the way My birthday is being celebrated, write letters of love and hope to soldiers away from home. They are terribly afraid and lonely this time of year. I know, they tell Me all the time.

➢ Visit someone in a nursing home. You don't have to know them personally. They just need to know that someone cares about them.

➢ Instead of writing George complaining about the wording on the cards his staff sent out this year, why don't you write and tell him that you'll be praying for him and his family this year. Then follow up. It will be nice hearing from you again.

➢ Instead of giving your children a lot of gifts you can't afford and they don't need, spend time with them. Tell them the story of My birth, and why I came to live with you down here. Hold them in your arms and remind them that I love them.

➢ Pick someone that has hurt you in the past and forgive him or her.

➢ Did you know that someone in your town will attempt to take their own life this season because they feel so alone and hopeless? Since you don't know who that person is, try giving everyone you meet a warm smile; it could make the difference. Also, you might consider supporting the local Hotline. They talk with people like that every day.

➢ Instead of nit picking about what the retailer in your town calls the holiday, be patient with the people who work there. Give them a warm smile and a kind word. Even if they aren't allowed to wish you a "Merry Christmas," that doesn't keep you from wishing them one. Then stop shopping there on Sunday. If the store didn't make so much money on that day, they'd close and let their employees spend the day at home with their families.

➤ If you really want to make a difference, support a missionary, especially one who takes My love and Good News to those who have never heard My name. You may already know someone like that.

➤ Here's a good one. There are individuals and whole families in your town who not only will have no "Christmas" tree, but neither will they have any presents to give or receive. If you don't know them (and I suspect you don't), buy some food and a few gifts and give them to the Marines, the Salvation Army or some other charity which believes in Me and they will make the delivery for you.

➤ Finally, if you want to make a statement about your belief in and loyalty to Me, then **behave like a Christian**. Let people know by your actions that you are one of mine.

P.S. Don't forget; I am God and can take care of Myself. Just love Me and do what I have told you to do. I'll take care of all the rest. Check out the list above and get to work; time is short. I'll help you, but the ball is now in your court. And do have a most blessed Christmas with all those whom you love and remember, I love you, Jesus.

Like I said, I can't improve upon that.

Merry Christmas!

Chapter Thirteen

ESTABLISHMENT:
COMMANDMENTS

"Ava, come on. It isn't like you to be so angry. What gives?"

Jackson had just picked up his wife from her first PTA meeting at Alyssa's elementary school and Ava was not a happy camper.

"You won't believe it, Jackson. You just won't. I have had it. We need to talk. I would like to look into homeschooling to see if I can prepare myself by next fall. I don't want Alyssa returning to the Berkley School District."

"I'm not surprised," Jackson said. "We could both see this coming. What happened?"

"Well, the teachers had their rooms decked out for parents to explore what the kids are learning, so I looked around prior to Alyssa's name being called. Alyssa took me to her desk and, as I sat down, I noticed an official looking document hanging on the wall right next to her desk. I thought it might be the Ten Commandments or the Declaration of Independence because it was printed on paper made to look like parchment. Remember the research I did when we were looking into school prayer here in Berkley?"

"Yes, I remember. Where are you going with this?" said Jackson.

"You guessed it. There it was – The Creed of the Church of Scientology – hanging to the left of our daughter's desk each and every school day this year."

"I know the school board cannot attempt to indoctrinate our child like that. This is unconstitutional, for sure, and I'm going to see to it that this subtle form of brainwashing is stopped," said Jackson.

"You do know, honey, that you have a great source upon which to model your case. I saved all of the paperwork from the lawsuit you defended in Lubbock when you were on the school board. You remember. I had never seen you so upset when you lost."

"Great. All I will need to do is study the pleadings of those atheist folks who were successful in making us take down the Ten Commandments from the walls of our public elementary schools."

What had Jackson just said? He and Ava had never realized what it could be like to be on the minority side of a battle between religion and government. How enlightening! He was about to learn as much as he could about that family's concerns so that he could support what he had fought so hard to reject. Perhaps there was something to at least a "short fence of separation." Could he win? Should he fight? What is a Christian to do?

I don't think we have been to Kentucky yet. Let's pay the Blue Grass State a visit.

STONE v. GRAHAM
SUPREME COURT OF THE UNITED STATES
449 U.S. 39
November 17, 1980
[6 – 3]

OPINION:…**A Kentucky statute requires the posting of a copy of the Ten Commandments, purchased with private contributions, on the wall of each public classroom in the State.** Petitioners, claiming that this statute violates the Establishment and Free Exercise Clauses of the First Amendment, sought an injunction against its enforcement. The state trial court upheld the statute, finding that its avowed purpose was secular and not religious, and that the statute would neither advance nor inhibit any religion or religious group nor involve the state excessively in religious matters. The Supreme Court of the Commonwealth of Kentucky affirmed…We reverse.

This Court has announced a three-part test for determining whether a challenged state statute is permissible under the Establishment Clause of the United States Constitution: (1) The statute must have a secular legislative purpose. (2) Its principal or primary effect must be one that neither advances nor inhibits religion…(3) The statute must not foster an excessive government entanglement with religion. *Lemon v. Kurtzman.*

If a statute violates any of these three principles, it must be struck down under the Establishment Clause. We conclude that Kentucky's statute requiring the posting of the Ten Commandments in public school rooms has no secular legislative purpose, and is therefore unconstitutional.

[Kentucky] insists that the statute in question serves a secular legislative purpose, observing that the legislature required the following notation in small print at the bottom of each display of the Ten Commandments: "The secular application of the Ten Commandments is clearly seen in its adoption as the fundamental legal code of Western Civilization and the common law of the United States."

The trial court found the "avowed" purpose of the statute to be secular, even as it labeled the statutory declaration "self-serving." Under this Court's rulings, however, such an "avowed" secular purpose is not sufficient to avoid conflict with the First Amendment. In *Abington v. Schempp*, this Court held unconstitutional the daily reading of Bible verses and the Lord's Prayer in the public schools, despite the school district's assertion of such secular purposes as "the promotion of moral values, the contradiction to the materialistic trends of our times, the perpetuation of our institutions and the teaching of literature."

The pre-eminent purpose for posting the Ten Commandments on schoolroom walls is plainly religious in nature. The Ten Commandments are undeniably a sacred text in the Jewish and Christian faiths, and no legislative recitation of a supposed secular purpose can blind us to that fact.

The Commandments do not confine themselves to arguably secular matters, such as honoring one's parents, killing or murder, adultery, stealing, false witness, and covetousness. Rather, the first part of the Commandments concerns the religious duties of believers: worshiping the Lord God alone, avoiding idolatry, not using the Lord's name in vain, and observing the Sabbath Day.

This is not a case in which the Ten Commandments are integrated into the school curriculum, where **the Bible may constitutionally be used in an appropriate study of history, civilization, ethics, comparative religion, or the like**. *Abington*. Posting of religious texts on the wall serves no such educational function. If the posted copies of the Ten Commandments are to have any effect at all, it will be to induce the school children to read, meditate upon, perhaps to venerate and obey, the Commandments. However desirable this might be as a matter of private devotion, it is not a permissible state objective under the Establishment Clause. It does not matter that the posted copies of the Ten Commandments are financed by voluntary private contributions, for the mere posting of the copies under the auspices of the legislature provides the "official support of the State...Government" that the Establishment Clause prohibits. Nor is it significant that the Bible verses involved in this case are merely posted on the wall, rather than read aloud as in *Schempp* and *Engel*, for "it is no defense to urge that the religious practices here may be relatively minor encroachments on the First Amendment." We conclude that [the Kentucky statute] violates the first part of the *Lemon* test, and thus the Establishment Clause of the Constitution...The judgment below is reversed.

DISSENT: Justice Rehnquist...The Court's summary rejection of a secular purpose articulated by the legislature and confirmed by the state court is without precedent in Establishment Clause jurisprudence. This Court regularly looks to legislative articulations of a statute's purpose in Establishment Clause cases and accords such pronouncements the deference they are due...The fact that the asserted secular purpose may overlap with what some may see as a religious objective does not render it unconstitutional. As this Court stated in *McGowan v. Maryland*, in upholding the validity of Sunday closing laws, "the present purpose and effect of most of these laws is to provide a uniform day of rest for all citizens; the fact that this day is Sunday, a day of particular significance for the dominant Christian sects, does not bar the state from achieving its secular goals."...The Court rejects the secular purpose articulated by the State because the Decalogue is undeniably a sacred text. It is equally undeniable, however, as the elected representatives of Kentucky determined, that the Ten Commandments have had a significant impact on the development of secular legal codes of the Western World. The trial court concluded that evidence submitted substantiated this determination...Certainly the State was permitted to conclude that a document with such secular significance should be placed before its students, with an appropriate statement of the document's secular import. ("It does not seem reasonable to require removal of a passive monument, involving no compulsion, because its accepted precepts, as a foundation for law, reflect the religious nature of an ancient era")...

The Establishment Clause does not require that the public sector be insulated from all things which may have a religious significance or origin. This Court has recognized that "religion has been closely identified with our history and government" and that "the history of man is inseparable from the history of religion." Kentucky has decided to make students aware of this fact by demonstrating the secular impact of the Ten Commandments...

"Against" wins this time.

> **First Amendment Scoreboard**
> Rulings "for" Religion: 18 --- Rulings "against" Religion: 11

Next up – Austin, Texas. Get ready for a surprise.

VAN ORDEN v. PERRY
SUPREME COURT OF THE UNITED STATES
125 S. Ct. 2854
June 27, 2005
[5 – 4]

OPINION: Chief Justice Rehnquist…The question here is whether the Establishment Clause of the First Amendment allows the display of a monument inscribed with the Ten Commandments on the Texas State Capitol grounds. We hold that it does.

The 22 acres surrounding the Texas State Capitol contain 17 monuments and 21 historical markers commemorating the "people, ideals, and events that compose Texan identity." The monolith challenged here stands 6 feet tall and 3 feet wide…, its primary content [being the Ten Commandments]… Below the text are two Stars of David and the superimposed Greek letters Chi and Rho, which represent Christ. The bottom of the monument bears the inscription "PRESENTED TO THE PEOPLE AND YOUTH OF TEXAS BY THE FRATERNAL ORDER OF EAGLES OF TEXAS 1961."

The monuments are: Heroes of the Alamo, Hood's Brigade, Confederate Soldiers, Volunteer Fireman, Terry's Texas Rangers, Texas Cowboy, Spanish-American War, Texas National Guard, <u>Ten Commandments</u>, Tribute to Texas School Children, Texas Pioneer Woman, The Boy Scouts' Statue of Liberty Replica, Pearl Harbor Veterans, Korean War Veterans, Soldiers of World War I, Disabled Veterans, and Texas Peace Officers.

…The Eagles paid the cost of erecting the monument, the dedication of which was presided over by two state legislators.

Thomas Van Orden is a native Texan and a resident of Austin…He testified that, since 1995, he has encountered the Ten Commandments monument during his frequent visits to the Capitol grounds…Forty years after the monument's erection and six years after Van Orden began to encounter the monument frequently, he [brought this action]…seeking both a declaration that the monument's placement violates the Establishment Clause and an injunction requiring its removal...The District Court held that the monument did not contravene the Establishment Clause. It found that the State had a valid secular purpose in recognizing and commending the Eagles for their efforts to reduce juvenile delinquency. The District Court also determined that a reasonable observer, mindful of the history, purpose, and context, would not conclude that this passive monument conveyed the message that the state was seeking to endorse religion. The Court of Appeals affirmed [and so do we].

Our cases, Januslike, point in two directions in applying the Establishment Clause. One face looks toward the strong role played by religious traditions throughout our nation's history...The other face looks toward the principle that governmental intervention in religious matters can itself endanger religious freedom.

This case, like all Establishment Clause challenges, presents us with the difficulty of respecting both faces. Our institutions presuppose a Supreme Being, yet these institutions must not press religious observances upon their citizens. One face looks to the past in acknowledgment of our nation's heritage, while the other looks to the present in demanding a separation between church and state. Reconciling these two faces requires that we neither abdicate our responsibility to maintain a division between church and state nor evince a hostility to religion by disabling the government from in some ways recognizing our religious heritage...

In this case we are faced with a display of the Ten Commandments on government property outside the Texas State Capitol. Such acknowledgments of the role played by the Ten Commandments in our nation's heritage are common throughout America. We need only look within our own Courtroom. Since 1935, Moses has stood, holding two tablets that reveal portions of the Ten Commandments written in Hebrew, among other lawgivers in the south frieze. Representations of the Ten Commandments adorn the metal gates lining the north and south sides of the Courtroom as well as the doors leading into the Courtroom. Moses also sits on the exterior east facade of the building holding the Ten Commandments tablets.

Similar acknowledgments can be seen throughout a visitor's tour of our nation's Capitol. For example, a large statue of Moses holding the Ten

Commandments, alongside a statue of the Apostle Paul, has overlooked the rotunda of the Library of Congress' Jefferson Building since 1897. And the Jefferson Building's Great Reading Room contains a sculpture of a woman beside the Ten Commandments with a quote above her from the Old Testament...A medallion with two tablets depicting the Ten Commandments decorates the floor of the National Archives. Inside the Department of Justice, a statue entitled "The Spirit of Law" has two tablets representing the Ten Commandments lying at its feet. In front of the Ronald Reagan Building is another sculpture that includes a depiction of the Ten Commandments. So too a 24-foot-tall sculpture, depicting, among other things, the Ten Commandments and a cross, stands outside the federal courthouse that houses both the Court of Appeals and the District Court for the District of Columbia. Moses is also prominently featured in the Chamber of the United States House of Representatives...

Of course, the Ten Commandments are religious...The monument, therefore, has religious significance. According to Judeo-Christian belief, the Ten Commandments were given to Moses by God on Mt. Sinai. But Moses was a lawgiver as well as a religious leader. And the Ten Commandments have an undeniable historical meaning, as the foregoing examples demonstrate. Simply having religious content or promoting a message consistent with a religious doctrine does not run afoul of the Establishment Clause. *Lynch v. Donnelly; Marsh v. Chambers; McGowan v. Maryland; Walz v. Tax Comm'n.*

> The majority looks to *Lynch, Marsh, McGowan,* and *Walz* for support. With the exception of *Walz* (which could have gone either way), I believe these cases were wrongly decided.

There are, of course, limits to the display of religious messages or symbols. For example, we held unconstitutional a Kentucky statute requiring the posting of the Ten Commandments in every public schoolroom. *Stone v. Graham*...We have "been particularly vigilant in monitoring compliance with the Establishment Clause in elementary and secondary schools."

Edwards v. Aguillard. Compare *Lee v. Weisman* (holding unconstitutional a prayer at a secondary school graduation) with *Marsh v. Chambers* (upholding a prayer in the state legislature)...Neither *Stone* itself nor subsequent opinions have indicated that *Stone's* holding would extend to a legislative chamber (*Marsh*) or to capitol grounds.

The placement of the Ten Commandments monument on the Texas State Capitol grounds is a far more passive use of those texts than was the case in *Stone*, where the text confronted elementary school students every day. Indeed, Van Orden, the petitioner here, apparently walked by the monument for a number of years before bringing this lawsuit. The monument is therefore also quite different from the prayers involved in *Abington* and *Lee*. Texas has treated her Capitol grounds monuments as representing the several strands in the state's political and legal history. The inclusion of the Ten Commandments monument in this group has a dual significance, partaking of both religion and government. We cannot say that Texas' display of this monument violates the Establishment Clause of the First Amendment...

CONCURRENCE: Justice Scalia ... There is nothing unconstitutional in a state's favoring religion generally, honoring God through public prayer and acknowledgment, or, in a nonproselytizing manner, venerating the Ten Commandments.

CONCURRENCE: Justice Thomas...Our task would be far simpler if we returned to the original meaning of the word "establishment" than it is under the various approaches this Court now uses. The Framers understood an establishment "necessarily to involve actual legal coercion." *Lee v. Weisman* ("The coercion that was a hallmark of historical establishments of religion was coercion of religious orthodoxy and of financial support by force of law and threat of penalty.") "In other words, establishment at the founding involved, for example, mandatory observance or mandatory payment of taxes supporting ministers."

And "government practices that have nothing to do with creating or maintaining...coercive state establishments" simply do not "implicate the possible liberty interest of being free from coercive state establishments."

There is no question that, based on the original meaning of the Establishment Clause, the Ten Commandments display at issue here is constitutional. In no sense does Texas compel petitioner Van Orden to do anything. The only injury to him is that he takes offense at seeing the monument as he passes it on his way to the Texas Supreme Court Library. He need not stop to read it or even to look at it, let alone to express support for it or adopt the Commandments as guides for his life. The mere presence of the monument along his path involves no coercion and thus does not violate the Establishment Clause.

Returning to the original meaning would do more than simplify our task. It also would avoid the pitfalls present in the Court's current approach to such challenges. This Court's precedent elevates the trivial to the proverbial "federal case," by making benign signs and postings subject to challenge. Yet even as it does so, the Court's precedent attempts to avoid declaring all religious symbols and words of longstanding tradition unconstitutional, by counterfactually declaring them of little religious significance. Even when the Court's cases recognize that such symbols have religious meaning, they adopt an unhappy compromise that fails fully to account for either the adherent's or the non-adherent's beliefs, and provides no principled way to choose between them. Even worse, the incoherence of the Court's decisions in this area renders the Establishment Clause impenetrable and incapable of consistent application...This Court's jurisprudence leaves courts, governments, and believers and nonbelievers alike confused...

First, this Court's precedent permits even the slightest public recognition of religion to constitute an establishment of religion. For example, individuals frequenting a county courthouse have successfully challenged as an Establishment Clause violation a sign at the courthouse alerting the public that the building was closed for Good Friday and containing a 4-inch high crucifix. Similarly, a park ranger has claimed that a cross erected to honor World War I veterans on a rock in the Mojave Desert Preserve violated the Establishment Clause, and won. If a cross in the middle of a desert establishes a religion, then no religious observance is safe from challenge. Still other suits have charged that city seals containing religious symbols violate the Establishment Clause. In every instance, the litigants are mere "passers-by...free to ignore such symbols or signs, or even to turn their backs, just as they are free to do when they disagree with any other form of government speech." *Allegheny*.

> It is important to note that Justice Thomas is referring to **lower court decisions** around the country and is not suggesting that the Supreme Court would have rendered similar results.

Second, in a seeming attempt to balance out its willingness to consider almost any acknowledgment of religion an establishment, in other cases Members of this Court have concluded that the term or symbol at issue has no religious meaning by virtue of its ubiquity or rote ceremonial invocation. *Lynch v. Donnelly*. **But words such as "God" have religious significance...The declaration that our country is "one Nation under God" necessarily "entails an affirmation that God exists."** This phrase is thus anathema to those who reject God's existence and a validation of His existence to those who accept it. Telling either non-believers or believers that the words "under God" have no meaning contradicts what they know to be true. Moreover, repetition does not deprive religious words or symbols of their traditional meaning. Words like "God" are not vulgarities for which the shock value diminishes with each successive utterance.

> I must say I value honesty even more than outcome sometimes.

Even when this Court's precedents recognize the religious meaning of symbols or words, that recognition fails to respect fully religious belief or disbelief. This Court looks for the meaning to an observer of indeterminate religious affiliation who knows all the facts and circumstances surrounding a challenged display...In looking to the view of this unusually informed observer, this Court inquires whether the sign or display "sends the ancillary message to...non-adherents 'that they are outsiders, not full members of the political community, and an accompanying message to adherents that they are insiders, favored members of the political community.'"

This analysis is not fully satisfying to either non-adherents or adherents. For the non-adherent, who may well be more sensitive than the hypothetical "reasonable observer," or who may not know all the facts, this test fails to capture completely the honest and deeply felt offense he takes from the government conduct. For the adherent, this analysis takes no account of the message sent by removal of the sign or display, which may well appear to him to be an act hostile to his religious faith. The Court's foray into religious meaning either gives insufficient weight to the views of non-adherents and adherents alike, or it provides no principled way to choose between those views. In sum, this Court's effort to assess religious meaning is fraught with futility...The inconsistency between the decisions the Court reaches today in this case and in *McCreary County v. ACLU* only compounds the confusion...

CONCURRENCE: Justice Breyer...In *Abington*, Justice Goldberg... wrote, in respect to the First Amendment's Religion Clauses, that there is "no simple and clear measure which by precise application can readily and invariably demark the permissible from the impermissible." One must refer instead to the basic purposes of those Clauses. They seek to "assure the fullest possible scope of the religious liberty and tolerance for all." They seek to avoid that divisiveness based upon religion that promotes social conflict, sapping the strength of government and religion alike. They seek to maintain that "separation of church and state" that has long been critical to the "peaceful dominion that religion exercises in this country," where the "spirit of religion" and the "spirit of freedom" are productively "united,"...but in separate spheres "on the same soil."

If our citizens would read what you have read thus far on this journey, at a minimum, they would better understand the issues faced by the Court.

...The Court has made clear...that the realization of these goals means that government must "neither engage in nor compel religious practices," that it must "effect no favoritism among sects or between religion and nonreligion," and that it must "work deterrence of no religious belief." *Abington; Lee; Everson.* The government must avoid excessive interference with, or promotion of, religion. *Allegheny.* But the Establishment Clause does not compel the government to purge from the public sphere all that in any way partakes of the religious. *Marsh.* Such absolutism is not only inconsistent with our national traditions, but would also tend to promote the kind of social conflict the Establishment Clause seeks to avoid...

Where the Establishment Clause is at issue, tests designed to measure neutrality alone are insufficient, both because it is sometimes difficult to determine when a legal rule is neutral, and because untutored devotion to the concept of neutrality can lead to invocation or approval of results which partake not simply of that noninterference and noninvolvement with the religious which the Constitution commands, but of a brooding and pervasive devotion to the secular and a passive, or even active, hostility to the religious.

Neither can this Court's other tests readily explain the Establishment Clause's tolerance, for example, of the prayers that open legislative meetings (*Marsh*); certain references to, and invocations of, the Deity in the public words of public officials; the public references to God on coins, decrees, and buildings; or the attention paid to the religious objectives of certain holidays, including Thanksgiving...

Here the tablets have been used as part of a display that communicates not simply a religious message, but a secular message as well. The circumstances surrounding the display's placement on the capitol grounds and its physical setting suggest that the state itself intended the latter, nonreligious aspects of the tablets' message to predominate. And the monument's 40-year history on the Texas state grounds indicates that that has been its effect...

The physical setting of the monument, moreover, suggests little or nothing of the sacred. The monument sits in a large park containing 17 monuments and 21 historical markers, all designed to illustrate the "ideals" of those who settled in Texas and of those who have lived there since that time. The setting does not readily lend itself to meditation or any other religious activity. But it does provide a context of history and moral ideals. It (together with the display's inscription about its origin) communicates to visitors that the State sought to reflect moral principles, illustrating a relation between ethics and law that the State's citizens, historically speaking, have endorsed. That is to say, the context suggests that the State intended the display's moral message – an illustrative message reflecting the historical "ideal" of Texans – to predominate...

Please, **let's get real**. One of those "historical ideals" is quite obviously the fact that mainstream "Texans" believe in the Judeo-Christian God. That is precisely why the Texas State Legislature does not have any monument to the Book of Mormon on its lawn. It is hard to understand why the Supreme Court feels the need to distance the Ten Commandments from what they say unless it is to distort what they say in order to achieve a result not otherwise achievable.

This case, moreover, is distinguishable from instances where the Court has found Ten Commandments displays impermissible. **The display is not on the grounds of a public school, where, given the impressionability of the young, government must exercise particular care in separating church and state.** This case also differs from *McCreary County*, where the short (and stormy) history of the courthouse Commandments' displays demonstrates the substantially religious objectives of those who mounted them, and the effect of this readily apparent objective upon those who view them. That history there indicates a governmental effort substantially to promote religion, not simply an effort primarily to reflect, historically, the secular impact of a religiously inspired document. And, in today's world, in a nation of so many different religious and comparable nonreligious fundamental beliefs, a more contemporary state effort to focus attention upon a religious text is certainly likely to prove divisive in a way that this longstanding, pre-existing monument has not.

For these reasons, I believe that the Texas display – serving a mixed but primarily nonreligious purpose, not primarily "advancing" or "inhibiting religion," and not creating an "excessive government entanglement with religion," – might satisfy this Court's more formal Establishment Clause tests. But, as I have said, in reaching the conclusion that the Texas display falls on the permissible side of the constitutional line, I rely less upon a literal application of any particular test than upon consideration of the basic purposes of the First Amendment's Religion Clauses themselves. This display has stood apparently uncontested for nearly two generations. That experience helps us understand that as a practical matter of degree this display is unlikely to prove divisive. And this matter of degree is, I believe, critical in a borderline case such as this one…

A contrary conclusion…would, I fear, lead the law to exhibit a hostility toward religion that has no place in our Establishment Clause traditions. Such a holding might well encourage disputes concerning the removal of longstanding depictions of the Ten Commandments from public buildings across the nation. And it could thereby create the very kind of religiously based divisiveness that the Establishment Clause seeks to avoid…

> Because this Court based its ruling in large part on the fact that this monument is only one such monument in a veritable "monument museum" several acres in size, no one should be misled. The Court has **not** determined how to handle this identical monument erected as the **only** monument outside the County Courthouse in Anytown, Anystate, U.S.A.

I recognize the danger of the slippery slope. Still, where the Establishment Clause is at issue, we must "distinguish between real threat and mere shadow." Here we have only the shadow…

DISSENT: Justice Stevens…The sole function of the monument on the grounds of Texas' State Capitol is to display the full text of one version of the Ten Commandments. The monument is not a work of art and does not refer to any event in the history of the State. It is significant because, and only because, it communicates the following message:

I am the Lord thy God.

Thou shalt have no other gods before me.

Thou shalt not make to thyself any graven images.

Thou shalt not take the Name of the Lord thy God in vain.

Remember the Sabbath day, to keep it holy.

Honor thy father and thy mother, that thy days may be long upon the land which **the Lord thy God** giveth thee.

Thou shalt not kill.

Thou shalt not commit adultery.

Thou shalt not steal.

Thou shalt not bear false witness against thy neighbor.

Thou shalt not covet thy neighbor's house.

Thou shalt not covet thy neighbor's wife, nor his manservant, nor his maidservant, nor his cattle, nor anything that is thy neighbor's.

> The Biblical source for this quote is not the New Living Translation published by Tyndale House Publishers, Inc. It is a direct quote from the Supreme Court opinion.

Viewed on its face, Texas' display has no purported connection to God's role in the formation of Texas or the founding of our nation; nor does it provide the reasonable observer with any basis to guess that it was erected to honor any individual or organization. The message transmitted by Texas' chosen display is quite plain: This State endorses the divine code of the "Judeo-Christian" God.

> Justice Stevens and I do not often agree, but his summary of the message appears to be accurate.

For those of us who learned to recite the King James version of the text long before we understood the meaning of some of its words, God's Commandments may seem like wise counsel. The question before this Court, however, is whether it is counsel that the State of Texas may proclaim without violating the Establishment Clause of the Constitution. If any fragment of Jefferson's metaphorical "wall of separation between church and State" is to be preserved – if there remains any meaning to the "wholesome 'neutrality' of which this Court's Establishment Clause cases speak" (*Abington*) – a negative answer to that question is mandatory...

At the very least, the Establishment Clause has created a strong presumption against the display of religious symbols on public property. The adornment of our public spaces with displays of religious symbols and messages undoubtedly provides comfort, even inspiration, to many individuals who subscribe to particular faiths. Unfortunately, the practice also runs the risk of "offending non-members of the faith being advertised as well as adherents who consider the particular advertisement disrespectful."

...The wall that separates the church from the State does not prohibit the government from acknowledging the religious beliefs and practices of the American people, nor does it require governments to hide works of art or historic memorabilia from public view just because they also have religious significance. This case, however, is not about historic preservation or the mere recognition of religion...The monolith displayed on Texas Capitol grounds cannot be discounted as a passive acknowledgment of religion, nor can the State's refusal to remove it...be explained as a simple desire to preserve a historic relic. This nation's resolute commitment to neutrality with respect to religion is flatly inconsistent with the plurality's wholehearted validation of an official state endorsement of the message that there is one, and only one, God...The State may admonish its citizens not to lie, cheat or steal, to honor their parents and to respect their neighbors' property; and it may do so by printed words, in television commercials, or on granite monuments in front of its public buildings. Moreover, **the State may provide its schoolchildren and adult citizens with educational materials that explain the important role that our forebears' faith in God played in their decisions to select America as**

267

a refuge from religious persecution, to declare their independence from the British Crown, and to conceive a new nation. The message at issue in this case, however, is fundamentally different from either a bland admonition to observe generally accepted rules of behavior or a general history lesson...

> Some believe the Supreme Court has prohibited even that which Justice Stevens says has not been prohibited. You are not delusional. You read correctly. Justice Stevens just said: "The State may provide its schoolchildren and adult citizens with educational materials that explain the important role that our forebears' faith in *God* played in their decisions to select America as a refuge from religious persecution, to declare their independence from the British Crown, and to conceive a new nation." See there, we can say "God." Who in the world started the rumor that we cannot?

Attempts to secularize what is unquestionably a sacred text defy credibility and disserve people of faith.

The profoundly sacred message embodied by the text inscribed on the Texas monument is emphasized by the especially large letters that identify its author: "I AM the LORD thy God." It commands present worship of Him and no other deity. It directs us to be guided by His teaching in the current and future conduct of all of our affairs. It instructs us to follow a code of divine law, some of which has informed and been integrated into our secular legal code ("Thou shalt not kill"), but much of which has not ("Thou shalt not make to thyself any graven images...")

...Even if, however, the message of the monument, despite the inscribed text, fairly could be said to represent the belief system of all Judeo-Christians, it would still run afoul of the Establishment Clause by prescribing a compelled code of conduct from one God, namely a Judeo-Christian God, that is rejected by prominent polytheistic sects, such as Hinduism, as well as nontheistic religions, such as Buddhism...And, at the very least, the text of the Ten Commandments impermissibly commands a preference for religion over irreligion...Any of those bases...would be sufficient to conclude that the message should not be proclaimed by the State of Texas on a permanent monument at the seat of its government...

Even more than the display of a religious symbol on government property,... displaying this sectarian text at the state capitol should invoke a powerful presumption of invalidity. As Justice Souter's opinion persuasively demonstrates, the physical setting in which the Texas monument is displayed – far from rebutting that presumption – actually enhances the religious content of its message. The monument's permanent fixture at the seat of Texas government is of immense significance. The fact that a monument "is installed on public property implies official recognition and reinforcement of its message. That implication is especially strong when the sign stands in front of the seat of government itself. The 'reasonable observer' of any symbol placed unattended in front of any capitol in the world will normally assume that the sovereign – which is not only the owner of that parcel of real estate but also the lawgiver for the surrounding territory – has sponsored and facilitated its message." *Pinette* (Stevens, J., dissenting).

Critical examination of the Decalogue's prominent display at the seat of Texas government, rather than generic citation to the role of religion in American life, unmistakably reveals on which side of the "slippery slope" this display must fall. God, as the author of its message, the Eagles, as the donor of the monument, and the State of Texas, as its proud owner, speak with one voice for a common purpose – to encourage Texans to abide by the divine code of a "Judeo-Christian" God. If this message is permissible, then the shining principle of neutrality to which we have long adhered is nothing more than mere shadow...

Thus, when public officials deliver public speeches, we recognize that their words are not exclusively a transmission from the government because those oratories have embedded within them the inherently personal views of the speaker as an individual member of the polity...

A reading of the First Amendment dependent on either of the purported original meanings expressed above would eviscerate the heart of the Establishment Clause. It would replace Jefferson's "wall of separation" with a perverse wall of exclusion – Christians inside, non-Christians out.

It would permit States to construct walls of their own choosing – Baptists inside, Mormons out; Jewish Orthodox inside, Jewish Reform out. A Clause so understood might be faithful to the expectation of some of our Founders, but it is plainly not worthy of a society whose enviable hallmark over the course of two centuries has been the continuing expansion of religious pluralism and tolerance...

It is our duty, therefore, to interpret the First Amendment's command that "Congress shall make no law respecting an establishment of religion" not by merely asking what those words meant to observers at the time of the founding, but instead by deriving from the Clause's text and history the broad principles that remain valid today...

The Eagles may donate as many monuments as they choose to be displayed in front of Protestant churches, benevolent organizations' meeting places, or on the front lawns of private citizens. The expurgated text of the King James version of the Ten Commandments that they have crafted is unlikely to be accepted by Catholic parishes, Jewish synagogues, or even some Protestant denominations, but the message they seek to convey is surely more compatible with church property than with property that is located on the government side of the... "wall." The judgment of the Court in this case stands for the proposition that the Constitution permits governmental displays of sacred religious texts. This makes a mockery of the constitutional ideal that government must remain neutral between religion and irreligion. **If a State may endorse a particular deity's command to "have no other gods before me," it is difficult to conceive of any textual display that would run afoul of the Establishment Clause**...I respectfully dissent.

DISSENT: Justice O'Connor...I respectfully dissent.

DISSENT: Justice Souter...The monument's presentation of the Commandments with religious text emphasized and enhanced stands in contrast to any number of perfectly constitutional depictions of them, the frieze of our own Courtroom providing a good example, where the figure of Moses stands among history's great lawgivers. While Moses holds the tablets of the Commandments showing some Hebrew text, no one looking at the lines of figures in marble relief is likely to see a religious purpose behind the assemblage or take away a religious message from it. Only one other depiction represents a religious leader, and the historical personages are mixed with symbols of moral and intellectual abstractions like Equity and Authority. Since Moses enjoys no especial prominence on the frieze, viewers can readily take him to be there as a lawgiver in the company of other lawgivers; and the viewers may just as naturally see the tablets of the Commandments (showing the later ones, forbidding things like killing and theft, but without the divine preface) as background from which the concept of law emerged, ultimately having a secular influence in the history of the nation. Government may, of course, constitutionally call attention to this influence, and may post displays or erect monuments recounting this aspect of our history no less than any other, so long as there is a context and that context is historical. Hence, a display of the Commandments accompanied by an exposition of how they have influenced modern law would most likely be constitutionally unobjectionable. **And the Decalogue could, as *Stone* suggested, be integrated constitutionally into a course of study in public schools...**

The Government of the United States does not violate the Establishment Clause by hanging Giotto's Madonna on the wall of the National Gallery. But 17 monuments with no common appearance, history, or esthetic role scattered over 22 acres is not a museum, and anyone strolling around the lawn would surely take each memorial on its own terms without any dawning sense that some purpose held the miscellany together more coherently than fortuity and the edge of the grass. One monument expresses admiration for pioneer women. One pays respect to the fighters of World War II. And one quotes the God of Abraham whose command is the sanction for moral law. The themes are individual grit, patriotic courage, and God as the source of Jewish and Christian morality; there is no common denominator. In like circumstances, we rejected an argument similar to the State's, noting in *Allegheny* that "the presence of Santas or other Christmas decorations elsewhere in the...courthouse, and of the nearby gallery forum, fail to negate the creche's endorsement effect... The record demonstrates...that the crèche, with its floral frame, was its own display distinct from any other decorations or exhibitions in the building."...To be sure, Kentucky's compulsory-education law meant that the schoolchildren were forced to see the display every day, whereas many see the monument by choice, and those who customarily walk the Capitol grounds can presumably avoid it if they choose. But in my judgment..., this distinction should make no difference. The monument in this case sits on the grounds of the Texas State Capitol. There is something significant in the common term "statehouse" to refer to a state capitol building; it is the civic home of every one of the State's citizens. If neutrality in religion means something, any citizen should be able to visit that civic home without having to confront religious expressions...meant to convey an official religious position that may be at odds with his own religion, or with rejection of religion...I would reverse...

Another score "for" religion.

First Amendment Scoreboard

Rulings "for" Religion: 19 --- Rulings "against" Religion: 11

For the final Ten Commandments case in this trilogy, we go to McCreary County, Kentucky.

McCREARY COUNTY v. ACLU
SUPREME COURT OF THE UNITED STATES
125 S. Ct. 2722
June 27, 2005
[5 – 4]

OPINION: Justice Souter...In the summer of 1999...McCreary County and Pulaski County, Kentucky,...put up in their respective courthouses large, gold-framed copies of an abridged text of the King James version of the Ten Commandments, including a citation to the Book of Exodus. In McCreary County, the placement of the Commandments responded to an order of the county legislative body requiring "the display to be posted in 'a very high traffic area' of the courthouse." In Pulaski County, amidst reported controversy over the propriety of the display, the Commandments were hung in a ceremony presided over by the county Judge-Executive, who called them "good rules to live by" and who recounted the story of an astronaut who became convinced "there must be a divine God" after viewing the Earth from the moon. The Judge-Executive was accompanied by the pastor of his church, who called the Commandments "a creed of ethics" and told the press after the ceremony that displaying the Commandments was "one of the greatest things the judge could have done to close out the millennium." In both counties, this was the version of the Commandments posted:

Thou shalt have no other gods before me.

Thou shalt not make unto thee any graven images.

Thou shalt not take the name of the Lord thy God in vain.

Remember the sabbath day, to keep it holy.

Honor thy father and thy mother.

Thou shalt not kill.

Thou shalt not commit adultery.

Thou shalt not steal.

Thou shalt not bear false witness.

Thou shalt not covet.

Exodus 20:3-17.

The Biblical source for this quote is not the New Living Translation published by Tyndale House Publishers, Inc. It is a direct quote from the Supreme Court opinion.

In each county, the hallway display was "readily visible to…county citizens who use the courthouse to conduct their civic business…"

In November 1999, the ACLU of Kentucky…sought a preliminary injunction against maintaining the displays…Within a month, and before the District Court had responded to the request for injunction, the legislative body of each County authorized a second, expanded display, by nearly identical resolutions reciting that the Ten Commandments are "the precedent legal code upon which the civil and criminal codes of...Kentucky are founded," and stating several grounds for taking that position: that "the Ten Commandments are codified in Kentucky's civil and criminal laws"; that the Kentucky House of Representatives had in 1993 "voted unanimously...to adjourn...in remembrance and honor of Jesus Christ, the Prince of Ethics"; that the "County Judge and...magistrates agree with the arguments set out by Judge Roy Moore" in defense of his "display of the Ten Commandments in his courtroom"; and that the "Founding Fathers had an explicit understanding of the duty of elected officials to publicly acknowledge God as the source of America's strength and direction."

As directed by the resolutions, the Counties expanded the displays of the Ten Commandments in their locations...In addition to the first display's large framed copy of the edited King James version of the Commandments, the second included eight other documents in smaller frames, each either having a religious theme or excerpted to highlight a religious element. The documents were the "endowed by their Creator" passage from the Declaration of Independence; the Preamble to the Constitution of Kentucky; the national motto, "In God We Trust"; a page from the Congressional Record of February 2, 1983, proclaiming the Year of the Bible and including a statement of the Ten Commandments; a proclamation by President Abraham Lincoln designating April 30, 1863, a National Day of Prayer and Humiliation; an excerpt from President Lincoln's "Reply to Loyal Colored People of Baltimore upon Presentation of a Bible," reading that "the Bible is the best gift God has ever given to man"; a proclamation by President Reagan marking 1983 the Year of the Bible; and the Mayflower Compact.

After argument, the District Court entered a preliminary injunction on May 5, 2000, ordering that the "display...be removed from each County Courthouse immediately" and that no county official "erect or cause to be erected similar displays." The court's analysis of the situation followed the three-part formulation first stated in *Lemon v. Kurtzman*. As to governmental purpose, it concluded that the original display "lacked any secular purpose" because the Commandments "are a distinctly religious document, believed by many Christians and Jews to be the direct and revealed word of God." Although the Counties had maintained that the original display was meant to be educational, "the narrow scope of the display – a single religious text unaccompanied by any interpretation explaining its role as a foundational document – can hardly be said to present meaningfully the story of this country's religious traditions." The court found that the second version also "clearly lacked a secular purpose" because the "Counties narrowly tailored their selection of foundational documents to incorporate only those with specific references to Christianity."

The Counties filed a notice of appeal from the preliminary injunction but voluntarily dismissed it after hiring new lawyers. They then installed another display in each courthouse, the third within a year. No new resolution authorized this one, nor did the Counties repeal the resolutions that preceded the second. The posting consists of nine framed documents of equal size, one of them setting out the Ten Commandments explicitly identified as the "King James Version" at Exodus 20:3-17 and quoted at greater length than before:

> **Thou shalt have no other gods before me.**
>
> **Thou shalt not make unto thee any graven image, or any likeness of any thing that is in heaven above, or that is in the earth beneath, or that is in the water underneath the earth: Thou shalt not bow down thyself to them, nor serve them: for I the LORD thy God am a jealous God, visiting the iniquity of the fathers upon the children unto the third and fourth generation of them that hate me...**
>
> **Thou shalt not take the name of the LORD thy God in vain: for the LORD will not hold him guiltless that taketh his name in vain.**
>
> **Remember the sabbath day, to keep it holy.**
>
> **Honour thy father and thy mother: that thy days may be long upon the land which the LORD thy God giveth thee.**
>
> Thou shalt not kill.

Thou shalt not commit adultery.

Thou shalt not steal.

Thou shalt not bear false witness against thy neighbour.

Thou shalt not covet thy neighbour's house, thou shalt not covet thy neighbour's wife, nor his manservant, nor his maidservant, nor his ox, nor his ass, nor anything that is thy neighbour's.

> This is the King James Version, not the New Living Translation published by Tyndale House Publishers, Inc. It is a direct quote from the Supreme Court opinion.

Assembled with the Commandments are framed copies of the Magna Carta, the Declaration of Independence, the Bill of Rights, the lyrics of the Star Spangled Banner, the Mayflower Compact, the National Motto, the Preamble to the Kentucky Constitution, and a picture of Lady Justice. The collection is entitled "The Foundations of American Law and Government Display" and each document comes with a statement about its historical and legal significance. The comment on the Ten Commandments reads:

> The Ten Commandments have profoundly influenced the formation of Western legal thought and the formation of our country. That influence is clearly seen in the Declaration of Independence, which declared that "We hold these truths to be self-evident, that all men are created equal, that they are endowed by their Creator with certain unalienable Rights, that among these are Life, Liberty, and the pursuit of Happiness." The Ten Commandments provide the moral background of the Declaration of Independence and the foundation of our legal tradition.

The ACLU moved to supplement the preliminary injunction to enjoin the Counties' third display, and the Counties responded with several explanations for the new version, including desires "to demonstrate that the Ten Commandments were part of the foundation of American Law and Government" and "to educate the citizens of the county regarding some of the documents that played a significant role in the foundation of our system of law and government." The court, however, took the objective of proclaiming the Commandments' foundational value as "a religious, rather than secular, purpose" under *Stone v. Graham* and found that the assertion that the Counties' broader educational goals are secular "crumbles…upon an examination of the history of this litigation." In light of the Counties' decision to post the Commandments by themselves in the first instance, contrary to *Stone*, and later to "accentuate" the religious objective by surrounding the Commandments with "specific references to Christianity," the District Court understood the Counties' "clear" purpose as being to post the Commandments, not to educate.

The Court also found that the effect of the third display was to endorse religion because the "reasonable observer will see one religious code placed alongside eight political or patriotic documents, and will understand that the counties promote that one religious code as being on a par with our nation's most cherished secular symbols and documents" and because the "reasonable observer would know something of the controversy surrounding these displays, which has focused on only one of the nine framed documents: the Ten Commandments."

…The Circuit majority stressed that under *Stone*, displaying the Commandments bespeaks a religious object unless they are integrated with other material so as to carry "a secular message." The majority judges saw no integration here because of a "lack of a demonstrated analytical or historical connection between the Commandments and the other documents." They noted in particular that the Counties offered no support for their claim that the Ten Commandments "provided the moral backdrop" to the Declaration of Independence or otherwise "profoundly influenced" it. The majority found that the Counties' purpose was religious, not educational, given the nature of the Commandments as "an active symbol of religion stating the religious duties of believers."…[We affirm]…

> Just to be clear, the Ten Commandments lost this round.

CONCURRENCE: Justice O'Connor … **Reasonable minds can disagree about how to apply the Religion Clauses in a given case. But the goal**

of the Clauses is clear: to carry out the Founders' plan of preserving religious liberty to the fullest extent possible in a pluralistic society... At a time when we see around the world the violent consequences of the assumption of religious authority by government, Americans may count themselves fortunate: Our regard for constitutional boundaries has protected us from similar travails, while allowing private religious exercise to flourish. The well-known statement that "we are a religious people" has proved true. Americans attend their places of worship more often than do citizens of other developed nations...and describe religion as playing an especially important role in their lives. **Those who would renegotiate the boundaries between church and state must therefore answer a difficult question: Why would we trade a system that has served us so well for one that has served others so poorly?**

It is true that many Americans find the Commandments in accord with their personal beliefs. But we do not count heads before enforcing the First Amendment...Nor can we accept the theory that Americans who do not accept the Commandments' validity are outside the First Amendment's protections. There is no list of approved and disapproved beliefs appended to the First Amendment – and the Amendment's broad terms ("free exercise," "establishment," "religion") do not admit of such a cramped reading. It is true that the Framers lived at a time when our national religious diversity was neither as robust nor as well recognized as it is now. They may not have foreseen the variety of religions for which this nation would eventually provide a home. They surely could not have predicted new religions, some of them born in this country. But they did know that line drawing between religions is an enterprise that, once begun, has no logical stopping point. **They worried that "the same authority which can establish Christianity, in exclusion of all other Religions, may establish with the same ease any particular sect of Christians, in exclusion of all other Sects."** The Religion Clauses, as a result, protect adherents of all religions, as well as those who believe in no religion at all...In my opinion, the display at issue was an establishment of religion in violation of our Constitution...

DISSENT: Justice Scalia...On September 11, 2001, I was attending in Rome, Italy, an international conference of judges and lawyers, principally from Europe and the United States. That night and the next morning virtually all of the participants watched, in their hotel rooms, the address to the nation by the President of the United States concerning the murderous attacks upon the Twin Towers and the Pentagon, in which thousands of Americans had been killed. The address ended, as Presidential addresses often do, with the prayer "God bless America." The next afternoon I was approached by one of the judges from a European country, who, after extending his profound condolences for my country's loss, sadly observed "How I wish that the Head of State of my country, at a similar time of national tragedy and distress, could conclude his address 'God bless _____.' It is of course absolutely forbidden."

As we have seen with all of our Presidents, such a conclusion to a speech is happily not forbidden in the U.S.A., thank **God**.

That is one model of the relationship between church and state – a model spread across Europe by the armies of Napoleon, and reflected in the Constitution of France, which begins "France is a...secular...Republic." Religion is to be strictly excluded from the public forum. This is not, and never was, the model adopted by America. George Washington added to the form of Presidential oath prescribed by Art. II, §1, cl. 8, of the Constitution, the concluding words "so help me God." The Supreme Court under John Marshall opened its sessions with the prayer, "God save the United States and this Honorable Court." The First Congress instituted the practice of beginning its legislative sessions with a prayer. The same week that Congress submitted the Establishment Clause as part of the Bill of Rights for ratification by the States, it enacted legislation providing for paid chaplains in the House and Senate. The day after the First Amendment was proposed, the same Congress that had proposed it requested the President to proclaim "a day of public thanksgiving and prayer, to be observed, by acknowledging, with grateful hearts, the many and signal favours of Almighty God." President Washington offered the first Thanksgiving Proclamation shortly thereafter, devoting November 26, 1789, on behalf of the American people "to the service of that great and glorious Being who is the beneficent author of all the good that is, that was, or that will be,"...thus beginning a tradition of offering gratitude to God that continues today...And of course the First Amendment itself accords religion (and no other manner of belief) special constitutional protection...

With all of this reality (and much more) staring it in the face, how can the Court possibly assert that "the First Amendment mandates governmental neutrality between...religion and nonreligion" and that "manifesting a purpose to favor...adherence to religion generally" is unconstitutional? Who says so? Surely not the words of the Constitution. Surely not the history and traditions that reflect our society's constant understanding of those words. Surely not even the current sense of our society, recently reflected in an Act of Congress adopted unanimously by the Senate and with only 5 nays in the House of Representatives, criticizing a Court of Appeals opinion that had held "under God" in the Pledge of Allegiance unconstitutional (reaffirming the Pledge of Allegiance and the National Motto ("In God We Trust") and stating that the Pledge of Allegiance is "clearly consistent with the text and intent of the Constitution.") Nothing stands behind the Court's assertion that governmental affirmation of the society's belief in God is unconstitutional except the Court's own say-so, citing as support only the unsubstantiated say-so of earlier Courts going back no farther than the mid-20th century...

Today's opinion...admits that it does not rest upon consistently applied principle...When the government relieves churches from the obligation to pay property taxes, when it allows students to absent themselves from public school to take religious classes, and when it exempts religious organizations from generally applicable prohibitions of religious discrimination, it surely means to bestow a benefit on religious practice – but we have approved it. *Walz. Zorach.* Indeed we have even approved (post-*Lemon*) government-led prayer to God. *Marsh*...The Court explained that "to invoke Divine guidance on a public body entrusted with making the laws is not...an 'establishment' of religion or a step toward establishment; it is simply a tolerable acknowledgment of beliefs widely held among the people of this country." (Why, one wonders, is not respect for the Ten Commandments a tolerable acknowledgment of beliefs widely held among the people of this country?)

...Besides appealing to the demonstrably false principle that the government cannot favor religion over irreligion, today's opinion suggests that the posting of the Ten Commandments violates the principle that the government cannot favor one religion over another. That is indeed a valid principle where public aid or assistance to religion is concerned or where the free exercise of religion is at issue (*Church of Lukumi Babalu Aye*), but it necessarily applies in a more limited sense to public acknowledgment of the Creator. If religion in the public forum had to be entirely nondenominational, there could be no religion in the public forum at all. One cannot say the word "God," or "the Almighty," one cannot offer public supplication or thanksgiving, without contradicting the beliefs of some people that there are many gods, or that God or the gods pay no attention to human affairs. With respect to public acknowledgment of religious belief, it is entirely clear from our nation's historical practices that the Establishment Clause permits this disregard of polytheists and believers in unconcerned deities, just as it permits the disregard of devout atheists. The Thanksgiving Proclamation issued by George Washington at the instance of the First Congress was scrupulously nondenominational – but it was monotheistic. In *Marsh* we said that the fact the particular prayers offered in the Nebraska Legislature were "in the Judeo-Christian tradition" posed no additional problem because "there is no indication that the prayer opportunity has been exploited to proselytize or advance any one, or to disparage any other, faith or belief."

Historical practices thus demonstrate that there is a distance between the acknowledgment of a single Creator and the establishment of a religion. The former is, as *Marsh* put it, "a tolerable acknowledgment of beliefs widely held among the people of this country." **The three most popular religions in the United States, Christianity, Judaism, and Islam – which combined account for 97.7% of all believers – are monotheistic. All of them, moreover (Islam included), believe that the Ten Commandments were given by God to Moses, and are divine prescriptions for a virtuous life. Publicly honoring the Ten Commandments is thus indistinguishable, insofar as discriminating against other religions is concerned, from publicly honoring God.** Both practices are recognized across such a broad and diverse range of the population – from Christians to Muslims – that they cannot be reasonably understood as a government endorsement of a particular religious viewpoint...

Finally, I must respond to Justice Stevens' assertion that I would "marginalize the belief systems of more than 7 million Americans" who adhere to religions that are not monotheistic. Surely that is a gross exaggeration. The beliefs of those citizens are entirely protected by the Free Exercise Clause and by those aspects of the Establishment Clause that do not relate to government acknowledgment of the Creator. Invocation of God despite their beliefs is permitted not because nonmonotheistic religions cease to be religions recognized by the religion clauses of the First Amendment, but because **governmental invocation of God is not an establishment.**

> I agree that governmental acknowledgment of God is not an establishment, but, again, isn't there a difference between "under God" in the Pledge and "Thou shall have no other Gods but the Judeo-Christian-Muslim God" in the First Commandment?

Justice Stevens fails to recognize that in the context of public acknowledgments of God there are legitimate competing interests: On the one hand, the interest of that minority in not feeling "excluded"; but on the other, the interest of the overwhelming majority of religious believers in being able to give God thanks and supplication as a people, and with respect to our national endeavors. Our national tradition has resolved that conflict in favor of the majority. It is not for this Court to change a disposition that accounts, many Americans think, for the phenomenon remarked upon in a quotation attributed to various authors, including Bismarck, but which I prefer to associate with Charles de Gaulle: "God watches over little children, drunkards, and the United States of America."

...The acknowledgment of the contribution that religion in general, and the Ten Commandments in particular, have made to our nation's legal and governmental heritage is surely no more of a step towards establishment of religion than was the practice of legislative prayer we approved in *Marsh*, and it seems to be on par with the inclusion of a crèche or a Menorah in a "Holiday" display that incorporates other secular symbols, see *Lynch; Allegheny*. The parallels between this case and *Marsh* and *Lynch* are sufficiently compelling that they ought to decide this case, even under the Court's misguided Establishment Clause jurisprudence.

Are there differences between a non-denominational prayer to open a legislative session, a nativity scene with Santa Claus junk around it, and the first two Commandments? Take a close look and decide whether, as Justice Scalia suggests, "the parallels are compelling." Finally, please picture yourself a follower of a non-Christian religion going into a courthouse where justice is expected to be blind, but you find that justice, if determined by what is hanging on the wall, is defined only in Christian terms. If that does not persuade, then picture yourself as a Christian seeking justice in a courthouse who's chief judge decides to place an image of Buddha on the wall behind him. Of course, I believe *Marsh* was wrongly decided and, even more so, that *Lynch* and *Allegheny* were very bad decisions. However, even that trilogy can be reconciled with a decision to deny the Ten Commandments display in a courthouse.

...The constitutional problem, the Court says, is with the Counties themselves. The Court adds in a footnote: "One consequence of taking account of the purpose underlying past actions is that the same government action may be constitutional if taken in the first instance and unconstitutional if it has a sectarian heritage." This inconsistency may be explicable in theory, but I suspect that the "objective observer" with whom the Court is so concerned will recognize its absurdity in practice...Displays erected in silence (and under the direction of good legal advice) are permissible, while those hung after discussion and debate are deemed unconstitutional. Reduction of the Establishment Clause to such minutiae trivializes the Clause's protection against religious establishment; indeed, it may inflame religious passions by making the passing comments of every government official the subject of endless litigation.

> Absolutely agreed on that point! The history of how these displays got on the wall should be irrelevant to the issues in this case.

...What Justice Kennedy said of the crèche in *Allegheny* is equally true of the Counties' original Ten Commandments displays:

> No one was compelled to observe or participate in any religious ceremony or activity. The counties did not contribute significant amounts of tax money to serve the cause of one religious faith. The Ten Commandments are purely passive symbols of the religious foundation for many of our laws and governmental institutions. Passersby who disagree with the message conveyed by the displays are free to ignore them, or even to turn their backs, just as they are free to do when they disagree with any other form of government speech.

Nor is it the case that a solo display of the Ten Commandments advances any one faith. They are assuredly a religious symbol, but they are not so closely associated with a single religious belief that their display can reasonably be understood as preferring one religious sect over another. The Ten Commandments are recognized by Judaism, Christianity, and Islam alike as divinely given...I would reverse the judgment of the Court of Appeals.

One more "against."

> ### First Amendment Scoreboard
> Rulings "for" Religion: 19 --- Rulings "against" Religion: 12

Again, let us summarize in chronological fashion.

1980: In *Stone v. Graham* we learned that government cannot post the Ten Commandments in public school rooms because they have no secular legislative purpose.

History Lessons: The Commandments do not confine themselves to arguably secular matters, such as honoring one's parents, killing or murder, adultery, stealing, false witness, and covetousness. Rather, the first part of the Commandments concerns the religious duties of believers: worshiping the Lord God alone, avoiding idolatry, not using the Lord's name in vain, and observing the Sabbath Day.

Dicta: The Ten Commandments may be integrated into the school curriculum, where the Bible may constitutionally be used in an appropriate study of history, civilization, ethics, or comparative religion.

2005: In *Van Orden v. Perry* we learned that the Ten Commandments placed amongst numerous other historical monuments on the Texas Capitol lawn is permissible.

Dicta: Words like "God" are not vulgarities for which the shock value diminishes with each successive utterance. The wall that separates the church from the state does not prohibit the government from acknowledging the religious beliefs and practices of the American people, nor does it require governments to hide works of art or historic memorabilia from public view just because they also have religious significance. **The state may provide its schoolchildren and adult citizens with educational materials that explain the important role that our forebears' faith in God played in their decisions to select America as a refuge from religious persecution, to declare their independence from the British Crown, and to conceive a new nation.**

2005: In *McCreary County v. ACLU* we learned that the Ten Commandments are prohibited from being hung in a courtroom.

Dicta (concurrence): Per Justice O'Connor, "Why would we trade a system that has served us so well for one that has served others so poorly?"

THE SUGGESTED CHRISTIAN RESPONSE

<u>Lost Causes</u>:

For the same reason that displaying the Ten Commandments in public grade schools and courthouses is a lost cause, Jackson and Ava Elliot will <u>win</u> in their quest to have the Creed of Scientology removed in Berkley, California.

<u>Causes to Champion</u>:

What do you think is more important - hanging the Ten Commandments in public schools or knowing them (and, then, living them)?

Do you know them?

Do you teach them to your children?

Do you have a copy hanging in your home?

Do you live them?

Please, people, let us focus on the mission of Christ. I am quite sure He does not need pieces of paper hung here and there nearly as much as He needs willing doers of His Word.

I love the Gideons. You know, the Bible-in-every-hotel folks. I think their mission is to be highly praised. However, let us Christians never rely upon Bible placement and Ten Commandment location to absolve us of the responsibility of spreading the Word of Christ with our tongues as well as the manner in which we live our lives.

Chapter Fourteen

ESTABLISHMENT:
EQUAL OPPORTUNITY

The Berkley School District has always enjoyed good public relations with the community. So much so that they decided there was no reason to let their building go unused after school hours. They adopted a resolution that permitted various not-for-profit community groups the scheduled use of their building free of charge. Groups sign up on a first-come first-served basis for up to two hours per week.

Ava soon found that she was not the only one upset with some of the anti-Christian goings-on in the schools. In her investigation to prepare herself for homeschooling, she ran across others (mostly non-natives of Berkley) who were looking into that as well. They decided to form a not-for-profit corporation for the purpose of supporting homeschoolers from a Christian perspective. At their meetings they prayed, studied the Bible, and even sought converts to the faith. As they grew in number, they needed a larger place to meet, so Ava suggested applying for a weekly spot at the very school where her daughter was enrolled.

Only one problem – her application was denied. As the superintendent put it, "separation of church and state" would not permit a "religious-based organization" to use public property.

"Oh, for heaven's sake," thought Ava. "Then, why are you praying in the schools? Why the Scientology Creed on the wall?" What to do?

We're going to the heartland - Kansas City.

WIDMAR v. VINCENT
SUPREME COURT OF THE UNITED STATES
454 U.S. 263
Dec. 8, 1981
[8 -1]

OPINION: Justice White...[A state university makes its facilities generally available for the activities of registered student groups. May it close its facilities to a registered student group desiring to use the facilities for religious worship and discussion?]

[The University's regulation prohibiting the use of University buildings for purposes of religious worship or teaching is invalid.]

[**Having once created a forum generally open for use by student groups**, the University of Missouri at Kansas City assumed an obligation to justify its discrimination and exclusions under applicable constitutional norms. In order to justify discriminatory exclusion from a public forum based on the religious content of a group's intended speech, it must show that its regulation is necessary to serve a compelling state interest and that it is narrowly drawn to achieve that end. The University claims a compelling state interest in maintaining strict separation of church and State. The parties agree that...an open forum policy (including nondiscrimination against religious speech) would have a secular purpose and would avoid entanglement with religion. The State argued, however, that allowing religious groups to share the limited public forum would have the "primary effect" of advancing religion. The question is not whether the creation of a religious forum would violate the Establishment Clause. The question is, given that the University has opened its facilities for use by student groups, can it now exclude groups because of the content of their speech? **An open forum does not confer any imprimatur of state approval on religious sects or practices.** The state's asserted interest of "separation" is limited by the Free Exercise and Free Speech Clauses.]

> In other words, the University of Missouri could not discriminate against this religious group. Hmm! Looks like university students can say "God."

DISSENT: Justice White...[Not Provided.]

Here is a score "for" religion that really *is* a good result.

> First Amendment Scoreboard
>
> Rulings "for" Religion: 20 --- Rulings "against" Religion: 12

Back to New York.

***Lamb's Chapel v. Center Moriches School District* (1993):** [9 – 0] Justice White...[New York law authorizes local school boards to adopt reasonable regulations for the use of school property when it is not in use for school purposes. Among the permitted uses is the holding of social, civic, and recreational meetings and entertainment pertaining to the welfare of the community. They shall be nonexclusive and open to the general public. Among the regulations adopted by this school board is a rule against use by any group for religious purposes. Whether it violates the Free Speech Clause to deny a church access to the property to exhibit for public viewing a film series dealing with family and child rearing issues faced by parents today?]

[Held: It is unconstitutional to deny this church group access.]

Although this was addressed primarily as a free speech issue, it is important because most of the population would likely be surprised that the Supreme

Court actually allows a church to use public school property for any reason. Are you surprised? If this happens in your community, someone will charge the school board with acting unconstitutionally and that someone would be flat wrong! **Please help stamp out ignorance with me.** It is also very important to understand that this church would not have been allowed to use the school for showing the film if the school had not opened its doors for public use in the first instance. Score one more "for" religion.

First Amendment Scoreboard

Rulings "for" Religion: 21 --- Rulings "against" Religion: 12

Staying in New York, let's go to Milford.

GOOD NEWS CLUB v. MILFORD CENTRAL SCHOOL
SUPREME COURT OF THE UNITED STATES
533 U.S. 98
June 11, 2001
[6 – 3]

OPINION: Justice Thomas...[1] Whether Milford Central School violated the free speech rights of the Good News Club when it excluded the Club from meeting after hours at the school? [2] Whether any such violation is justified by Milford's concern that permitting the Club's activities would violate the Establishment Clause? We conclude that Milford's restriction violates the Club's free speech rights and that no Establishment Clause concern justifies that violation.

[A New York State statute] authorizes local school boards to adopt regulations governing the use of their school facilities [and] enumerates several purposes for which local boards may open their schools to public use. In 1992, Milford Central School enacted a community use policy adopting seven of [the statute's] purposes for which its building could be used after school, [two of which are relevant here.]

> Let us not forget that if the school had never permitted any groups to use its facilities, then it would not have to permit this group to use it. The starting point is a policy of opening up schools for public after-hours use.

First, district residents may use the school for "instruction in any branch of education, learning or the arts." Second, the school is available for "social, civic and recreational meetings and entertainment events, and other uses pertaining to the welfare of the community, provided that such uses shall be nonexclusive and shall be opened to the general public."

...The...local Good News Club is a private Christian organization for children ages 6 to 12. Pursuant to Milford's policy,...the GNC... submitted a request to Dr. Robert McGruder, interim superintendent of the district, in which they sought permission to hold the Club's weekly after-school meetings in the school cafeteria [which McGruder formally denied] on the ground that the proposed use – to have "a fun time of singing songs, hearing a Bible lesson and memorizing scripture" – was "the equivalent of religious worship." According to McGruder, the community use policy, which prohibits use "by an individual or organization for religious purposes," foreclosed the Club's activities...

The Club sent a set of materials used or distributed at the meetings and the following description of its meeting [to Milford's attorney to explain who they are and what they do]:

[As attendance is taken, if a child who is called] recites a Bible verse the child receives a treat. After attendance, the Club sings songs. Next, Club members engage in games that involve learning Bible verses...A Bible story [is told with explanation as to how it applies to Club members' lives.] The Club closes with prayer...

...[Milford concluded that the proposed activities] were not a discussion of secular subjects such as child rearing, development of character and development of morals from a religious perspective, but were in fact the equivalent of religious instruction itself. [The GNC request was denied] "for the purpose of conducting religious instruction and Bible study." GNC...filed an action...against Milford...alleging that Milford's denial of its application violated its free speech rights under the First and Fourteenth Amendments and its right to equal protection...

The District Court [held in favor of Milford and] found that the Club's "subject matter is decidedly religious in nature, and not merely a discussion of secular matters from a religious perspective that is otherwise permitted under Milford's use policies." Because the school had not permitted other groups that provided religious instruction to use its limited public forum, the court held that the school could deny access to the Club without engaging in unconstitutional viewpoint discrimination. The court also rejected the Club's equal protection claim...

The Court of Appeals...affirmed. First, the court rejected the Club's contention that Milford's restriction against allowing religious instruction in its facilities is unreasonable. Second, it held that, because the subject matter of the Club's activities is "quintessentially religious" and the activities "fall outside the bounds of pure 'moral and character development,'" Milford's policy of excluding the Club's meetings was constitutional subject discrimination, not unconstitutional viewpoint discrimination... [We reverse.]

When the State establishes a limited public forum, the State is not required to...allow persons to engage in every type of speech. The State may be justified "in reserving its forum for certain groups or for the discussion of certain topics." *Rosenberger v. Rector; Lamb's Chapel.* The State's power to restrict speech, however, is not without limits. The restriction must not discriminate against speech on the basis of viewpoint (*Rosenberger*) and the restriction must be "reasonable in light of the purpose served by the forum." *Cornelius v. NAACP* (1985).

Applying this test, we first address whether the exclusion constituted viewpoint discrimination...In *Lamb's Chapel,* we held that a school district violated the Free Speech Clause of the First Amendment when it excluded a private group from presenting films at the school based solely on the films' discussion of family values from a religious perspective...In *Rosenberger,* we held that a university's refusal to fund a student publication because the publication addressed issues from a religious perspective violated the Free Speech Clause. Concluding that Milford's exclusion of the Good News Club based on its religious nature is indistinguishable from the exclusions in these cases, we hold that the exclusion constitutes viewpoint discrimination [and, therefore, do not] need to decide whether it is unreasonable in light of the purposes served by the forum.

Milford has opened its limited public forum to activities that serve a variety of purposes, including events "pertaining to the welfare of the community." Milford interprets its policy to permit discussions of subjects such as child rearing, and of "the development of character and morals from a religious perspective." For example, this policy would allow someone to use Aesop's Fables to teach children moral values. Additionally, a group could sponsor a debate on whether there should be a constitutional amendment to permit prayer in public schools and the Boy Scouts could meet "to influence a boy's character, development and spiritual growth." In short, any group that "promotes the moral and character development of children" is eligible to use the school building.

Just as there is no question that teaching morals and character development to children is a permissible purpose under Milford's policy, it is clear that the Club teaches morals and character development to children. For example, no one disputes that the Club instructs children to overcome feelings of jealousy, to treat others well regardless of how they treat the children, and to be obedient, even if it does so in a nonsecular way. Nonetheless, because Milford found the Club's activities to be…"the equivalent of religious instruction itself" – it excluded the Club…

Applying *Lamb's Chapel*, we find it quite clear that Milford engaged in viewpoint discrimination when it excluded the Club from the after school forum. In *Lamb's Chapel*, the local New York school district similarly had adopted §414's "social, civic or recreational use" category as a permitted use in its limited public forum. The district also prohibited use "by any group for religious purposes." Citing this prohibition, the school district excluded a church that wanted to present films teaching family values from a Christian perspective. We held that, because the films "no doubt dealt with a subject otherwise permissible" under the rule, the teaching of family values, the district's exclusion of the church was unconstitutional viewpoint discrimination.

Like the church in *Lamb's Chapel*, the Club seeks to address a subject otherwise permitted under the rule, the teaching of morals and character, from a religious standpoint. Certainly, one could have characterized the film presentation in *Lamb's Chapel* as a religious use, as the Court of Appeals did. And one easily could conclude that the film's purpose to instruct that "society's slide toward humanism...can only be counterbalanced by a loving home where Christian values are instilled from an early age" was "quintessentially religious." The only apparent difference between the activity of Lamb's Chapel and the activities of the Good News Club is that the Club chooses to teach moral lessons from a Christian perspective through live storytelling and prayer, whereas Lamb's Chapel taught lessons through films. This distinction is inconsequential. Both modes of speech use a religious viewpoint. Thus, the exclusion of the GNC activities, like the exclusion of Lamb's Chapel's films, constitutes unconstitutional viewpoint discrimination...

The Court of Appeals...believed that its characterization of the Club's activities as religious in nature warranted treating the Club's activities as different in kind from the other activities permitted by the school (i.e., the Club "is doing something other than simply teaching moral values"). The "Christian viewpoint" is unique, according to the court, because it contains an "additional layer" that other kinds of viewpoints do not. That is, the Club "is focused on teaching children how to cultivate their relationship with God through Jesus Christ," which it characterized as "quintessentially religious." With these observations, the court concluded that, because the Club's activities "fall outside the bounds of pure 'moral and character development,'" the exclusion did not constitute viewpoint discrimination.

We disagree that something that is "quintessentially religious"...cannot also be characterized properly as the teaching of morals and character development from a particular viewpoint...What matters for purposes of the Free Speech Clause is that we can see no logical difference in kind between the invocation of Christianity by the Club and the invocation of teamwork, loyalty, or patriotism by other associations to provide a foundation for their lessons. It is apparent that the unstated principle of the Court of Appeals' reasoning is its conclusion that any time religious instruction and prayer are used to discuss morals and character, the discussion is simply not a "pure" discussion of those issues. According to the Court of Appeals, reliance on Christian principles taints moral and character instruction in a way that other foundations for thought or viewpoints do not. We, however, have never reached such a conclusion. Instead, we reaffirm...that speech discussing otherwise permissible subjects cannot be excluded from a limited public forum on the ground that the subject is discussed from a religious viewpoint. Thus, we conclude that Milford's exclusion of the Club from use of the school, pursuant to its community use policy, constitutes impermissible viewpoint discrimination.

Milford argues that, even if its restriction constitutes viewpoint discrimination, its interest in not violating the Establishment Clause outweighs the Club's interest in gaining equal access to the school's facilities...We disagree [and conclude] that the school has no valid Establishment Clause interest...In *Lamb's Chapel*, we explained that "the showing of the film series would not have been during school hours, would not have been sponsored by the school, and would have been open to the public, not just to church members." Accordingly, we found that "there would have been no realistic danger that the community would think that the District was endorsing religion or any particular creed." Likewise, in *Widmar*, where the university's forum was already available to other groups, this Court concluded that there was no Establishment Clause problem...

As in *Lamb's Chapel*, the GNC meetings were held after school hours, not sponsored by the school, and open to any student who obtained parental consent, not just to Club members. As in *Widmar*, Milford made its forum available to other organizations. The Club's activities are materially indistinguishable from those in *Lamb's Chapel* and *Widmar*. Thus, Milford's reliance on the Establishment Clause is unavailing.

Milford attempts to distinguish *Lamb's Chapel* and *Widmar* by emphasizing that Milford's policy involves elementary school children. According to

Milford, children will perceive that the school is endorsing the Club and will feel coercive pressure to participate, because the Club's activities take place on school grounds, even though they occur during non-school hours. This argument is unpersuasive.

First, we have held that "a significant factor in upholding governmental programs in the face of Establishment Clause attack is their neutrality towards religion."…Milford's implication that granting access to the Club would do damage to the neutrality principle defies logic. For the "guarantee of neutrality is respected, not offended, when the government, following neutral criteria and even-handed policies, extends benefits to recipients whose ideologies and viewpoints, including religious ones, are broad and diverse." **The Good News Club seeks nothing more than to be treated neutrally and given access to speak about the same topics as are other groups.** Because allowing the Club to speak on school grounds would ensure neutrality, not threaten it, Milford faces an uphill battle in arguing that the Establishment clause compels it to exclude the Good News Club.

Second, to the extent we consider whether the community would feel coercive pressure to engage in the Club's activities, the relevant community would be the parents, not the elementary school children. It is the parents who choose whether their children will attend the Good News Club meetings. Because the children cannot attend without their parents' permission, they cannot be coerced into engaging in the Good News Club's religious activities. Milford does not suggest that the parents of elementary school children would be confused about whether the school was endorsing religion. Nor do we believe that such an argument could be reasonably advanced.

Third, whatever significance we may have assigned in the Establishment Clause context to the suggestion that elementary school children are more impressionable than adults,…we have never extended our Establishment Clause jurisprudence to foreclose private religious conduct during non-school hours merely because it takes place on school premises where elementary school children may be present…

Milford cites *Lee v. Weisman* for the proposition that "there are heightened concerns with protecting freedom of conscience from the subtle coercive pressure in the elementary and secondary public schools." In *Lee*, however, we concluded that attendance at the graduation exercise was obligatory. See also *Santa Fe Independent School Dist. v. Doe* (holding the school's policy of permitting prayer at football games unconstitutional where the activity took place during a school-sponsored event and not in a public forum). We did not place independent significance on the fact that the graduation exercise might take place on school premises. Here, where the school facilities are being used for a non-school function and there is no government sponsorship of the Club's activities, *Lee* is inapposite...

We cannot say the danger that children would misperceive the endorsement of religion is any greater than the danger that they would perceive a hostility toward the religious viewpoint if the Club were excluded from the public forum...We conclude that permitting the Club to meet on the school's premises would not have violated the Establishment Clause...[The judgment of the Court of Appeals is reversed.]

CONCURRENCE: Justice Scalia...The disagreement...regards the portions of the Club's meetings that are not "purely" "discussions" of morality and character from a religious viewpoint. The Club, for example, urges children "who already believe in the Lord Jesus as their Savior" to "stop and ask God for the strength and the 'want'...to obey Him," and it invites children who "don't know Jesus as Savior" to "trust the Lord Jesus to be their Savior from sin." The dissenters and the Second Circuit say that the presence of such additional speech, because it is purely religious, transforms the Club's meetings into something different in kind from other, nonreligious activities that teach moral and character development. Therefore, the argument goes, excluding the Club is not viewpoint discrimination. I disagree...

From no other group does respondent require the sterility of speech that it demands of petitioners. The Boy Scouts could undoubtedly buttress their exhortations to keep "morally straight" and live "clean" lives...by giving reasons why that is a good idea – because parents want and expect it, because it will make the scouts "better" and "more successful" people, because it will emulate such admired past Scouts as former President Gerald Ford.

The Club, however, may only discuss morals and character, and cannot give its reasons why they should be fostered – because God wants and expects it, because it will make the Club members "saintly" people, and because it emulates Jesus Christ. The Club may not, in other words, independently discuss the religious premise on which its views are based – that God exists and His assistance is necessary to morality. It may not defend the premise, and it absolutely must not seek to persuade the children that the premise is true. The children must, so to say, take it on faith. This is blatant viewpoint discrimination…

The dissenters emphasize that the religious speech used by the Club as the foundation for its views on morals and character is not just any type of religious speech – although they cannot agree exactly what type of religious speech it is. In Justice Stevens' view, it is speech "aimed principally at proselytizing or inculcating belief in a particular religious faith." This does not, to begin with, distinguish *Rosenberger*, which also involved proselytizing speech…But, in addition, it does not distinguish the Club's activities from those of the other groups using respondent's forum – which have not, as Justice Stevens suggests, been restricted to roundtable "discussions" of moral issues. Those groups may seek to inculcate children with their beliefs, and they may furthermore "recruit others to join their respective groups." The Club must therefore have liberty to do the same, even if, as Justice Stevens fears…, its actions may prove (shudder) divisive…

Justice Souter, while agreeing that the Club's religious speech "may be characterized as proselytizing," thinks that it is even more clearly excludable from respondent's forum because it is essentially "an evangelical service of worship." But we have previously rejected the attempt to distinguish worship from other religious speech, saying that "the distinction has no intelligible content," and further, no "relevance" to the constitutional issue. *Murdock v. Pennsylvania* (refusing to distinguish evangelism from worship). Those holdings are surely proved correct today by the dissenters' inability to agree, even between themselves, into which subcategory of religious speech the Club's activities fell. If the distinction did have content, it would be beyond the courts' competence to administer. *Widmar v. Vincent; Lee v. Weisman.* ("I can hardly imagine a subject less amenable to the competence of the federal judiciary, or more deliberately to be avoided where possible," than "comparative theology.") And if courts (and other government officials) were competent, applying the distinction would require state monitoring of private, religious speech with a degree of pervasiveness that we have previously found unacceptable. *Rosenberger; Widmar.* I will not endorse an approach that suffers such a wondrous diversity of flaws. With these words of explanation, I join the opinion of the Court...

DISSENT: Justice Stevens...[Not provided.]

DISSENT: Justice Souter [joined by Justice Ginsburg]...It is beyond question that Good News intends to use the public school premises not for the mere discussion of a subject from a particular, Christian point of view, but for an evangelical service of worship calling children to commit themselves in an act of Christian conversion...

We can add the information in *Widmar* to the list of things the Supreme Court has not done. In other words, a religious student group cannot be denied a place to meet at a university even if it meets to "worship" under the facts of that case. Who knew?

In *Widmar*, we held that the Establishment Clause did not bar a religious student group from using a public university's meeting space for worship as well as discussion. As for the reasonable observers who might perceive government endorsement of religion, we pointed out that the forum was used by university students, who "are, of course, young adults," and, as such, "are less impressionable than younger students and should be able to appreciate that the University's policy is one of neutrality toward religion."... And if all that had not been enough to show that the university-student use would probably create no impression of religious endorsement, we pointed out that the university in that case had issued a student handbook with the explicit disclaimer that "the University's name will not 'be identified in any way with the aims, policies, programs, products, or opinions of any organization or its members.'"

Lamb's Chapel involved an evening film series on child-rearing open to the general public (and, given the subject matter, directed at an adult audience).

There, school property "had repeatedly been used by a wide variety of private organizations," and we could say with some assurance that "under these circumstances...there would have been no realistic danger that the community would think that the District was endorsing religion or any particular creed..."

What we know about this case looks very little like *Widmar* or *Lamb's Chapel*. The cohort addressed by Good News is not university students with relative maturity, or even high school pupils, but elementary school children as young as six. The Establishment Clause cases have consistently recognized the particular impressionability of school children...and the special protection required for those in the elementary grades in the school forum. We have held the difference between college students and grade school pupils to be a "distinction that warrants a difference in constitutional results."

...In *Widmar*, the nature of the university campus and the sheer number of activities offered precluded the reasonable college observer from seeing government endorsement in any one of them, and so did the time and variety of community use in the *Lamb's Chapel* case.

See also *Rosenberger*. ("Given this wide array of nonreligious, antireligious and competing religious viewpoints in the forum supported by the University, any perception that the University endorses one particular viewpoint would be illogical.")...The timing and format of Good News's gatherings, on the other hand, may well affirmatively suggest the imprimatur of officialdom in the minds of the young children...

Justices Souter and Ginsburg actually believe that **elementary** school children take time to contemplate who authorizes the GNC meetings, much less that "government" must be the one "approving" of them. Perhaps they have lost touch with reality on this one.

This is a good victory "for" religion.

```
┌─────────────────────────────────────────────────────┐
│                                                     │
│              First Amendment Scoreboard             │
│   Rulings "for" Religion: 22 --- Rulings "against" Religion: 12   │
│                                                     │
└─────────────────────────────────────────────────────┘
```

Again, let's summarize in chronological fashion.

1981: In *Widmar v. Vincent* we learned that once a university opens its doors for use by student groups, it cannot exclude religious groups even if their purpose is to worship God.

Principles: At the university level, the Court concludes that the appearance of state approval for a religious group or any group is not justified.

1993: In *Lamb's Chapel v. Center Moriches School District* we learned that once a local public school board opens its doors for use by community groups, it cannot exclude churches whose purpose is obviously religious in nature.

2001: In *Good News Club v. Milford Central School* we learned that the principles of *Lamb's Chapel* were upheld even for a religious club whose subjects are elementary school children.

THE SUGGESTED CHRISTIAN RESPONSE

Causes to Champion:

This topic, happily, is a *good news* story, pun intended. The message to Christians is simple. Correct your fellow citizens when they criticize the use of public property for religious purposes if government has opened its doors to use by community groups. Show them these cases and, perhaps, they will absolve themselves of at least some degree of misinformation. And, by the way, Ava will win her claim to equal access to school property use in Berkley. This is the type of cause worth fighting for.

Chapter Fifteen

ESTABLISHMENT:
COMMON RESPECT

Last stop! Elk Grove, California.

ELK GROVE UNIFIED SCHOOL DISTRICT v. NEWDOW
SUPREME COURT OF THE UNITED STATES
542 U.S. 1
June 14, 2004
[8 – 0]

OPINION: Justice Stevens...[Justice Scalia did not participate.] Each day elementary school teachers in the Elk Grove Unified School District lead their classes in a group recitation of the Pledge of Allegiance...Michael A. Newdow is an atheist whose daughter participates in that daily exercise. Because the Pledge contains the words "under God," he views the School District's policy as a religious indoctrination of his child that violates the First Amendment. A divided panel of the Court of Appeals...agreed... We...conclude that Newdow lacks standing and therefore reverse the Court of Appeals' decision...

> Not just anyone can file a lawsuit. You have to have some "skin in the game."

The Pledge of Allegiance was initially conceived more than a century ago. As part of the nationwide interest in commemorating the 400th anniversary of Christopher Columbus' discovery of America, a widely circulated national magazine for youth proposed in 1892 that pupils recite the following affirmation: "I pledge allegiance to my Flag and the Republic for which it stands: one Nation indivisible, with Liberty and Justice for all." In the 1920s, the National Flag Conferences replaced the phrase "my Flag" with "the flag of the United States of America."

In 1942, in the midst of World War II, Congress adopted, and the President signed, a Joint Resolution codifying a detailed set of "rules and customs pertaining to the display and use of the flag of the United States of America." Section 7 of this codification provided in full:

> That the pledge of allegiance to the flag, "I pledge allegiance to the flag of the United States of America and to the Republic for which it stands, one Nation indivisible, with liberty and justice for all," be rendered by standing with the right hand over the heart; extending the right hand, palm upward, toward the flag at the words "to the flag" and holding this position until the end, when the hand drops to the side. However, civilians will always show full respect to the flag when the pledge is given by merely standing at attention, men removing the headdress. Persons in uniform shall render the military salute.

This resolution...confirmed the importance of the flag as a symbol of our nation's indivisibility and commitment to the concept of liberty.

Congress revisited the Pledge of Allegiance 12 years later when it amended the text to add the words "under God." The House Report that accompanied the legislation observed that, "from the time of our earliest history our peoples and our institutions have reflected the traditional concept that our nation was founded on a fundamental belief in God." The resulting text is the Pledge as we know it today.

...Under California law, "every public elementary school" must begin each day with "appropriate patriotic exercises." The statute provides that "the giving of the Pledge of Allegiance to the Flag of the United States of America shall satisfy" this requirement. The Elk Grove Unified School District has implemented the state law by requiring that "each elementary school class recite the pledge of allegiance to the flag once each day." Consistent with our case law, the School District permits students who object on religious grounds to abstain from the recitation. *West Virginia Bd. of Education v. Barnette.*

In March 2000, Newdow filed suit...At the time of filing, Newdow's daughter was enrolled in kindergarten in the Elk Grove Unified School District and participated in the daily recitation of the Pledge...The complaint explains that Newdow is an atheist who was ordained more than 20 years ago in a ministry that "espouses the religious philosophy that the true and eternal bonds of righteousness and virtue stem from reason rather than mythology." The complaint seeks a declaration that the 1954 Act's addition of the words "under God" violated the Establishment and Free Exercise Clauses of the United States Constitution, as well as an injunction against the School District's policy requiring daily recitation of the Pledge...

In our view, it is improper for the federal courts to entertain a claim by a plaintiff whose standing to sue is founded on family law rights that are in dispute when prosecution of the lawsuit may have an adverse effect on the person who is the source of the plaintiff's claimed standing...There is a vast difference between Newdow's right to communicate with his child – which both California law and the First Amendment recognize – and his claimed right to shield his daughter from influences to which she is exposed in school despite the terms of the custody order. We conclude that...Newdow lacks prudential standing to bring this suit in federal court. The judgment of the Court of Appeals is reversed.

> Newdow did not have custody of his daughter, so he was not the proper person to bring suit on his daughter's behalf. The majority, therefore, reversed his case without ruling on the question he wanted addressed.

CONCURRENCE: Chief Justice Rehnquist...On the merits, I conclude that the Elk Grove Unified School District policy that requires teachers to lead willing students in reciting the Pledge of Allegiance, which includes the words "under God," does not violate the Establishment Clause of the First Amendment...

> Justice Rehnquist, however, wanted to state how he felt about the question Newdow wanted answered. All of his concurrence is, therefore, dicta.

Congress amended the Pledge to include the phrase "under God" in 1954. The amendment's sponsor...said its purpose was to contrast this country's belief in God with the Soviet Union's embrace of atheism... Following the decision of the Court of Appeals in this case, Congress passed legislation that made extensive findings about the historic role of religion in the political development of the nation and reaffirmed the text of the Pledge. To the millions of people who regularly recite the Pledge, and who have no access to, or concern with, such legislation or legislative history, "under God" might mean several different things: that God has guided the destiny of the United States, for example, or that the United States exists under God's authority. How much consideration anyone gives to the phrase probably varies, since the Pledge itself is a patriotic observance focused primarily on the flag and the nation, and only secondarily on the description of the nation.

The phrase "under God" in the Pledge seems, as a historical matter, to sum up the attitude of the nation's leaders...Examples of patriotic invocations of God and official acknowledgments of religion's role in our nation's history abound. [Justice Rehnquist refers to Washington's inaugural prayer, Thanksgiving proclamations of numerous presidents, and Lincoln's Gettysburg Address.] The motto "In God We Trust" first appeared on the country's coins during the Civil War...In 1956, Congress declared that the motto of the United States would be "In God We Trust." Our Court Marshal's opening proclamation concludes with the words "God save the United States and this honorable Court." The language goes back at least as far as 1827. All of these events strongly suggest that our national culture allows public recognition of our nation's religious history and character...

Notwithstanding the voluntary nature of the School District policy, the Court of Appeals, by a divided vote, held that the policy violates the Establishment Clause of the First Amendment because it "impermissibly coerces a religious act." To reach this result, the court relied primarily on our decision in *Lee v. Weisman*. That case arose out of a graduation ceremony for a public high school in Providence, Rhode Island. The ceremony was begun with an invocation, and ended with a benediction, given by a local rabbi. The Court held that even though attendance at the ceremony was voluntary, students who objected to the prayers would nonetheless feel coerced to attend and to stand during each prayer. But the Court throughout its opinion referred to the prayer as "an explicit religious exercise" and "a formal religious exercise."

I do not believe that the phrase "under God" in the Pledge converts its recital into a "religious exercise" of the sort described in *Lee*. Instead, it is a declaration of belief in allegiance and loyalty to the United States flag and the Republic that it represents. The phrase "under God" is in no sense a prayer, nor an endorsement of any religion, but a simple recognition of the fact...that: "From the time of our earliest history our peoples and our institutions have reflected the traditional concept that our nation was founded on a fundamental belief in God." Reciting the Pledge, or listening to others recite it, is a patriotic exercise, not a religious one; participants promise fidelity to our flag and our nation, not to any particular God, faith or church.

There is no doubt that respondent is sincere in his atheism and rejection of a belief in God. But the mere fact that he disagrees with this part of the Pledge does not give him veto power over the decision of the public schools that willing participants should pledge allegiance to the flag in the manner prescribed by Congress. There may be others who disagree, not with the phrase "under God," but with the phrase "with liberty and justice for all." However, surely that would not give such objectors the right to veto the holding of such a ceremony by those willing to participate. Only if it can be said that the phrase "under God" somehow tends to the establishment of a religion in violation of the First Amendment can respondent's claim succeed, where one based on objections to "with liberty and justice for all" fails. Our cases have broadly interpreted this phrase, but none have gone anywhere near as far as the decision of the Court of Appeals in this case. The recital, in a patriotic ceremony pledging allegiance to the flag and to the nation, of the descriptive phrase "under God" cannot possibly lead to the establishment of a religion, or anything like it...

The Constitution only requires that schoolchildren be entitled to abstain from the ceremony if they choose to do so. To give the parent of such a child a sort of "heckler's veto" over a patriotic ceremony willingly participated in by other students, simply because the Pledge of Allegiance contains the descriptive phrase "under God," is an unwarranted extension of the Establishment Clause, an extension which would have the unfortunate effect of prohibiting a commendable patriotic observance.

CONCURRENCE: Justice O'Connor...[Not provided.]

CONCURRENCE: Justice Thomas...[Not provided.]

This is a good victory "for" religion, even if it is just dicta.

First Amendment Scoreboard

Rulings "for" Religion: 23 --- Rulings "against" Religion: 12

THE SUGGESTED CHRISTIAN RESPONSE

Causes to Champion:

"Common Respect" is the chosen title of this final chapter on the substantive law. There are some topics that should never rise to the level of debate, much less litigation.

As I said in the Preface, I am hard pressed to understand what a person who professes the "virtues" of believing in nothing has to gain by fighting for the loss of what the rest of us "fools" hold dear. Why do atheists care if the majoritarian profession of trust in God remains on our coins? Why is it not counted a virtue by atheists to maintain respectful acknowledgment for what the rest of us do believe?

Issues such as presidents adding "so help me God" to the end of their oath of office or elected representatives ending a speech with "God bless America" do not fall under this title. These are matters of free speech for the speaker – end of issue. The difference with the phrases "under God" in the Pledge and "In God We Trust" on our coins is that in these instances government is the fundamental author of the words, not the individual.

I had a discussion recently with a man who professes to be an atheist. He is both highly intelligent and a truly good man. The topic was whether or not I felt the Constitution required our government to stop minting our nation's motto on our coins.

If you can believe it, the discussion started getting heated because he was so highly offended by having to look at "In God We Trust" on the coins of our nation. When I pointed out that this was simply a statement by the majority that we believe in a higher being and everyone knows it is not meant to apply to all of us, his response was that the ranks of atheists are growing, are larger than might be expected, and everyone understands the "God" of our coins to be the Judeo-Christian God of Abraham. I simply believe that is unreasonable.

We also believe in the freedom a representative democracy provides. That does not mean that for those who believe a dictatorship is the way to go, we must remove the "land of the free" from our anthem. With all due respect, please "get over it."

Recently, the very liberal Ninth Circuit Court of Appeals in San Francisco upheld the use of "under God" in the Pledge as well as the motto on our coins. Guess who the complainant was? Right – Michael Newdow, the perennial-atheist plaintiff. If common respect issues of this type ever do reach the Supreme Court on their merits, I will go out on a limb and predict they will all be upheld, thank God.

In yet another recent example of the extreme, a small group of atheists got in a tizzy over the plan of the U.S. Postal Service to issue a Mother Teresa stamp. Amanda, Charley, and Sean may well respond, "Isn't it a shame the Postal Service will not likely issue the stamp because we can't say 'God' anymore." And the truth is, of course, the stamp was subsequently issued. Why? **Because we <u>can</u> say "God" in America!** Christians must stop with the false rumors and defeatist attitudes and get educated!

Subjecting a minor child in a public school to a prayer of one particular God or the first four commandments of the Decalogue is a far cry from a majoritarian motto or a majoritarian acknowledgment in a patriotic pledge. Surely, any adult atheist who is otherwise rational is not likely to have a breakdown over these minor intrusions into his world of unbelief.

Justice Scalia had it right in his dissent in *Lee*: "Maintaining respect for the religious observances of others is a fundamental civic virtue that government…can and should cultivate – so that even if it were the case that the displaying of such respect might be mistaken for taking part in a prayer, I would deny that the dissenter's interest in avoiding even the false appearance of participation constitutionally trumps the government's interest in fostering respect for religion generally." Although that was said in the context of public school prayer at graduation, his message rings true for these types of issues, as well.

I suggest you atheists who are not willing to take on the virtue of respectful silence (and, I know many of you do), if you absolutely must, simply tell your children how foolish the majority of Americans are to believe in a God, inclusive of all past presidents and Albert Einstein. That is, unless you think that is so unpersuasive as to offend your child. Then, perhaps you should just remain respectfully silent.

Chapter Sixteen

SO, IS IT OK TO SAY "GOD"?

French political historian Alexis de Tocqueville was quoted in the *Marsh* case (see chapter nine). I am compelled to quote him again. He wrote the following concerning his travels through this land in the early 1830s:

> The religious atmosphere of the country was the first thing that struck me on arrival in the United States...In France I had seen the spirits of religion and of freedom almost always marching in opposite directions. In America I found them intimately linked together in joint reign over the same land. My longing to understand the reason for this phenomenon increased daily. To find this out, I questioned the faithful of all communions; I particularly sought the society of clergymen, who are the depositories of the various creeds and have a personal interest in their survival...; **all thought that the main reason for the quiet sway of religion over their country was the complete separation of church and state.** I have no hesitation in stating that throughout my stay in America I met nobody, lay or cleric, who did not agree about that.

Well, as we have seen, "complete separation" is an overstatement. I do not believe the separation principle has changed so much as the fact that some people today are willing to go to outrageous extents to challenge our heritage. For example, I doubt there were many citizens in de Tocqueville's world who believed that a city-owned nativity scene in Pleasantville, U.S.A., was a form of church/state intimacy that came anything close to something that needed separating.

However, please understand that we are not living in de Tocqueville's world. And, while I call upon Christians to speak up and revive our historical Christian beginnings in the minds of our youth and all of our citizenry, we cannot forget there are movements afoot today by people who unashamedly attack Christianity and godliness in general. In the 1830s, if such voices existed, they weren't very loud, probably because Christians weren't afraid to live their faith out loud. These groups are challenging our nation's core values and the outer limits of our Constitution like never before. How we handle the onslaught will determine the direction our country takes.

Extreme liberals and the atheist fringe shout "separation of church and state" at the mere mention of God in a public forum. I hope you can see that our Supreme Court has denied their historically false position at every turn. We must never accept (or repeat) their rantings as fact.

On the other hand, far too many Christians seek to tear down every last brick in the metaphorical "wall of separation." Woe to this nation, to Christianity, and all religions if they are ever successful.

From my perspective, what the Supreme Court of the United States has actually said "separation" means through their interpretation of the establishment clause is miles apart from what well-intended, but misinformed, Christians believe they have said. We must get our facts straight, for only then can we effectively handle false and damaging rumor.

New attacks seem to pop up every day, some from within, some from without. Here are four examples.

1: Red Skelton Video

You may have seen the internet video of Red Skelton, an American icon, performing a dramatic reading of the Pledge of Allegiance. He recites it and interprets it as it was written when he was a child in grade school. He reminds us that the phrase "under God" was added in 1954 and closes by saying, "Wouldn't it be a pity if someone said that was a prayer and the Pledge would be eliminated from schools, too?"

I suppose there are several versions on the internet. The one that caught my eye has an accompanying comment:

Help spread this important message. Red Skelton – from his television show in 1969. Wow! Just think. He said this on his television show in 1969 and really had no clue it would ever come about. Sad, isn't it? What a wonderful and worthwhile clip to watch and share with all your friends and acquaintances!

As I said in chapter two, "words matter." This comment was no doubt said by someone who loves this country and his God and believes, in so many words, that we should all wake up by spreading this sad tale. Let's examine, shall we?

Observation #1: Check out chapter nine (Prayer). Red likely was keenly aware of *Engel v. Vitale*, decided in 1962, seven years prior to Red's television show. You now know that *Engel* was the first case to hold that government-sponsored prayer in public schools was a violation of the Constitution.

He also likely knew about the *Barnette* case decided in 1943 (see chapter five). As you recall, this case held that the state could not punish a Jehovah's Witness student for not participating in the Pledge of Allegiance when the student believed it to be the worship of a graven image and, thus, in violation of the student's (and his parents') interpretation of the Ten Commandments.

So, in retrospect, this was not a "wow" moment. Red likely *did* have a clue that "under God" might be challenged someday, if not as a prayer, as an establishment of religion. You would have, too, in 1969. Anyone who kept themselves educated about our Supreme Court and our Constitution at that time would have known, at a minimum, that it might be challenged.

Observation #2: More importantly, when the author says Red "really had no clue it would ever come about. Sad, isn't it?," one implication is that the Pledge *has* both been challenged and that it lost; that is, that the Pledge has been taken out of schools because of the "under God" phrase.

You have seen the only three cases on the Pledge that have reached the Supreme Court: *Minersville School District v. Gobitis; West Virginia Board of Education v. Barnette;* and, *Elk Grove Unified School District v. Newdow.*

I wanted to see just how "sad" the implication of the comment is, so I also looked into all of the Pledge cases in the lower federal courts. Here are the chronological results of my study.

1940: *Minersville School District v. Gobitis* (Supreme Court) held that a student or parent could be punished for not reciting the Pledge.

1943: *West Virginia Board of Education v. Barnette* (Supreme Court) reversed *Minersville.* This decision did not take "under God" out of the Pledge - in 1943, it wasn't in the Pledge. It also did not take the Pledge out of schools. All it did was permit a Jehovah's Witness student to refrain from reciting it because it was against his religious beliefs to do so.

2004: *Elk Grove Unified School District v. Newdow* (Supreme Court) reversed the 9th Circuit Court of Appeals decision that struck down the Pledge because of the "under God" phrase, but did so for technical unrelated reasons.

2004: *The Circle School v. Pappert* (3rd Circuit Court of Appeals). The Pledge and "under God" phrase in public schools was upheld.

2005: *Myers v. Loudon County Public Schools United* (4th Circuit Court of Appeals). The Pledge and "under God" phrase in public schools was upheld.

2008: *Frazier v. Winn* (11th Circuit Court of Appeals). The Pledge and "under God" phrase in public schools was upheld.

2010: *Newdow v. Rio Linda Union Schools District* (9th Circuit Court of Appeals). The Pledge and "under God" phrase in public schools was upheld.

2010: *Croft v. Perry* (5th Circuit Court of Appeals). The Pledge and "under God" phrase in public schools was upheld.

2010: *Freedom From Religion Foundation v. Hanover School District* (1ˢᵗ Circuit Court of Appeals). The Pledge and "under God" phrase in public schools was upheld.

That's it, folks. Two Supreme Court and six Court of Appeals cases upholding the Pledge and one Supreme Court case reversing the only case that ever held the "under God" phrase in the Pledge to be unconstitutional.

So, I agree. Watch the video. It is "worthwhile and wonderful" and it is sad that anyone would challenge the Pledge. However, don't forward the video unless you also spread the message that the true ending is not sad. The one and only time the Pledge lost was not because it was considered a prayer; but, rather, because it was considered a violation of the establishment clause. More importantly, it was reversed and all other cases challenging the Pledge in our public schools have failed. It should be a message of victory!

If you do not also share the good news along with the video, then please do not spread it further because "a lie told often enough becomes the truth," doesn't it? School Boards who hear false reports will start believing the Pledge cannot be recited and, you guessed it, out of nowhere – **It's not OK to say "God."** We can't let that happen anymore.

2: President Obama's Inauguration

You may have heard that a lawsuit was filed seeking to require that then President-Elect Obama's inauguration ceremony (January 2009) leave out all references to God and religion. The suit demanded that Obama be forbidden from adding "So help me God" to his oath of office and that no invocation or benediction be delivered that referenced God or religion. Michael Newdow instigated the lawsuit along with several atheist organizations.

This inaugural lawsuit alleged in part: "There can be no purpose for placing 'so help me God' in an oath or sponsoring prayers to God, other than promoting the particular point of view that God exists." It was alleged that such references to God violate the Constitution's ban on the establishment of religion.

The plaintiffs contended that having to watch a ceremony with religious components would make them feel excluded and stigmatized, and, therefore, put them in a position of having to choose between not watching the presidential inauguration or being forced to countenance endorsements of purely religious notions that they expressly deny.

The Reverends Rick Warren and Joseph Lowery were also named in the lawsuit, as they were the two ministers scheduled to participate in the ceremony. The complaint included criticism of a quote from Warren on atheists: "I could not vote for an atheist because an atheist says, 'I don't need God.'" This, of course, is the same message conveyed by President Lincoln (see chapter five), repeated here:

> I do not think I could myself, be brought to support a man for office, whom I knew to be an open enemy of, and scoffer at, religion.

See how important it is to study history?

Mr. Newdow said religious references in the inauguration ceremony send a message to non-believers that "we who believe in God are the righteous, the real Americans" and that it is unconstitutional to imply that atheists and others are not as good. Of course, it is absurd to suggest that no public office-holder can ever say anything unless all are in agreement with his message. And it is more than absurd for atheists to conclude they are being told they are "not as good as believers." In fact, Christian believers would tell Mr. Newdow that their message is not at all about Christians being better than anyone else. The argument is ridiculous.

This "inaugural" lawsuit was dismissed for procedural reasons, but I ask all of you to please get the following down into your very soul. As long as a president takes the oath as specifically stated in the Constitution, he has every right to add "So help me God" if he wishes to do so. It is called freedom of speech, also made sacrosanct in the same First Amendment where we find the religion clauses, and has absolutely nothing to do with the establishment clause. In fact, a president has the absolute free exercise right to pray at his inaugural, as well. And, as I have said before, a sense of common respect for these rights would be a trait one would hope to see in all people, including atheists. No law commands our leaders to be atheists and no law commands them to believe in a Creator.

Mr. Newdow and his ilk should understand this: If an atheist is ever elected president and announces he will not add "so help me God" to his oath, no Christian is going to be filing a lawsuit demanding that he does. First, I would hope people of faith would respect his right to his views and, second, such a lawsuit would be frivolous – just as frivolous as many of the atheists' perennial claims.

When folks like Newdow file such lawsuits, the media reports them out of proportion to their weight and misinformed people (as well as some with a clear agenda) begin talking to Christians in coffee shops around the country. After several years of this progressive agenda, Christians start believing it. After all, we have heard that phrase "separation of church and state." We start thinking, "Maybe the Newdows of the world are onto something. Maybe our presidents shouldn't be saying 'God' anymore and maybe prayers should not be said at inaugurations." Or, to put it more accurately, regardless of what Christians believe "should" or "should not be," we somehow permit ourselves to become the victims of brainwashing.

3: The National Day of Prayer

When the National Day of Prayer was struck down by Federal District Judge Crabb in 2010, I wrote an op-ed column for the St. Louis Post-Dispatch, republished with permission here:

"Pray for the Day of Prayer"
St. Louis Post-Dispatch
Tad Armstrong
Wednesday, May 5, 2010

Something's in the air. Few discuss it, but most everyone knows it's out there somewhere. Whether it comes in the form of another terror attack or severe depression or the chaos of Arizona on a national scale, most of us have had the sense for quite some time that our nation is out of control. Indeed, our world is out of control.

Right is wrong. Wrong is right. Hate-crime statutes precipitate hate. Illegal immigrants rape, kidnap and murder in Arizona and mindless city governments boycott against Arizona from afar for attempting to right such injustice.

David Letterman shed a tear for his country on 9/12/01 and on 6/09/09 described a vice-presidential candidate as having a "slutty flight attendant" look and made an inappropriate sexual joke about the candidate's daughter and a Yankee player. And his audience laughed. And he still has a job. And I weep for my country and my grandchildren.

Our Vice-President dropped the "F" bomb at a microphone poised to a worldwide audience and the Democratic Party responded with T-shirts sporting "BFD" (Big F---ing Deal) to raise money for its cause. The Republican Party spent $2,000 on erotic entertainment, and people buy T-shirts and quickly forget. And I weep for my country and my grandchildren.

We cannot expect one person or group to make it all go away. We have relied on government to take care of us for far too long. It's time to rely on God. It's time to pray. Perhaps Congress should designate an annual day of prayer.

Congress did that in 1952, but, alas, three weeks ago we were told by Federal District Judge Barbara Crabb that our Constitution does not permit it.

You can read *"Freedom From Religion Foundation, Inc. v. Obama"* for yourself if you browse its name. If you are too lazy to read it, you are not entitled to criticize it. Wallowing in ignorance in the midst of the information age is the downfall of our great nation.

I predict Judge Crabb's well-reasoned opinion will be reversed on appeal, but it is of little consequence to me, either way.

A challenge by atheists to a simple "declaration" is silly, and I bet that most atheists have the common decency to stand in silent respect for the views of others on this occasion, although common respect is yet another virtue of the past for many, including I'm afraid, some Christians.

There is a place for religion in the public square. It is that narrow place where the freedom of speech and the freedom to exercise one's religion trump governmental intrusion into a holy domain. It is a president's personal right to add "so help me God" to his oath and, so long as public funds are not tapped, it is his right to invite ministers to pray at his inauguration. On the other hand, there is a proper time for religion to distance itself from government for the sake of its own survival.

Judge Crabb's decision will not be enforced this year while on appeal. If it is reversed, next year believers of all faiths can continue to pray in earnest on that one day a year when Congress – which 70% of us say we do not trust and many of us feel is corrupt – says it's OK. How comforting.

If you get a chance, I urge you to attend a National Day of Prayer breakfast tomorrow, May 6th. But, in the land of the free, we do not need nor should we seek the blessing of Congress before organizing such an event ourselves. Christianity hardly needed the blessing of Rome to survive.

If you have studied the Supreme Court decisions on this subject, you probably understand that at least a "short fence of separation," as opposed to an impenetrable "wall," is one reason why this nation has been spared the religious turmoil and bloodshed we have seen in every other corner of the world. If you have not, I am certain you would be very surprised at how friendly the judiciary has been to religion.

As Judge Crabb said, "The same law that prohibits the government from declaring a National Day of Prayer also prohibits it from declaring a National Day of Blasphemy." To my fellow Christians and to people of all faiths, please be ever so careful what you ask government to be for religion – what you ask government to provide for religion – and what you ask government to sanction on behalf of religion. You just might get it.

Since the foregoing article appeared in the newspaper (and just before this book going to print), I learned that the ruling in *"Freedom From Religion Foundation, Inc. v. Obama"* has been reversed for lack of standing, much the same as the Michael Newdow Pledge of Allegiance case. Therefore, the National Day of Prayer will continue to be organized by government. But, no matter, if we Christians cannot organize our own national day of prayer without the help of government, God help us. I'm not going to rely on government to schedule my praying. How about you?

4: The Cross at Ground Zero

This book had almost gone to print when another attack on Christianity hit the news in August of 2011. American Atheists, Inc. filed a lawsuit seeking what has been dubbed the "World Trade Center Cross" to be either removed from the National September 11 Memorial and Museum or to be joined by their symbol, along with other non-Christian symbols.

In their complaint, they attack the cross as "an insult to every non-Christian survivor of the attack."

As I warned in chapter twelve, these extremists get their encouragement to file such a lawsuit from the majority opinion in *Lynch v. Donnelly* and from the opinions in *Allegheny County v. ACLU* that supported either the Menorah alone or both the Menorah and the nativity scene in Pittsburgh.

Frank Silecchia, working with the New York City Fire Department, discovered this steel beam structure in the form of a cross in the rubble of the Twin Towers at the intersection of Liberty and Church, NYC, USA. It became a place for Christian workers to meet and pray. I predict this lawsuit will not be successful, but the reason the cross should remain at the museum has nothing to do with the foregoing wrongly decided religious symbol cases and everything to do with the undeniable fact that this cross is a historical artifact, not unlike the Bible President Lincoln used to take his oath of office. And, because it is a part of history, that does not give atheists or any other religion the right to equal space in the museum.

Jane Everhart, one of the plaintiffs, called the cross an "ugly piece of wreckage" that "does not represent anything...but horror and death."

Some will view it as nothing more, but that does not make it something we should forget. The cremation ovens at Auschwitz are preserved precisely to remember the Holocaust.

In addition to Ms Everhart's accurate description, others view it as representing hope and everlasting life on the heels of the most horrific undeserved death ever known.

These atheist plaintiffs have indicated they would settle for removing the cross from the museum; in other words, they aren't committed to demanding their own symbol, the atom, being somehow represented in the museum. It appears their ultimate goal is not equal time with Christianity; but, rather, to eliminate Christianity from our culture.

I believe the greatest insult is not to them, as they have alleged, nor to Christianity (we can survive this nonsense), but to their fellow atheists who have the common decency to respect this slice of history.

––––––––

What lawsuit will challenge Christianity next week? I believe our worst enemy is ourselves, as postulated in chapter two. I am not nearly as concerned about enemies from without, such as those that challenge the Pledge of Allegiance, the Ground Zero American Atheist, Inc. plaintiffs, and the inauguration-lawsuit-plaintiff-types. They all lose. These groups do not seek tolerance of their beliefs. They seek elimination of Christianity from our culture. Their claims have no merit because **"It is OK to say 'God'"** almost anywhere almost any time in almost any manner we wish because of our Constitution and the manner in which it has been interpreted by our Supreme Court. One cannot credibly deny that, with the most glaring exception of the evolution/creation science cases, the High Court has been very favorable to religion, and to Christianity in particular.

When it comes to enemies from without, my greatest fear is that Christians will give up and yield to the heavy toll in time and money to defend the outrageous demands made in these frivolous lawsuits. For example, if the defendants in the Ground Zero case yield and remove the cross from the museum, it would not bode well for winning the culture wars. Consider contributing to the defense fund of defendants who find themselves in the line of fire, for unlike Amanda and Charley at the WWII Memorial, we simply cannot "shake our heads sadly and walk away" from these particular fights.

As for enemies from within, what problems will Christians bring upon themselves next week in the form of ill-conceived lawsuits of their own?

As a follow-up to the case that permitted prayer to stand in the Nebraska legislature (*Marsh v. Chambers*), in chapter nine I said:

> Although I am hard pressed to criticize the outcome of this case, I feel its foundation in logic is lacking. Saying a prayer to adults who are not compelled to be present for the first few seconds of the day, in itself, does not "appear" to be a problem. The problem lies in spending the tax money of constituents of all faiths to hire a chaplain of one faith. **Something doesn't feel right about the outcome, though. I suppose we have to score this one "for" religion, but I predict problems ahead.**

As we go to print, my prediction has come true in the case of *Joyner v. Forsyth County, North Carolina* (out of the United States Court of Appeals for the Fourth Circuit), not because of the holding in *Marsh*, but because the Christians of Forsyth County are taking *Marsh* to a new level. Unfortunately, they have decided to seek an appeal of their loss in the *Joyner* case to the United States Supreme Court. Not unlike the religious symbol cases, it is my firm belief they are fighting the wrong battle. Let me show you what I mean.

With *Marsh* as their rallying cry, the good folks on the Forsyth County Board of Commissioners had a long-standing policy of opening government sessions with prayer. The Clerk maintained a list of all religious congregations in the community and invited a leader from each congregation to deliver an invocation at the start of meetings on a first-come, first-served basis. The invitation letter closed as follows:

This opportunity is voluntary, and you are free to offer the invocation according to the dictates of your own conscience. To maintain a spirit of respect and ecumenism, the Board requests only that the prayer opportunity not be exploited as an effort to convert others to the particular faith of the invocational speaker, nor to disparage any faith or belief different than that of the invocational speaker.

There were other parameters, but the reality is that for a year and a half prior to this lawsuit, 80% of the prayers referred to Jesus Christ and none of them mentioned non-Christian deities.

In striking down this program, the Fourth Circuit majority said:

> ...[I]n order to survive constitutional scrutiny, invocations must consist of the type of nonsectarian prayers that solemnize the legislative task and seek to unite rather than divide. Sectarian prayers must not serve as the gateway to citizen participation in the affairs of local government. To have them do so runs afoul of the promise of public neutrality among faiths that resides at the heart of the First Amendment's religion clauses...[W]hile legislative prayer has the capacity to solemnize the weighty task of governance and encourage ecumenism among its participants, it also has the potential to generate sectarian strife. Such conflict rends communities and does violence to the pluralistic and inclusive values that are a defining feature of American public life.

The *Forsyth* Court noted that Nebraska's invocations in *Marsh* fell within constitutional parameters, "going so far as to remove 'all references to Christ after a 1980 complaint from a Jewish legislator' in order to ensure that the prayers represented a 'tolerable acknowledgment of beliefs widely held among the people of this country.'"

Take a look at the closing paragraph of the majority opinion in *Marsh v. Nebraska* from chapter nine: **"The content of the prayer is not of concern to judges where, as here, there is no indication that the prayer opportunity has been exploited to proselytize or advance any one, or to disparage any other, faith or belief. That being so, it is not for us to embark on a sensitive evaluation or to parse the content of a particular prayer."**

If the Supreme Court takes this appeal, I predict Forsyth County will lose precisely because these prayer opportunities have been exploited to proselytize and advance one faith – the Christian faith. The salutation to the Board by the pastor that offered the prayer at the opening of business in Forsyth County on December 17, 2007, is illustrative of the reason why such prayers will not likely stand. He said:

> Before we pray, I would like to say my appreciation to the ones that serve here on the Board. I'm a lifelong resident of Forsyth County...and I appreciate your service to me and also the stand the Board took as a whole allowing me, a minister of the Gospel of the Lord Jesus Christ, to be able to pray as the New Testament instructs. And I appreciate that.

He knows, of course, he is speaking to a Christian Board and, therefore, that he is "the favored one" of their constituents, the very thing the establishment clause was meant to avoid. Lest all the unwarranted "blame" be cast upon poor Thomas Jefferson for his 1802 "wall of separation" letter, please consult item number three in Madison's 1785 Memorial and Remonstrance, written three years before the Constitution was ratified. You will find it in the Appendix where it states as follows:

> Who does not see that the same authority which can establish Christianity, in exclusion of all other Religions, may establish with the same ease any particular sect of Christians, in exclusion of all other Sects?

In other words, the Constitution protects all religions, not just the majoritarian Christian religion.

For the same reason I predicted problems to follow in the wake of the *Marsh* decision, there can be no good outcome in Forsyth County. If the Supreme Court does not take their appeal, the Christians pushing their cause will feel betrayed by their judicial system. If they prevail, Christianity will have won the right to be the bully on the block, just as they were in Pawtucket, Rhode Island, with their shabby nativity scene.

Additionally, you recall that our forefathers fled England, in part, because **"controversies over the Common Book of Prayer regarding its content repeatedly threatened to disrupt the peace of that country as the accepted forms of prayer in the established church changed with the views of the particular ruler that happened to be in control at the time."** See *Engel v. Vitale* in chapter nine. Aside from the unavoidable necessity to check prayers like those in Forsyth County for proselytizing, we never – I mean never – should want to see the day when our judicial branch starts to determine which details of specific prayers are acceptable and which ones are not. That is why we fled England.

On a personal note, I am so very dismayed over these kinds of fights. I believe the Christians that pursue them are well-intended; however, to me, the goal comes off as extraordinarily arrogant. I am reminded of the following portions of a letter from the Apostle Paul to the Philippians:

> **Your attitude should be the same as that Christ Jesus had. Though he was God, he did not demand and cling to his rights as God. He made himself nothing; he took the humble position of a slave and appeared in human form. And in human form he obediently humbled himself even further by dying a criminal's death on a cross. Because of this, God raised him up to the heights of heaven and gave him a name that is above every other name, so that at the name of Jesus every knee will bow, in heaven and on earth and under the earth, and every tongue will confess that Jesus Christ is Lord, to the glory of God the Father.**
>
> **Philippians 2:5-11**

I mean no disrespect to the good folks of Forsyth County when I suggest that, contrary to my Pastor's admonition to "Live life by making God look good" (see the preface), I do not believe these are the skirmishes that accomplish that goal.

———

So, Charley, who said we (metaphorically) can't say "God" anymore? The Supreme Court most certainly has not done so.

And, Mr. Hannity, who said we can't say "God" in our schools? You have, but the Supreme Court definitely has not.

And, Mr. O'Reilly, please don't give the atheists any more worldwide free advertising this Christmas when, because of the ill-conceived decisions in the religious symbol cases, they will have the absolute right to their display on government property if government opens their property up to another faith's symbols.

There is a way to constitutionally get God back into government and back into a society that seems to have lost its faith in much of anything. It's really quite simple. Elect people of faith to public office and hold them accountable. And, help me educate others to stop repeating false information because if the ignorant keep repeating lies, then government, whose leaders are also in the dark, will begin believing them and acting upon them. They will believe that the Bible cannot be taught in schools or that students can't say "God" in school hallways or that we cannot even voluntarily pray on school property. In other words, we Christians need to educate ourselves, get over (understand) what, in truth, is a very valuable metaphor (whether we call it a "wall" or a "short fence"), and *live our faith instead of complaining about mythical villains whom we falsely believe are out to destroy our faith.*

You have studied the actual Supreme Court decisions that have shaped our Constitution instead of relying on sound bites, headlines, and e-mails. You have learned the truth from the source. **Please refer to the review of decisions and dicta in the appendix often. There you will find the ammunition you need to counter false rumor.**

––––––

Christians of goodwill everywhere, I encourage you to live your faith in God out loud. Do not "shake your head sadly and walk away" when faced with the myth that separation of church and state means utter and complete avoidance of one from the other. Do not invite self-imposed defeat. Politely and in a manner pleasing to Christ, lead those in the dark into the light of knowledge. Show them these cases and the words uttered by the Supreme Court Justices and, if you get the chance, consider introducing them to Jesus Christ. And, oh, by the way, let them know **"It's OK to say 'God.'"**

> **And you will know the truth,**
> **and the truth will set you free.**

> **Jesus Christ**
> **John 8:32**

AFTERWORD

Once again, Albert Einstein, perhaps our most famous naturalized citizen, had this to say about our Constitution:

The strength of the Constitution lies entirely in the determination of each citizen to defend it. Only if every single citizen feels duty bound to do his share in this defense are the constitutional rights secure.

However, we cannot defend that which we do not understand. Depending upon the publisher, the pocket-size versions of the Constitution (with amendments) are approximately 30 pages in length. This book has focused on 16 words that comprise the religion clauses of the First Amendment. Hopefully, you have found the journey to be both enlightening and empowering.

What if you had this same level of knowledge under your belt for the rest of the Constitution? If just 40-100 citizens in every community in this nation possessed such knowledge, how much of an impact do you think it would have in a nation designed to be steered by its own citizens in conformance with the Constitution?

I submit it would have an overwhelmingly favorable impact, for each group would share their newfound knowledge with family and friends on the right or left, conservative or liberal, progressive or tea party type. We would have a better understanding of how freedom nurtured an American spirit that took us to the pinnacle of hope in a world starved for leadership to advance all of humankind.

And, while it might come in handy at a fund-raising trivia contest to know that we presently have 27 amendments to the Constitution or that two presidents have been impeached (none convicted) or that over 11,000 bills have been introduced in Congress to amend our founding document, knowledge of such constitutional trivia will get us nowhere. The only meaningful way to gain the knowledge is to study the work of the Supreme Court.

There are plenty of deep, philosophical books about the Constitution written for lawyers and plenty written for the lay public that only skim the surface. Newspapers, television, and radio provide headlines and sound bites that respective media outlets want you to see and hear, but no one provides the material necessary to arm the lay public with the constitutional knowledge it will take for "We, the People" to take back our country and regain our position of American exceptionalism like ELL Constitution Clubs™.

As we go to print, nine community clubs have formed, one high school club has formed and we are in the process of forming new clubs at Ramstein Air Base in Germany and in Minnesota, Colorado, Missouri and Florida and at another high school in our area. We have been very successful with our clubs in the St. Louis Metro East area. There is no reason why we cannot expand to form 10,000 clubs across the nation. What impact do you believe that would have on future laws passed by Congress?

You can help us. You can be the spark that helps birth a new club in your hometown.

Please consider learning how you can be the catalyst in forming a new club at www.ellconstitutionclubs.com.

Daniel Webster, acclaimed orator and constitutional lawyer, thought the Framers' work was fairly important when he said, "Hold on to the Constitution, for if the American Constitution should fail, there will be anarchy throughout the world." We have memorialized Webster in bronze at the State Houses of Massachusetts and New Hampshire, in New York's Central Park, and each of Webster and Einstein in the District of Columbia. It seems our nation once thought they had something important to say.

The Federalist Papers, written to persuade New Yorkers to ratify the original Constitution, were published anonymously in the newspapers of that state in the years 1787 and 1788. If you have consumed just some of them, you know that, while they are very informative, they are not exactly light reading.

Folks, there was a time in this country when a substantial portion of our electorate were educated enough to run the ship of state. It is time we had a revival of learning and culture when it comes to our form of government. Thank you so very much for taking the time to educate yourself on these short, but important provisions of the First Amendment. Hopefully, you will agree it is now time to roll up your sleeves and become part of a true American Constitutional Renaissance.

"The End…
Of the Beginning."

CONSTITUTION
CLUBS®

Appendix

1. Religion Clause Scoreboard.

RELIGION CLAUSE SCOREBOARD	
Rulings "for" Religion	Rulings "against" Religion
22	12
1	Pierce v. Society of Sisters	Reynolds v. United States
2	Cantwell v. Connecticut	McCollum v. Board of Education
3	Martin v. City of Struthers	Lemon v. Kurtzman
4	Murdock v. Pennsylvania	Engel v. Vitale
5	West Va. Bd. of Ed. v. Barnette	Abington School Dist. v. Schempp
6	Torcaso v. Watkins	Wallace v. Jaffree
7	Walz v. Tax Commission	Lee v. Weisman
8	Clay v. United States	Epperson v. Arkansas
9	Wisconsin v. Yoder	Edwards v. Aguillard
10	McDaniel v. Paty	Allegheny County v. ACLU
11	Church of the LBA v. Hialeah	Stone v. Graham
12	Everson v. Ewing Township	McCreary County v. ACLU
13	Zorach v. Clauson	
14	Board of Education v. Allen	
15	McGowan v. Maryland	
16	Marsh v. Chambers	

17	Lynch v. Donnelly	
18	Allegheny County v. ACLU	
19	Van Orden v. Perry	
20	Widmar v. Vincent	
21	Lamb's Chapel v. Moriches District	
22	Good News Club v. Milford	
23	Elk Grove Unified School Dist. v. Newdow	

2. Memorial and Remonstrance.

MEMORIAL AND REMONSTRANCE
AGAINST RELIGIOUS ASSESSMENTS, 1785

To the Honorable the General Assembly of the Commonwealth of Virginia

A Memorial and Remonstrance
Against Religious Assessments

We the subscribers, citizens of the said Commonwealth, having taken into serious consideration, a Bill printed by order of the last Session of General Assembly, entitled "A Bill establishing a provision for Teachers of the Christian Religion," and conceiving that the same if finally armed with the sanctions of a law, will be a dangerous abuse of power, are bound as faithful members of a free State, to remonstrate against it, and to declare the reasons by which we are determined. We remonstrate against the said Bill,

1. Because we hold it for a fundamental and undeniable truth, "that Religion or the duty which we owe to our Creator and the manner of discharging it, can be directed only by reason and conviction, not by force or violence." The Religion then of every man must be left to the conviction and conscience of every man; and it is the right of every man to exercise it as these may dictate. This right is in its nature an unalienable right. It is unalienable; because the opinions of men, depending only on the evidence contemplated

by their own minds cannot follow the dictates of other men: It is unalienable also; because what is here a right towards men, is a duty towards the Creator. It is the duty of every man to render to the Creator such homage, and such only, as he believes to be acceptable to him. This duty is precedent both in order of time and in degree of obligation, to the claims of Civil Society. Before any man can be considered as a member of Civil Society, he must be considered as a subject of the Governor of the Universe: And if a member of Civil Society, who enters into any subordinate Association, must always do it with a reservation of his duty to the general authority; much more must every man who becomes a member of any particular Civil Society, do it with a saving of his allegiance to the Universal Sovereign. We maintain therefore that in matters of Religion, no man's right is abridged by the institution of Civil Society, and that Religion is wholly exempt from its cognizance. True it is, that no other rule exists, by which any question which may divide a Society, can be ultimately determined, but the will of the majority; but it is also true, that the majority may trespass on the rights of the minority.

2. Because if religion be exempt from the authority of the Society at large, still less can it be subject to that of the Legislative Body. The latter are but the creatures and vicegerents of the former. Their jurisdiction is both derivative and limited: it is limited with regard to the co-ordinate departments, more necessarily is it limited with regard to the constituents. The preservation of a free government requires not merely, that the metes and bounds which separate each department of power be invariably maintained; but more especially, that neither of them be suffered to overleap the great Barrier which defends the rights of the people. The Rulers who are guilty of such an encroachment, exceed the commission from which they derive their authority, and are Tyrants. The People who submit to it are governed by laws made neither by themselves, nor by an authority derived from them, and are slaves.

3. Because, it is proper to take alarm at the first experiment on our liberties. We hold this prudent jealousy to be the first duty of

citizens, and one of the noblest characteristics of the late Revolution. The freemen of America did not wait till usurped power had strengthened itself by exercise, and entangled the question in precedents. They saw all the consequences in the principle, and they avoided the consequences by denying the principle. We revere this lesson too much soon, to forget it. Who does not see that the same authority which can establish Christianity, in exclusion of all other Religions, may establish with the same ease any particular sect of Christians, in exclusion of all other Sects? That the same authority which can force a citizen to contribute three pence only of his property for the support of any one establishment, may force him to conform to any other establishment in all cases whatsoever?

4. Because the Bill violates the equality which ought to be the basis of every law, and which is more indispensable, in proportion as the validity or expediency of any law is more liable to be impeached. If "all men are by nature equally free and independent," all men are to be considered as entering into Society on equal conditions; as relinquishing no more, and therefore retaining no less, one than another, of their natural rights. Above all are they to be considered as retaining an "equal title to the free exercise of Religion according to the dictates of Conscience." Whilst we assert for ourselves a freedom to embrace, to profess and to observe the Religion which we believe to be of divine origin, we cannot deny an equal freedom to those whose minds have not yet yielded to the evidence which has convinced us. If this freedom be abused, it is an offence against God, not against man: To God, therefore, not to men, must an account of it be rendered. As the Bill violates equality by subjecting some to peculiar burdens; so it violates the same principle, by granting to others peculiar exemptions. Are the Quakers and Menonists the only sects who think a compulsive support of their religions unnecessary and unwarrantable? Can their piety alone be intrusted with the care of public worship? Ought their Religions to be endowed above all others, with extraordinary privileges, by which proselytes may be enticed from all others. We think too

favorably of the justice and good sense of these denominations, to believe that they either covet pre-eminences over their fellow citizens, or that they will be seduced by them, from the common opposition to the measure.

5. Because the bill implies either that the Civil Magistrate is a competent Judge of Religious truth; or that he may employ Religion as an engine of Civil policy. The first is an arrogant pretension falsified by the contradictory opinions of Rulers in all ages, and throughout the world: The second an unhallowed perversion of the means of salvation.

6. Because the establishment proposed by the Bill is not requisite for the support of the Christian Religion. To say that it is, is a contradiction to the Christian Religion itself; for every page of it disavows a dependence on the powers of this world: it is a contradiction to fact; for it is known that this Religion both existed and flourished, not only without the support of human laws, but in spite of every opposition from them; and not only during the period of miraculous aid, but long after it had been left to its own evidence, and the ordinary care of Providence: Nay, it is a contradiction in terms; for a Religion not invented by human policy, must have pre-existed and been supported, before it was established by human policy. It is moreover to weaken in those who profess this Religion a pious confidence in its innate excellence, and the patronage of its Author; and to foster in those who still reject it, a suspicion that its friends are too conscious of its fallacies, to trust it to its own merits.

7. Because experience witnesseth that ecclesiastical establishments, instead of maintaining the purity and efficacy of Religion, have had a contrary operation. During almost fifteen centuries, has the legal establishment of Christianity been on trial. What have been its fruits? More or less in all places, pride and indolence in the Clergy; ignorance and servility in the laity; in both, superstition, bigotry and persecution. Enquire of the Teachers of Christianity for the ages in which it appeared in its greatest lustre; those of

every sect, point to the ages prior to its incorporation with Civil policy. Propose a restoration of this primitive state in which its Teachers depended on the voluntary rewards of their flocks; many of them predict its downfall. On which side ought their testimony to have greatest weight, when for or when against their interest?

8. Because the establishment in question is not necessary for the support of Civil Government. If it be urged as necessary for the support of Civil Government only as it is a means of supporting Religion, and it be not necessary for the latter purpose, it cannot be necessary for the former. If Religion be not within the cognizance of Civil Government, how can its legal establishment be said to be necessary to civil Government? What influence in fact have ecclesiastical establishments had on Civil Society? In some instances they have been seen to erect a spiritual tyranny on the ruins of the Civil authority; in many instances they have been seen upholding the thrones of political tyranny; in no instance have they been seen the guardians of the liberties of the people. Rulers who wished to subvert the public liberty, may have found an established clergy convenient auxiliaries. A just government, instituted to secure & perpetuate it, needs them not. Such a government will be best supported by protecting every citizen in the enjoyment of his Religion with the same equal hand which protects his person and his property; by neither invading the equal rights of any Sect, nor suffering any Sect to invade those of another.

9. Because the proposed establishment is a departure from that generous policy, which, offering an asylum to the persecuted and oppressed of every Nation and Religion, promised a lustre to our country, and an accession to the number of its citizens. What a melancholy mark is the Bill of sudden degeneracy? Instead of holding forth an asylum to be persecuted, it is itself a signal of persecution. It degrades from the equal rank of Citizens all those whose opinions in Religion do not bend to those of the Legislative authority. Distant as it may be, in its present form, from the Inquisition it differs from it only in degree. The one is the first step, the other the last in the career of intolerance. The magnanimous

338

sufferer under this cruel scourge in foreign Regions, must view the Bill as a Beacon on our Coast, warning him to seek some other haven, where liberty and philanthropy in their due extent may offer a more certain repose from his troubles.

10. Because, it will have a like tendency to banish our Citizens. The allurements presented by other situations are every day thinning their number. To superadd a fresh motive to emigration, by revoking the liberty which they now enjoy, would be the same species of folly which has dishonoured and depopulated flourishing kingdoms.

11. Because, it will destroy that moderation and harmony which the forbearance of our laws to intermeddle with Religion, has produced among its several sects. Torrents of blood have been spilt in the old world, by vain attempts of the secular arm to extinguish Religious discord, by proscribing all difference in Religious opinions. Time has at length revealed the true remedy. Every relaxation of narrow and rigorous policy, wherever it has been tried, has been found to assuage the disease. The American Theatre has exhibited proofs, that equal and compleat liberty, if it does not wholly eradicate it, sufficiently destroys its malignant influence on the health and prosperity of the State. If with the salutary effects of this system under our own eyes, we begin to contract the bounds of Religious freedom, we know no name that will too severely reproach our folly. At least let warning be taken at the first fruits of the threatened innovation. The very appearance of the Bill has transformed that "Christian forbearance, love and charity," which of late mutually prevailed, into animosities and jealousies, which may not soon be appeased. What mischiefs may not be dreaded should this enemy to the public quiet be armed with the force of a law?

12. Because, the policy of the bill is adverse to the diffusion of the light of Christianity. The first wish of those who enjoy this precious gift, ought to be that it may be imparted to the whole race of mankind. Compare the number of those who have as yet received it with the number still remaining under the dominion of false

Religions; and how small is the former! Does the policy of the Bill tend to lessen the disproportion? No; it at once discourages those who are strangers to the light of revelation from coming into the Region of it; and countenances, by example the nations who continue in darkness, in shutting out those who might convey it to them. Instead of levelling as far as possible, every obstacle to the victorious progress of truth, the Bill with an ignoble and unchristian timidity would circumscribe it, with a wall of defence against the encroachments of error.

13. Because attempts to enforce by legal sanctions, acts obnoxious to so great a proportion of Citizens, tend to enervate the laws in general, and to slacken the bands of Society. If it be difficult to execute any law which is not generally deemed necessary or salutary, what must be the case where it is deemed invalid and dangerous? and what may be the effect of so striking an example of impotency in the Government, on its general authority.

14. Because a measure of such singular magnitude and delicacy ought not to be imposed, without the clearest evidence that it is called for by a majority of citizens: and no satisfactory method is yet proposed by which the voice of the majority in this case may be determined, or its influence secured. "The people of the respective counties are indeed requested to signify their opinion respecting the adoption of the Bill to the next Session of Assembly." But the representation must be made equal, before the voice either of the Representatives or of the Counties, will be that of the people. Our hope is that neither of the former will, after due consideration, espouse the dangerous principle of the Bill. Should the event disappoint us, it will still leave us in full confidence, that a fair appeal to the latter will reverse the sentence against our liberties.

15. Because, finally, "the equal right of every citizen to the free exercise of his Religion according to the dictates of conscience" is held by the same tenure with all our other rights. If we recur to its origin, it is equally the gift of nature; if we weigh its importance, it cannot be less dear to us; if we consult the Declaration of those rights

which pertain to the good people of Virginia, as the "basis and foundation of Government," it is enumerated with equal solemnity, or rather studied emphasis. Either then, we must say, that the will of the Legislature is the only measure of their authority; and that in the plenitude of this authority, they may sweep away all our fundamental rights; or, that they are bound to leave this particular right untouched and sacred: Either we must say, that they may controul the freedom of the press, may abolish the trial by jury, may swallow up the Executive and Judiciary Powers of the State; nay that they may despoil us of our very right of suffrage, and erect themselves into an independent and hereditary assembly: or we must say, that they have no authority to enact into the law the Bill under consideration. We the Subscribers say, that the General Assembly of this Commonwealth have no such authority: And that no effort may be omitted on our part against so dangerous an usurpation, we oppose to it, this remonstrance; earnestly praying, as we are in duty bound, that the Supreme Lawgiver of the Universe, by illuminating those to whom it is addressed, may on the one hand, turn their councils from every act which would affront his holy prerogative, or violate the trust committed to them: and on the other, guide them into every measure which may be worthy of his [blessing, may re] dound to their own praise, and may establish more firmly the liberties, the prosperity, and the Happiness of the Commonwealth.

3. Thomas Jefferson's letter to the Danbury Baptist Association.

"Believing with you that religion is a matter which lies solely between man and his god; that he owes account to none other for his faith or his worship; that the legislative powers of the government reach actions only, and not opinions, -- I contemplate with sovereign reverence that act of the whole American people which declared that their legislature should 'make no law respecting an establishment of religion or prohibiting the free exercise thereof,' thus building a wall of separation between church and state. Adhering to this expression of the supreme will of the nation in behalf of the rights of conscience, I shall see with sincere satisfaction the progress of those sentiments which tend to restore man to all his natural rights, convinced he has no natural right in opposition to his social duties."

4. **Christmas Symbol Scorecard.**

CHRISTMAS SYMBOL SCORECARD			
JUSTICE *not on the Court at the time	LYNCH NATIVITY SCENE 5/4	ALLEGHENY MENORAH 6/3	ALLEGHENY NATIVITY SCENE 5/4
BURGER	STAYS	*	*
O'CONNOR	STAYS	STAYS	GOES
WHITE	STAYS	STAYS	STAYS
POWELL	STAYS	*	*
REHNQUIST	STAYS	STAYS	STAYS
BRENNAN	GOES	GOES	GOES
MARSHALL	GOES	GOES	GOES
BLACKMUN	GOES	STAYS	GOES
STEVENS	GOES	GOES	GOES
KENNEDY	*	STAYS	STAYS
SCALIA	*	STAYS	STAYS

5. **Review.**

We learned the truth about Supreme Court rulings:

We began by asking the question in chapter five: "Just how free is the free exercise of religion?" The Supreme Court told us that government may not intrude upon matters of opinion or conscience, but actions that exceed the bounds of social duty and good order can be punished. *Reynolds v. United States.*

The practice of religion is not so free as to permit the practice of polygamy. *Reynolds v. United States.*

States cannot require your children to attend public schools and, therefore, they can attend private religious schools. *Pierce v. Society of Sisters.*

Government cannot condition the act of preaching and soliciting for religious purposes upon the prior proof to government that the speaker represents a valid religion (*Cantwell v. Connecticut*), nor can it forbid religious solicitors from knocking on doors of residents (*Martin v. Struthers*), nor can it condition the distribution of religious material upon the payment of a license fee. *Murdock v. Pennsylvania.*

If you believe that pledging your allegiance to a piece of cloth violates a religious commitment not to worship a graven image, you cannot be punished for refusing to do so in the land of the free. *West Virginia Board of Education v. Barnette.*

No one has to declare a belief in God to hold public office. That shouldn't come as a surprise, given Article VI of the Constitution: "No religious Test shall ever be required as a Qualification to any Office or public Trust under the United States." *Torcaso v. Watkins.*

Persons with sincerely held religious beliefs against war cannot be forced into the military. *Clay v. United States.*

We learned the Constitution does not require Amish students to be "conformed to this world" by attending the last two years of public high school in violation of their religious beliefs. *Wisconsin v. Yoder.*

A state may not forbid clergy from holding public office (*McDaniel v. Paty*) and a city may not target religion to its exclusion for practicing a form of animal sacrifice. *Church of the Lukumi Babalu Aye v. Hialeah.*

How could anyone conclude "religion" did not come out the winner with these very representative free exercise decisions?

After introducing the dreaded "wall of separation" in chapter six, we learned in chapter seven that a tax to reimburse parents for the costs of bussing their children to private religious schools was not an establishment of religion (*Everson v. Board of Education*) and, thus, not forbidden, but the uses of public schools for religious proselytizing during school hours was forbidden. *McCollum v. Board of Education.* Moving the religious classes off campus solved the *McCollum* problem in *Zorach v. Clauson.* Taxes can be used to purchase secular books to **loan** to religious schools (*Board of*

Education v. Allen), but subsidizing the salaries of religious teachers and **giving** secular textbooks to religious schools went too far in *Lemon v. Kurtzman.*

Because of *McGowan v. Maryland* in chapter eight, we know that government can make it a crime to work on Sunday in obvious deference to the Christian religion.

Perhaps chapter nine (Prayer) is the least understood constitutional topic on religion. Yes, we did learn that government-sponsored official prayer as part of a religious program carried on in public schools is constitutionally prohibited. *Engel v. Vitale.* It was not surprising, thereafter, to learn that government-required reading of 10 verses from the Holy Bible daily without commentary and of the Lord's Prayer in public school is also unconstitutional. *Abington School Dist. v. Schempp.* And, an official period of silence for "meditation or prayer" in public schools is not permitted. *Wallace v. Jaffree.*

In a 5-4 decision, we learned that a government-sponsored prayer at a graduation ceremony in elementary and secondary school is prohibited (*Lee v. Weisman*); therefore, many were likely surprised to learn that opening legislative sessions with official government-sponsored prayer is not prohibited. *Marsh v. Chambers.*

Religion was not victorious in chapter ten where we learned that government may not ban the teaching of evolution in public schools (*Epperson v. Arkansas*) and that a state cannot condition the teaching of evolution upon the teaching of creation science. *Edwards v. Aguillard.*

Exempting religion from taxation is okay in chapter eleven (*Walz v. Tax Commission*) and chapter twelve informs that city ownership/involvement with religious symbols is okay in some situations (*Lynch v. Donnelly*), but not in others (*Allegheny County v. ACLU*).

We learned in chapter thirteen that displaying the Ten Commandments is okay in some settings (*Van Orden v. Perry* – Texas State Capitol lawn amidst other monuments), but not in others (*Stone v. Graham* – public schools and *McCreary County v. ACLU* – a courthouse).

Chapter fourteen brought several winners to religion as we learned that once a university opens its doors for use by student groups, it cannot exclude religious groups even if their purpose is to worship God. *Widmar v. Vincent.* The same rule of law applies to the use of local public schools. *Lamb's Chapel v. Center Moriches School District* and *Good News Club v. Milford Central School.*

And, finally, in chapter fifteen, we learned that, although the constitutionality of the Pledge of Allegiance "under God" provision has never been determined in the Supreme Court on the merits (as you recall, Mr. Newdow's case was dismissed and, therefore, reversed, on lack of standing grounds in *Elk Grove Unified School District v. Newdow*, so the ultimate issue was not determined), all other federal appellate cases that have addressed the issue have upheld the Pledge, granting a pass only to those persons whose religious convictions forbid them to recite it.

We know that atheists continue to challenge the motto on our coins and currency (In God We Trust), prayers at inaugural events and presidents who dare add "So help me, God" to their oath or "God bless America" to their speeches. None of these questions have been decided in the Supreme Court, but I contend that all of these matters deserve the simple common respect of the minority and that is the way I believe each of these questions will ultimately be resolved if the High Court ever does address them.

We learned insights of the Justices through dicta:

Many of you, no doubt found these principles, enunciated by our Justices, to be both encouraging and surprising. I urge you to sit down with your family, make them aware of these gems and discuss them in your home.

"No official, high or petty, can prescribe what shall be orthodox in politics, nationalism, religion, or other matters of opinion or force citizens to confess by word or act their faith therein.

"There is before us the right of freedom to believe, freedom to worship one's Maker according to the dictates of one's conscience, a right which the Constitution specifically shelters.

"Official compulsion to affirm what is contrary to one's religious beliefs is the antithesis of freedom of worship." *West Virginia Board of Education v. Barnette.*

"Religious ideas, no less than any other, may be the subject of debate which is uninhibited, robust and wide-open.

"Religious discussion, association, or political participation is not a less preferred status than rights of discussion, association, and political participation generally.

"Churches as much as secular bodies and private citizens have the right to take strong positions on public issues.

"Government may not inquire into the religious beliefs and motivations of officeholders – it may not remove them from office merely for making public statements regarding religion, or question whether their legislative actions stem from religious conviction.

"Religionists no less than members of any other group enjoy the full measure of protection afforded speech, association, and political activity generally." *McDaniel v. Paty.*

"We are a religious people whose institutions presuppose a Supreme Being." *Zorach v. Clauson.*

"The study of art without its religious influence is absurd. The same is true for music and sacred music. Gospel music had a major influence on all American music. Our children should never study architecture without studying the cathedrals of Rome or study English literature without studying references to the Bible." Concurring opinion of Justice Jackson in *McCollum v. Board of Education.*

"One of the greatest dangers to the freedom of the individual to worship in his own way lies in the government's placing its official stamp of approval upon one particular kind of prayer or one particular form of religious services.

"Our Founders were no more willing to let the content of their prayers and their privilege of praying whenever they pleased be influenced by the ballot box than they were to let these vital matters of personal conscience depend upon the succession of monarchs.

"A union of government and religion tends to destroy government and to degrade religion.

"Religion is too personal, too sacred, too holy, to permit its unhallowed perversion by a civil magistrate." *Engel v. Vitale.*

"Government may not establish a religion of secularism in the sense of affirmatively opposing religion, thus preferring those who believe in no religion to those who do.

"One's education is not complete without a study of comparative religion. The Bible is worthy of study for its literary and historic qualities.

"Not every involvement of religion in public life is unconstitutional. Provisions may be made by government for churches and chaplains at military establishments or for chaplains in penal institutions because folks could not otherwise practice their religion freely.

"Government may allow temporal use of public buildings by religious organizations when their churches are unavailable because of disaster or emergency.

"Any attempt to use rigid limits upon the mere mention of God or references to the Bible would be fraught with dangers." *Abington School Dist. v. Schempp.*

"Legislators may say prayers on the floor or form voluntary prayer groups.

"Bona fide classes in comparative religion can be offered in the public schools.

"The text of Abraham Lincoln's Second Inaugural Address... inscribed on a wall of the Lincoln Memorial need not be purged of its profound theological content." *Marsh v. Chambers.*

"Nothing in the Constitution prohibits public school students from voluntarily praying on their own at any time before, during or after the school day." *Wallace v. Jaffree.*

"Some devout Christians believe the crèche should be placed only in reverential settings, not as an aid to commercialism." Dissent in *Allegheny County v. ACLU.*

"The Ten Commandments may be integrated into the school curriculum, where the Bible may constitutionally be used in an appropriate study of history, civilization, ethics or comparative religion." *Stone v. Graham.*

"Words like 'God' are not vulgarities for which the shock value diminishes with each successive utterance.

"The wall that separates the church from the state does not prohibit the government from acknowledging the religious beliefs and practices of the American people.

"Nor does it require governments to hide works of art or historic memorabilia from public view just because they also have religious significance.

"The state may provide its schoolchildren and adult citizens with educational materials that explain the important role that our forbears' faith in God played in their decisions to select America as a refuge from religious persecution, to declare their independence from the British Crown, and to conceive a new nation." *Van Orden v. Perry.*

INDEX